Raspberry Pi OS
ASSEMBLY LANGUAGE

Hands-on-Guide

Fourth Edition

www.brucesmith.info

Raspberry Pi OS Assembly Language
Hands On Guide

© Bruce Smith
Editions 1 ,2 3, Previously published as *Raspberry Pi Assembly Language Raspbian* ISBN 9781492135289

Fourth edition Revised and updated: March 2021 [0004]
iSBN: 978-0-6480987-3-7

Editor: Alan Ford Edits, Melanie Smith
Cover: Sumit Shringi, Graphic Designer (Book Cover-Design)
Typeset by BSB using Affinity Publisher

All Trademarks and Registered Trademarks are hereby acknowledged. Within this *Hands On Guide* the term BBC refers to the British Broadcasting Corporation. Raspberry Pi and the Raspberry Pi logos are registered trademarks of the Raspberry Pi Foundation.

Raspberry Pi OS Assembly Language: Hands On Guide is not endorsed by the Raspberry Pi Foundation.

All rights reserved. No part of this book (except brief passages quoted for critical purposes) or any of the computer programs to which it relates may be reproduced or translated in any form, by any means mechanical electronic or otherwise without the prior written consent of the copyright holder.

Disclaimer: Whilst every effort has been made to ensure that the information in this publication (and any programs and software) is correct and accurate, the author and publisher can accept no liability for any consequential loss or damage, however caused, arising as a result of the information printed in this book and on any associated websites. Because neither BSB nor the author have any control over the way in which the contents of this book is used, no warranty is given or should be implied as to the suitability of the advice or programs for any given application. No liability can be accepted for any consequential loss or damage, however caused, arising as a result of using the programs or advice printed in this book.

Published by BSB. www.brucesmith.info.

Table of Contents

    Table of Program Listings 10

1: Introduction 15
    Imagination Unlimited 16
    Start Experimenting 17
    GNU C Compiler 17
    Learn by Example 18
    What Will You Learn? 18
    Fourth Edition and Compatibility 19
    Raspberry Pi OS 20
    What About 64-bit? 20
    Keyboard Computing 21
    The Significance of ARM 21
    Raspberry Pi Through the Ages 22
    Compute Modules 22
    Notation in Use 23
    Table Terminology 24
    Centre for Computing History 24
    Companion Website and Free Books 26
    Acknowledgements 26

2: Starting Out 27
    Numbers with Meaning 27
    ARM Instructions 28
    The Transformation Process 29
    Why Machine Code? 30
    Language Levels 30
    Into Orbit 31
    RISC and Instruction Sets 32
    Assembler Structure 32
    Error Of Your Ways 33
    Cross Compilers 33

  The Raspberry Pi ARM Chip(s) 34

3: First Time Out 35
  The Command Line 35
  Creating A Source File 36
  Come to the Execution 39
  Assembler Errors 40
  The Components 41
  Lack of _start 43
  Linking Files 44
  Tidying Up 46
  A Comment on Comments 46
  Geany Programmer's Editor 47

4: Bits of a RISC Machine 49
  Binary to Decimal 50
  Decimal to Binary 51
  Binary to Hex 52
  Hex to Decimal and Back 53
  Binary Addition 54
  Subtraction 55
  Twos Complement Numbers 56
  When Twos Don't Add Up 57
  Desktop Calculator 58

5: ARM Arrangements 59
  Word Lengths 59
  Byte and Word Accessed Memory 60
  Registers 61
  R15 - Program Counter 63
  Current Program Status Register 63
  Bits and Flags 63
  Setting Flags 64
  S Suffix 65
  R14: The Link Register 66
  R13: Stack Pointer 66

6: Data Processing 67
  Addition Instructions 68
  Subtraction 71
  Multiplication 73
  Divide Arrives 75
  Move Instructions 76

22: Disassembling C 205
GCC The Swiss Army Knife 205
A Simple C Framework 206
Sourcing the Assembler 208
Building Blocks 209
A printf Example 211
Frame Pointer Variables 213
Disassembling System Calls 213

23: GPIO Functions 215
Memory Mapping 215
The GPIO Controller 217
GPIO In and Outs 219
Other GPIO Functions 230
GPIO Pins Explained 231

24: Floating-Point 233
VFP Architecture 233
The Register File 236
Managing and Printing 237
Assembling and Debugging VFP with GDB 238
Load, Store and Move 240
Precision Conversion 242
Vector Arithmetic 243

25: VFP Control Register 245
Conditional Execution 245
Scalar and Vector Operations 248
Which Type of Operator? 250
Len and Stride 251

26: Neon 255
Neon Assembler 257
Neon Instructions and Data Types 259
Addressing Modes 261
VLD and VST in their Stride 261
Load of Others 264
Neon Intrinsic 264
Neon Arrays 265
Order Correctly 270
Matrix Math 271
Multi Matrix 274

Compare Instructions 76
Ordering Numbers 77

7: ROS Ins and Outs 79
SWI and SVC Commands 79
Writing to the Screen 80
Reading from the Keyboard 82
eax and Others 84
Makefile 84

8: Logical Operations 87
Logical AND 87
Logical OR 88
Logical EOR 88
Logical Instructions 89
ORR to Convert Character Case 90
Bit Clear with BIC 91
Flag Tests 92
System Call Registers 95

9: Conditional Execution 97
Single Flag Condition Codes 99
EQ: Equal 99
NE: Not Equal 99
VS: Overflow Set 99
VC: Overflow Clear 100
MI: Minus Set 100
PL: Plus Clear 100
CS: Carry Set (HS: Higher or Same) 101
CC: Carry Clear (LO: Lower) 101
AL: Always 101
NV: Never 102
Multiple Flag Condition Code 102
HI: Higher (Unsigned) 102
LS: Lower Than or Same (Unsigned) 102
GE: Greater or Equal (Signed) 103
LT: Less Than (Signed) 103
GT: Greater Than (Signed) 103
LE: Less Than or Equal To (Signed) 103
Mixing the S Suffix 104

10: Branch and Compare 105
- Branch Instructions 105
- The Link Register 106
- Using Compare Instructions 106
- Compare Forward Thinking 107
- Using Conditionals Effectively 108
- Branch Exchange 110

11: Shifts and Rotates 111
- Logical Shifts 111
- Logical Shift Right 113
- Arithmetic Shift Right 113
- Rotations 114
- Extended Rotate 114
- Uses of Shifts and Rotates 115
- Immediate Constant Range 115
- Top Move 118

12: Smarter Numbers 119
- Long Multiplication 119
- Long Accumulation 121
- Division and Remainder 122
- Smarter Simple Multiplication 123
- Much More Inside 124

13: Program Counter R15 125
- Pipelining 126
- Calculating Branches 127

14: Debugging with GDB 129
- Frozen Cases 129
- Assembling for GDB 131
- The Disassembler 133
- Breakpoints 134
- Breakpoint Labels 137
- Memory Dump 138
- Shortcuts 139
- GDB Make Options 140

15: Data Transfer 143
- ADR Directive 143
- Indirect Addressing 146
- ADR and LDR 147

- Pre-Indexed Addressing
- Accessing Memory Bytes
- Address Write Back
- Post-Indexed Addressing
- Byte Conditions
- PC Relative Addressing

16: Block Transfer
- Write Back
- Block Copy Routine

17: Stacks
- Push and Pull
- Stack Growth
- Stack Application
- Framed Work
- Frame Pointer

18: Directives and Macros
- Data Storage Directives
- Aligning Data
- Macros
- Including Macros

19: File Handling
- File Permissions

20: Using libc
- Using C Functions in Assembler
- Source File Structure
- Investigating the Executable
- Number Input with Scanf
- Getting This Information

21: Coding Functions
- Function Standards
- Register Use
- More Than Three
- Preserving Links and Flags
- Robust Print Routines
- Bubbble Sort

Macro Matrix Example 279

27: Thumb Code 281
Differences 281
Assembling Thumb 283
Stack Operators 288
Single and Multi-Register 288
Functions in Thumb 289
ARMv7 Thumb Instructions 289

28: Unified Language 291
Thumb Changes 293
New A32 Instructions 293
Compare by Zero 294
Assembling UAL 295

29: Exception Handing 297
Modes of Operation 297
Vectors 298
Register Arrangements 300
Exception Handling 302
MRS and MSR 303
Interrupts When? 304
Your Interrupt Decisions 305
Returning from Interrupts 306
Writing Interrupt Routines 306

30: System on a Chip 307
The ARM Chip & Instruction Sets 308
Co-processors 309
Pipeline 309
Memory & Caches 310
The GPU 310
ARMv8 Overview 311
Raspberry Pi OS 64-Bit 312
In Summary 312
Archimedes Principle 312

A: ASCII character Set 314

B: ARM Instruction Set 316
Compare and Test Instructions 317
Branch Instructions 317

9

    Arithmetic Instructions 317
    Logical Instructions 318
    Data Movement Instructions 318

C: ROS Syscalls 319

Index 323

Table of Program Listings

Program 3a. A simple source file.	39
Program 3b. Part 1 of the source file.	44
Program 3c. Part 2 of the source file.	45
Program 6a. Simple 32-bit addition.	69
Program 6b. 64-bit addition.	70
Program 6c. 32-bit multiplication.	73
Program 6d. Using MLA - Multiply with Accumulate.	74
Program 6e. Signed Division with SDIV.	75
Program 7a. Syscall 4 to write a string to the screen.	81
Program 7b. Syscall 3 to write a string to the screen.	82
Program 7c. Automate assembly and linking with Make.	85
Program 8a. Converting character case.	90
Program 8b. Printing a number as a binary string.	92
Program 10a. Conditional execution to improve program size.	109
Program 12a. Long multiplication 'the hard way'	120
Program 12b. Division the long way.	122
Program 14a. Flexible makefile for debugging code.	139
Program 15a. Use of the ADR directive.	142
Program 15b. Use of pre-indexed indirect addressing.	147
Program 15c. Using post-indexed addressing.	150
Program 16a. Moving Blocks of Memory	157
Program 18a. Use of .byte and .equ directives	166
Program 18b. Implementing a simple macro.	169
Program 18c. Multi-calling a macro.	170

Program 18d. AddMult macro file	172
Program 18e. Macro Include Test	172
Program 19a. File Creation and Access.	176
Program 20a. GCC source file structure.	185
Program 20b. Passing parameters to printf.	187
Program 20c. Reading and converting a number with scanf.	189
Program 20d. Combining scanf and printf.	191
Program 21a. Passing function values via the stack.	196
Program 21b. Print vector of words	198
Program 21c. Test printw	199
Program 21d. Bubble Sort Routine	200
Program 21e. Bubble Sort Test	201
Program 22a. A simple C program to print an asterisk.	205
Program 22b. The final putchar listing.	208
Program 22c. C listing for the 'hello world' program.	209
Program 22d. A C listing for using the scanf function.	210
Program 23a. File access to GPIO memory.	219
Program 24a. Printing a floating-point value with printf.	235
Program 24b. Manipulating and printing two or more fp values.	239
Program 25a. Conditional VFP-based execution.	246
Program 25b. Using LEN and STRIDE to sum vectors.	251
Program 26a. A Simple Neon Test.	255
Program 26b. Rotate a 2D matrix by 90 degrees (clockwise).	264
Program 26c. Adding two 4x4 Matrices together.	270
Program 26d. Single-Precision Matrix Multiplication	274
Program 26e. Single-Precision Matrix Multi - Using Macro Version	277
Program 27a. How to invoke Thumb State and run Thumb code.	282
Program 27b. Using external functions by inter-working code.	286
Program 28a. Unified Assembly Language	294

**The source files from this book are available to download at the author's website:
www.brucesmith.info**

Dedicated to all the health care workers, nurses, doctors and carers around the world.

To the ones that gave their all in a time of need during the pandemic. Their memory will be embedded into our hearts for years to come.
Thank you

About the Author

Bruce Smith purchased his first computer—an Acorn Atom — in 1980. He was immediately hooked, becoming a regular contributor to the mainstream computer press including 'Computing Today' and 'Personal Computer World'. With the arrival of the BBC Micro his magazine work expanded into books and his 1982 title 'Interfacing Projects for the BBC Micro' has become regarded as a classic of the time as the first book showing home users how to connect the computer to the outside world. He was one of the first to write about the ARM chip when it was released on the Acorn Archimedes in 1987.

Bruce has written about all aspects of computer use. His friendly, lucid style of writing caused one reviewer to write, *'This is the first computer book I have read in bed for pleasure rather than to cure insomnia!'* Bruce's books have been translated into many languages and sold across the world. His publishers have included BBC Books, Collins, Virgin Books and Rough Guides.

Originally from London's East End, he now lives in Sydney, NSW.

Amazon 5-Star Reviews for earlier editions of this book:

"Excellent little book. Would thoroughly recommend this to anyone looking to learn ARM assembly language."

"This book is not just for beginners, it also contains information for those at the intermediate level, and it touches on some advanced topics. In my opinion this book is 10/10 and a must for anybody starting off or getting back into assembly language programming on the ARM v6 processor (Raspberry Pi). It's saved me a lot of time by having all the required information I needed in one place. Thanks Bruce for this valuable resource!"

"This is a great book for budding programmers who want to dig deeper into the Raspberry Pi to really understand how the computer works. Great step by step examples."

"Smith provides not only the necessary coaching and instruction in assembly language for the Raspberry Pi's ARM processor, but also gives clear practical instructions for getting everything to work… Whether you are looking just to have some fun learning assembly language with your Raspberry Pi or whether you view the Pi as a stepping-stone to greater things ARM, Bruce Smith's book definitely belongs on your shelf."

www.brucesmith.info

1: Introduction

It didn't surprise me when, early in 2013, it was announced that the Raspberry Pi had sold one million units. And counting... It took me back more years — decades even — than I care to remember when it was announced that the BBC Micro had done the same. Both came out of businesses based in Cambridge in the UK and there were even more links between the two than you might imagine.

Both systems fascinated me and literally millions of other people. The first system took every penny of my savings at the time, but the Raspberry Pi didn't even drain the cash in my wallet. But whist the ticket price for each was vastly different, pretty much everything else about them was so familiar. Not least their ability to run a wide range of software and educational tools and how easy it was to connect external devices and control the outside world. I would suspect that most people who own one Raspberry Pi, own several.

Figure 1a. Raspberry Pi Model B.

For the first time since the BBC Micro there is an affordable and infinitely accessible system that just about anyone can use. Meanwhile, the PC and Mac have dominated the market and other more games-orientated boxes have been available. But none of these have impacted the technical home hobbyist user. The *techsperts* have had a variety of development boards to experiment and fiddle with, again mostly beyond the scope of the home hobbyist computer market. For the cost of a couple of CDs or new release DVD, the Raspberry Pi has changed all that.

The launch of the Raspberry Pi Zero in November 2015 took cheapness to a new level. A fully-fledged ARM-driven computer for just $5. Insane! And if that wasn't enough the December 2015 issue of MagPi (the official Raspberry Pi magazine) had it bound on the cover as a free give away. Could the Raspberry Pi be classed as the world's first disposable computer?

At the time of updating this introduction for the fourth edition (December 2020) sales had surpassed 30 million across the various models available. Indeed, that figure was reported to have been passed by the start of 2020 with a variety of organisations using at the very heart of their infrastructure and development. Oracle hailed its cluster of 1,060 Raspberry Pi boards the 'world's largest' Pi supercomputer, sporting 4,240 cores. The Jet Propulsion Laboratory (JPL) also uses the boards for its Mars mission.

Imagination Unlimited

One reason for the birth of the Raspberry Pi was to make it easy for people to take up programming, with the aid of a competitively priced computer system whose use was limited only by the user's imagination. I hope this book will help many of you reading it realise that dream. In fact, it isn't a dream. It is a probability if you continue your way through the pages that follow — a first step on a rewarding and educational pastime. And, who knows, you may become part of a new generation of computer programmers working at the sharp end of what is possible.

The purpose of this book is to give the reader a better understanding of how computers really work at a lower level than in programming languages like C or Python. By gaining a deeper understanding of how computers work, you can often be much more productive developing software in higher level languages such C and Python. Learning to program in assembly language is an excellent way to achieve this goal.

This book provides an introductory tutorial in writing assembly language on the Raspberry Pi and specifically using the Raspberry Pi OS (Raspbian Operating System). Assembly language generates machine code that can be run directly on your computer.

I first learnt to program assembly language on early Acorn designed machines and ultimately watched the ARM chip develop on their Archimedes and BBC Micro Second-Processor systems. Ultimately that assembly language was the forerunner of what the Raspberry Pi uses today. If anything, that proves that what you learn here should stand you in good step for many years to come. So, it's been a significant investment.

Start Experimenting

While this is not a book for the complete novice, you certainly do not require any experience with assembly language or machine code to be able to pick it up and start reading and experimenting. Programming experience would be beneficial, and any structured language will have provided the groundwork for many of the fundamental concepts required.

This is a *Hands-on-Guide*, so there are plenty of programs for you to try for yourself. Learning to program is about experimenting, making mistakes, and then learning from them. Experimenting by changing values and information is without doubt the best way to understand what is happening and is to be encouraged. All programs are available to download from the companion website. The book is equally applicable to all versions of the Raspberry Pi. More on this shortly.

GNU C Compiler

There are several operating systems (programming environments) available to download for using with the Raspberry Pi. As the title suggests, the one we're using here is called the Raspberry Pi OS (formerly Raspbian), and this comes with everything you'll need to write and run your programs..

The software we will utilise is GCC, the GNU Compiler Collection. The original author of the GNU C Compiler (GCC) was Richard Stallman, the founder of the GNU Project. The GNU project was started in 1984 to create a complete operating system as free software, to promote freedom and cooperation among computer users and programmers. Every operating system needs a C compiler, and as there were no free compilers in existence at that time, the GNU Project had to develop one from scratch.

You may be aware that C is an extremely popular programming language; it is also one that is very closely tied to the Advanced RISC Machine (ARM) microprocessor which the Raspberry Pi uses at its very core. You do not need to know C to write assembly language programs, so don't be too concerned about that.

GCC is a very clever piece of software and can be used in many ways. One of its key components is as an assembler, and this is the part of GCC we shall be primarily interested in.

The work was funded by donations from individuals and companies to the Free Software Foundation, a non-profit organisation set up to support the work of the GNU Project. The first release of GCC came in 1987. Since that time GCC has become one of the most important tools in the development of free software and is available on almost every operating system platform in existence.

GCC is free software, distributed under the GNU General Public License (GNU GPL). This means you have the freedom to use and to modify GCC, as with all GNU software. If you need support for a new type of CPU, a new language, or a new feature you can add it yourself, or get someone to do it for you.

Learn by Example

The programs presented in this book are provided to illustrate concepts being explained with a simple and — where possible — practical application. I will not try to baffle you with long and complex listings; there is no need to. I will leave it to you to take the examples and information and combine them two, three, four and more at a time to create a useful outcome, learning a great deal along the way.

Some degree of 'chicken and egg' syndrome has been unavoidable, but I have tried to keep it to a minimum. Concepts are introduced in an order that goes with knowledge so far acquired. However, sometimes this is not always possible; in such cases I will highlight the fact. In such cases, you need to accept that it works, and you will understand the how and why later in the day!

Programming really is fun. I have written a tonne of books on the subject and a good percentage of them have been about home computers — how to program and use them. I have never had a computer lesson in my life. If I can do it, so can anyone. It is also frustrating! There is not a programmer who ever lived, novice or expert, who has not spent an inordinate amount of time trying to solve a programming problem, just to realise later that the issue was right there in front of them all along. I would go so far as to say the real satisfaction comes when you solve problems for yourself.

One word of advice: If you can't solve something, walk away, and do something else for a while. It's amazing how often the solution comes to you when you are doing something else. A good rule for life in general!

What Will You Learn?

In a nutshell, you will learn to become a proficient assembly language programmer. By the end of this book, provided you have worked through and applied the example programs and small snippets of programs that are dotted through the text, you will be able to design, write and produce machine code programs to undertake any number of tasks. You will also have the grounding to allow you to delve into the more generic texts relating to the ARM chip and system programming.

You will also become familiar with using GCC in a whole variety of ways including writing for the Raspberry Pi Operating System and by combining your assembled programs with libraries of standalone functions.

You will learn how to interpret and manipulate what your Raspberry Pi is doing at its most fundamental level. You will be right in there programming, deep inside the ARM chip.

Problem solving is something you will also need to learn. When a machine code program will not work as you intended it is often a simple logical flaw that is the root cause. GCC comes with its own debugging tools and we'll see how to use these to good effect. I'll also provide some useful tips on the best way you can narrow down your search area to the source of the problem.

Fourth Edition and Compatibility

By and large this book is compatible with the full range of Raspberry Pi computers. One of the mantras of those developing the hardware and software for the system is to ensure that it remains backwards compatible (as far as possible). That essentially means that what works on one Raspberry Pi will work on another, provided it is written correctly (in terms of software). Hardware should work also, aside from some of the physical changes that have taken place. For example, the HDMI port works, but the type of lead required to connect to the outside world may change (standard to micro, for instance).

Figure 1b. Raspberry Pi 4 Model B.

Physically, the difference between models and versions is generally obvious. And for the purposes of this book I would assume you have a model that has a GPIO port fitted as standard, and this is largely where some of the changes come in from this books point of view, of you are intending to use some of the examples there that show how use your coding to connect to attached devices. Where required changes are noted in the text of the book.

Several different versions of the ARM chip have been used in the evolution of the Raspberry Pi to date, and that may continue in the future as well. For now, just be aware that differences may exist, but these will become apparent as your knowledge grows. As this is essentially a beginner's book, it does not change the fundamentals of the programming experience herein. As such, the contents of this book can be considered applicable as an introduction to ARM assembly language regardless of the model Raspberry Pi you are using.

Raspberry Pi OS

When the 8GB Raspberry Pi 4 was announced (May 2020), the Raspberry Pi Foundation revealed that it was changing the name of its official operating system from Raspbian to Raspberry Pi OS. This is with a view to providing a similar, and stable operating system and windows-style desktop environment across all platforms and to ensure on-going backwards compatibility with software and applications as far as possible.

The two main categories of processors are 32-bit and 64-bit. By supporting both 32-bit and 64-bit operating systems, and taking charge of the operating system build, the look and feel of OS's can be maintained. Simply put, a 64-bit processor is more capable than a 32-bit processor because it can handle more data at once. A 64-bit processor is capable of storing more computational values, including memory addresses, which means it can access over four billion times the physical memory of a 32-bit processor. That's just as big as it sounds!

From a user point of view, utilising the standard 32-bit operating system, there is no functional difference in what this book covers. For *'Raspbian'* read *'Raspberry Pi OS'* and vice versa. More importantly, the OS remains backwards compatible so that Raspberry Pi OS will run on all versions of the Raspberry Pi. You can update and upgrade your current operating system to the latest Raspberry Pi OS at any point.

The Raspbian project will continue and will undoubtedly continue to be used to build the 32-bit version of Raspberry Pi OS. Considering that several models of Raspberry Pi, including the very-popular Raspberry Pi Zero, will never work with a 64-bit OS, the 32-bit platform will continue to be important if not dominant for years to come. It's the common denominator.

What About 64-bit?

The Raspberry Pi 2B (v1.2) was the first to use an ARM 64-bit processor, yet there wasn't an official 64-bit OS available for it. That's because the Raspberry Pi Foundation has focused instead on making its 32-bit Raspbian OS run on all generations of the RPi. Since the aforementioned Raspberry Pi 2B (v1.2), all RPi releases have been based on 64-bit processors, which can also run in 32-bit mode.

The 32-bit state of the ARM chip is called AArch32 (or A32) and the 64-bit is AArch64 or A64. This means that 32-bit software can be run on a 64-bit ARM chip in AArch32 state–the reverse is not true.

At the time of writing there is a beta-version of the 64-bit Raspberry Pi OS available for download and use. Once this is out of beta it will be released and run on all 64-bit capable versions (see Chapter 30). Note that the 32-bit version (A32) of ARM assembly language is different to the 64-bit version (A64), therefore code written in A32 will not run without modification in A64 state.

Keyboard Computing

The inevitable happened in November 2020 when desktop computing finally arrived for the Raspberry Pi the board being re-engineered and packaged inside a red and white keyboard for the launch of the Raspberry Pi 400.

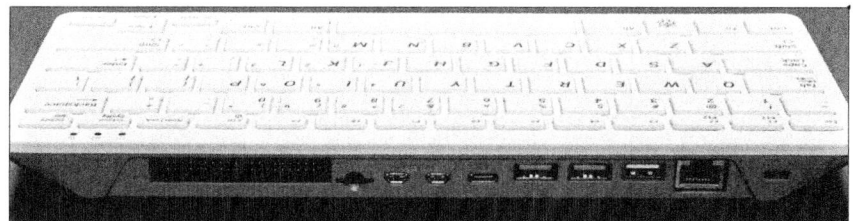

Figure 1c. The Raspberry Pi 400 the ultimate in keyboard computing.

The Significance of ARM

All microprocessors are based on a specific instruction set architecture (ISA), and the most significant of these down the years has been x86-based which has dominated the desktop and laptop marketplace (PC and Apple). Most recently this includes the 64-bit version called x86-64 or AMD64.

However most Apple and Android tablets and smart phones have ARM processors within, which is incompatible with x86. These devices use the ARM chip because of its low energy consumption, as in longer battery life. However, the incompatibility means that software compiled for desktops and laptops cannot be directly run on ARM-controlled mobile devices.

Reduced Instruction Set Computing or RISC processors, used in ARM devices, execute a lot of simple instructions to complete task. The x86 processors use CISC or a Complex Instruction Set and execute a series of more complex instructions to complete an identical task.

ARM chips therefore achieve their lower power consumption as they have fewer transistors in their core structure than CISC based ones. It also means from a programmers' point of view you have less instructions to learn as an ARM programmer!

The other very significant difference is that ARM Holdings is not a chip manufacture. It designs the chips and then licenses these core designs for others to include in their own purpose build chips.

In mid-2020 Apple Computers announced it will be going full tilt with self-manufactured ARM chips included in its full range of new computers, therefore ensuring applications can run across its range of devices. Microsoft 365, Adobe Creative Cloud and like software are likely to be available for a new range of ARM Macs. It doesn't take a great stretch of the imagination to see they could also be available for other ARM-based computers too.

While the x86 based laptops and desktops will continue in the short term at least dominate the marketplace in terms of installed numbers ARM-based Apple Macs should bring ARM-based laptops/desktops computers into the mainstream market place, and may tempt other players as well.

All this adds to another reason to learn ARM assembly language programming.

Raspberry Pi Through the Ages

The Raspberry Pi has been evolving ever since it was first released in 2012. With each generation there is often significant improvement, in the type of the central processing unit, memory capacity, networking support, and peripheral-device support.

The table shown in Figure 1d lists some of the basic specifications for each of the Raspberry Pi formats. As a rule, Raspberry Pi comes in three different formats:

Model B: these are the 'full size' boards which include Ethernet and USB ports. The B+ versions often add enhancements or specific differences.

Model A: these are the square shape boards. Consider these a 'lighter' version of the Raspberry Pi, usually with lower specifications than the headline Model B, with less USB ports and often no Ethernet. As such they retail at a lower price point.

Zero: Smallest Raspberry Pi available. Zeros have less computing processing power than the Model B but use less power as well. No USB, no Ethernet, just a nice simple package!

The amount of memory available on each Raspberry Pi should have no real significance for the requirements of this book, just be aware that the memory addresses you see when you run or list a particular program may differ from what is shown herein. That should not hinder the program operation though.

Compute Modules

The Compute Module is a stripped-down Raspberry Pi which is intended for industrial or commercial applications. The idea being that they can be used in development projects by anyone who wants them. (Ultimately you purchase the boards and finalise them yourself for whatever need you might have.) As such the Compute Modules don't have the connection bells and whistles that you may find on the equivalent Raspberry Pi, equally they are not as robust. As such, and although they do contain ARM processors as they are based on the Raspberry Pi, they are not covered herein.

But then came the Computer Module 4. Unlike previous Compute Modules this by purchasing the updated IO Board you get easy access to all the interfaces standard connectors, providing a ready made development platform and a starting point for your own designs.

Notation in Use

A standard notation has been adopted throughout this book. Number types and certain operations on numbers are commonplace in programming books such as this, and it is important to distinguish among them. The short list here is for reference. Their exact meaning will be described as we encounter them within the text of the book.

% or 0b	Denotes that the number that follows it is in binary or base 2. For example: %11110000 or 0b11110000
0x	Denotes that the number that follows it is hexadecimal or base16. For example: 0xCAFE
< >	Angle brackets or chevrons are used extensively to enclose a word that should not be taken literally but read as the object to use with the command. For example, <Register> means a register name, R0 for example, should be used in the angled brackets and not the word 'Register' itself.
Dest	Short for destination.
Operand1	The commentary in the text often talks about Operand1 and its use. The relevant values for Operand1 as defined at that point should be used. For Operand1, this is normally a register.
Operand2	The commentary in the text often talks about Operand2 and its use. The relevant values for Operand2 as defined at that point should be used. For Operand2, this is normally either a register or an immediate value.
Op1	Shorthand format for <Operand1> when space is tight.
Op2	Shorthand format for <Operand2> when space is tight.
( )	Brackets show that the item within is optional and may be omitted if not needed. For example, ADD (S) means that S may or may not be included.

Table Terminology

The table in Figure 1d utilises many acronyms that may or may not be new to you. We'll examine each of these briefly now and re-address them at the appropriate points in the book, as required.

SOC: System-on-Chip. One of the key elements of the Raspberry Pi design and generally the largest chip on the board, it contains all the significant components in one package. This includes the ARM processor or processors and graphics processing units. Note that each SoC is defined by a number - viz BCM2771 for the Raspberry Pi 4 B.

CPU: This is the ARM processor or processors used, integrated into the SoC. The table lists the specific ARM chip along with the number of included cores and the speed of operation. Thus, on the original Raspberry Pi B, the table tells us that a single ARM 1176JZF-S running at 700MHz was supplied. More recently the Raspberry Pi 4 B utilises four Cortex-A72 ARM cores running at 1.5GHz.

FPU: Floating-Point Unit or maths co-processor which provides complex math functions. This is also part of the SoC and later editions of the SoC include a Neon co-processor allowing the FPU to undertake multiple operations in parallel. VFP is short for vector floating-point.

GPU: Graphics Processing Unit. Included as part of the Broadcom SoC, this is also manufactured by Broadcom and is typically a VideoCore IV, changing to VideoCore VI with the Raspberry Pi 4 B. Effectively it is a multimedia processor that can decode the various graphics and sound formats (codecs) to ensure great output on your monitor, maintaining low power consumption.

The final column of the table lists the Instruction Set Architecture implemented and whether it is 32-bit or 64-bit. As you can see, and referring the item on 64-bits earlier, a 64-bit instruction set has been available on the Raspberry Pi since the RPi 2 B v1.2, effectively October 2016.

Centre for Computing History

The Centre for Computing History (CCH) is a pioneering educational charity that opened at its current site in Cambridge in August 2013. CCH was established as an educational charity to tell the story of the Information Age through exploring the historical, social, and cultural impact of developments in personal computing. It maintains a long-term collection of objects to tell this story and exploits them through education and events programmes.

CCH aims to deliver inspirational learning opportunities to a wide range of audiences – from pre-schoolers to the over-70s – so people become confident and creative users of information and digital technology. It offers a range of education services on site including programming and electronics workshops and other interactive learning using 1980s BBC Micros and Raspberry Pi.

www.computinghistory.org.uk

Model RPi	Release	SOC	CPU	FPU	GPU	ARM IS
400	Nov 2020	BCM 2711C0	4x Cortex-A72 @ 1.8GHz	VFPv4 + NEON	Broadcom VideoCore VI	ARMv8-A (64/32-bit)
4B	June 2019; May 2020 (8GB)	BCM2711 B0	4x Cortex-A72 @ 1.5GHz	VFPv4 + NEON	Broadcom VideoCore VI	ARMv8-A (64/32-bit)
3B+	May 2018	BCM2837B0	4x Cortex-A53 @ 1.4GHz	VFPv4 + NEON	Broadcom VideoCore IV	ARMv8-A (64/32-bit)
3B	Feb 2016	BC2837	4x Cortex-A53 @ 1.2GHz	VFPv4 + NEON	Broadcom Videocore IV	ARMv8-A (64/32-bit)
3A+	Nov 2018	BCM2837B0	4x Cortex-A53 @1.4GHz	VFPv4 + NEON	Broadcom Videocore IV	ARMv8-A (64/32-bit)
2B v1.2	Oct 2016	BCM2837	4x Cortex-A53 @ 900MHz	VFPv4 + NEON	Broadcom Videocore IV	ARMv8-A (64/32-bit)
2B	Feb 2015	BCM2836	4x Cortex-A7 @ 900MHz	VFPv3 + NEON	Broadcom Videocore IV	ARMv7-A (32-bit)
1B+	July 2014	BCM2835	1x ARM 1176JZF-S @ 700MHz	VFPv2	Broadcom Videocore IV	ARMv6Z (32-bit)
1B	May 2012	BCM2835	1x ARM 1176JZF-S @ 700MHz	VFPv2	Broadcom Videocore IV	ARMv6Z (32-bit)
1A+	Nov 2014	BCM2835	1x ARM 1176JZF-S @ 700MHz	VFPv2	Broadcom Videocore IV	ARMv6Z (32-bit)
1A	Feb 2013	BCM2835	1x ARM 1176JZF-S @ 700MHz	VFPv2	Broadcom Videocore IV	ARMv6Z (32-bit)
Zero W/WH	Feb 2017	BCM2835	1x ARM 1176JZF-S @ 1GHz	VFPv2	Broadcom VideoCore IV	ARMv6Z (32-bit)
Zero v1.3	May 2016	BCM2835	1x ARM 1176JZF-S @ 1GHz	VFPv2	Broadcom VideoCore IV	ARMv6Z (32-bit)
Zero v.1.2	Nov 2015	BCM2835	1x ARM 1176JZF-S @ 1GHz	VFPv2	Broadcom VideoCore IV	ARMv6Z (32-bit)

Figure 1d. Raspberry Pi formats - some base specifications.

Companion Website and Free Books

Go to www.brucesmith.info and follow the directions to the book companion pages. From the site, you can download all the programs and access updates to the book and additional information and features. In addition, links to other support websites and useful downloads can be found, along with details of forthcoming Bruce Smith Books publications covering the Raspberry Pi.

PDFs for several of my original books can be found to download free-of-charge via my website. These are books that were published prior to 2004 before the whole eBook and self-publishing era got full on. Whilst I did author many of them (all but two in fact) using a wordprocessor the original text has long since washed away (the first two were written longhand – blue ink on A4 ruled pages!).

Figure 1e. The author website. You can click on a book cover for more information.

Acknowledgements

Thanks go to Richard Khoury for his help with the C segments within this book and the finer art of using GCC and GDB. Thanks to Mike Ginns for the concepts of several programs listed here. Some listings originate from his book Archimedes Assembly Language which was first published by Dabs Press in 1988. (A key to how old the ARM is!) Also, I am grateful to Brian Scallan, Steve Cirelli and Tony Palmer for their feedback and updates. I am also indebted to the many readers who have written with suggestions to improve this book.

2: Starting Out

Assembly language gives you access to the native language of the Raspberry Pi – machine code. This is the tongue of the ARM chip which is the heart and brain of your computer system. ARM stands for stands for Advanced RISC Machine, and it ultimately controls everything that takes place on your Raspberry Pi.

Microprocessors such as the ARM, control the use and flow of data. The processor is also often called the CPU – Central Processing Unit – and data the CPU processes are digested as a continuous, almost never-ending stream of 1s and 0s. The order of these 1s and 0s has meaning to the ARM, and a particular sequence of them will be translated into a series of actions. Just like Morse Code where a series of dots and dashes in the correct order has meaning if you know how each letter is represented.

$$\bar{\cdot}.\bar{\cdot}.\ .\bar{\cdot}..\ .\ ...\bar{\ }\ .\ .\bar{\cdot}.$$

Numbers with Meaning

As a machine code program code program is a sequence of endless strings of 1s and 0s. For example:

```
11010111011011100101010100001011
01010001011100100110100011111010
01010100011001111111001010010100
10011000011101010100011001010001
```

It would be almost impossible — or at the very least extremely time-consuming — to interpret what these numbers mean. Assembly language helps to overcome these issues.

Assembly language is a form of shorthand that allows machine code programs to be written using an English style lexicon. An assembler is a program which translates the assembly language program into the machine code, thereby taking away what would otherwise be a laborious process. The assembly language program is often just a text file, and this is read by the assembler before being converted into its binary (1s and 0s) equivalent. The assembly language program is called the input or source file, and the machine code program the object file. The assembler translates (or compiles) the source file into an object file.

Assembly language is written using mnemonics. A mnemonic is a device that aids learning or acts as a reminder. This relies upon associations among easy-to-remember letter sequences that can be related back to the information to be remembered. You've probably encountered these at some point as acronyms. For example, to remember the colours of the rainbow you could take the phrase:

'Richard Of York Gave Battle In Vain'

And use the first letter of each word. Or use the fictitious name:

'Roy G. Biv'

A mnemonic language has developed around SMS messages sent on mobile phones. These enable text messages to be shorter and more compact. For example, 'L8R' for later', 'GR8' for Great and '2mrw' for 'tomorrow'.

ARM Instructions

The ARM chip has a specific set of machine code instructions that it understands. These operation codes or 'opcodes' and their use are really what this book is about. The ARM is just one type of microprocessor; there are many different types, and each has its own unique set of instructions.

You cannot take a machine code program written for ARM and run it successfully on a different microprocessor. It simply would not work as expected, if at all. That said, the concepts introduced here can be applied with a broad brush to most other microprocessors available and are consistent in application. If you learn to program in one, you are well on your way to programming others. Essentially you just need to learn a new set of mnemonics, and most likely many will be like the ones you are about to learn.

Microprocessors move and manipulate data, so not surprisingly many of the machine code commands deal with this control, and most instruction sets (the collective term for these mnemonics), include commands to add and subtract numbers. The assembly language mnemonics used to represent these tasks are typically in the form:

```
ADD
SUB
```

These examples are straightforward as are many other ARM mnemonics, However, they can also appear complex when combined in a single line sequence. By breaking them down into their component parts their action can be determined without any real difficulty.

An assembly language mnemonic is normally three characters in length, but there are occasions when it may be longer. Like anything new, this may take a bit of 'getting used to', but if you work through the examples given in this book, and apply them in your own examples you should not have too much trouble.

MOV is the mnemonic for the MOVe command. It takes information from one place and moves it to another place. How hard was that?

The Transformation Process

Once you have developed your assembly language program you have to convert it into machine code using the assembler. For example, when the assembler encounters the MOV mnemonic it will generate the correct number that represents the instruction. It stores the assembled machine code as a sequential file in memory and then allows you to run or execute it. In the process of assembling the program, the assembler also checks its syntax to ensure it is correct. If it spots an error, it will identify it to you and allow you to correct it. You can then try and assemble the program again. Note that this syntax check will only ensure that you have used the assembler instructions correctly. It cannot check their logic so if you have written something that has used instructions correctly, but not in the way that achieves what you wanted, it will assemble without error but will produce an unwanted result. For example, you may need to do an addition but programmed a subtraction instead!

There are various ways to write an assembly language program. The first ARM chips were designed by Acorn and so not surprisingly appeared on a range of Acorn-based computers running RISC OS. This included the Archimedes and RISC PC. These machines ran BBC BASIC, which was innovative in that it allowed you to write assembly language programs as an extension of BBC BASIC. This method is still available to you today should you install RISC OS on your Raspberry Pi.

As we have already identified, this book assumes you are using the Raspberry Pi Operating System and the GNU GCC software. Other assembler software does exist — much of it free — and a quick search on the internet will reveal what the offerings are. A major advantage of GCC Programming is that it can also assemble programs written in the C programming language.

Although this book is not about programming C, there are reasons why some familiarity with the infrastructure it employs is advantageous, and with just a bit of knowledge this can help make programming easier. We'll discuss this with examples later in the book.

The bottom line is that there is nothing to stop you trying any or all these other assemblers, and certainly what you learn here will be beneficial in that process.

Why Machine Code?

This is an easy question to answer. Essentially everything your Raspberry Pi does is done using machine code. By programming in machine code, you are working at the most fundamental level of the Raspberry Pi operation.

If you are using a language such as BBC BASIC or Python, then ultimately all its operations have to be converted into machine code every time you run the program. This takes a finite amount of time – in human terms lightning fast – but still time. This conversion or interpretation process does therefore slow the operation of the software down. In fact, even the most efficient languages can be over 30 times slower than their machine code equivalent, and that's on a good day!

If you program in machine code, your programs will run much faster as there is no conversion being undertaken. There is a conversion process when you run the assembler, but once you have created the machine code you can execute this directly — it is a one-off process. You do not have to run the assembler every time. Once you are happy with your program you can save the machine code and use it directly. You can also keep the assembly language source program and use it again, or perhaps make changes at some later point.

Language Levels

Languages such as C or Python are called high-level languages. High-level languages are often easier to write as they have a more English-like syntax and also include commands that do a complex sequence of actions using one command that would otherwise take a long list of machine code instructions to perform. Machine code is a low-level language level language as it is working amongst the 'nuts and bolts' of the computer: it spells out every technical step and detail and as a result is harder to understand.

This is the advantage of a high-level language as opposed to a low-level one. That said, as you become more proficient in assembly language, there is nothing stopping you from building libraries of routines to do a specific task and just adding them to your programs as you write them. As you dig deeper into the world of the ARM, you will find that such libraries already exist out there in cyberspace.

By writing in assembler you can also transport your assembly language programs onto other computers or systems that use the ARM chip. You simply load the assembly language file into an assembler at the new destination, assemble it and run the machine code program.

The GNU GCC compiler is available for just about all flavours of microprocessor, so being familiar with the use of GCC will allow you to transport your new-found skill onto other systems should you so desire.

Provided you take full advantage of the ARM chip's facilities you can even transfer and run the machine code directly. This has exciting possibilities when you consider that just about every Smart Phone and Tablet device available these days utilises ARM chips!

Into Orbit

Just to underline the power of the ARM chip and indeed smart phones in general, a whole new generation of satellites called CubeSats, have been placed into orbit around the Earth. They are small (about 10cms square) and have specific tasks. The Surrey Space Centre in the south of England has designed several CubeSats that are powered by Android phones. At around $100,000 each, these satellites are a fraction of the cost of previous machines. At the same time, the computing power of a single smart phone is perhaps tens of thousands of times more than could be found in the computers on all the Apollo moon missions put together! This is all at your disposal on your Raspberry Pi.

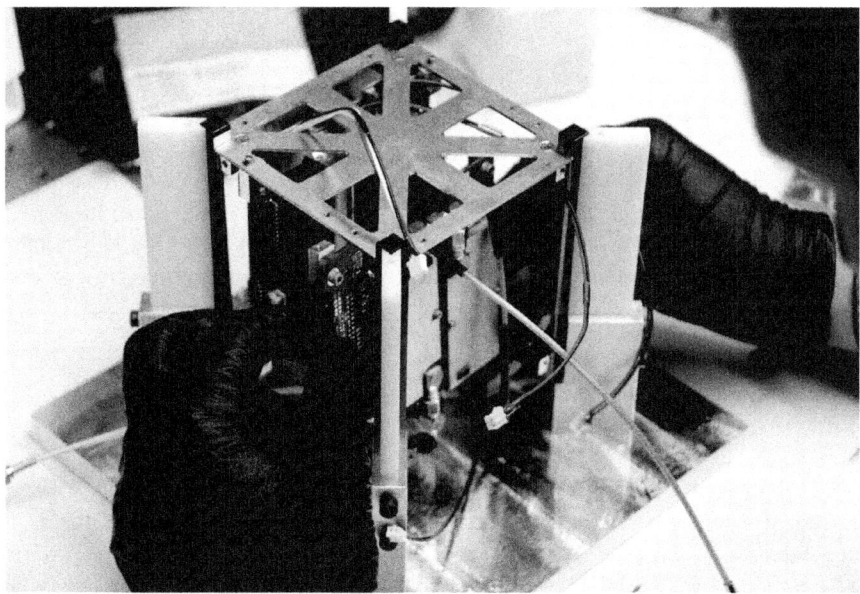

Figure 2a. A CubeSat under construction.

Surprise, surprise, the world is not all rosy! There are differences in the CPU releases. As with software, the ARM chip has gone through continual development and has had new version issues. But the base instruction set remains the same so 'porting' is not as hard as it might seem. It only becomes an issue if you are using more advanced features of the microprocessor. For this introductory guide, these changes are not relevant. Everything in these pages is applicable to your Raspberry Pi.

RISC and Instruction Sets

The R in ARM stands for RISC. This is an acronym for Reduced Instruction Set Computing. All CPUs operate using machine code and each of these machine code instructions or opcodes has a specific task. Together these instructions form the instruction set.

The philosophy behind RISC has been to create a small, highly optimised set of instructions. This has several advantages — fewer instructions to learn for one — but obviously greater variation in their use.

Assembler Structure

Programming in any language, just like speaking in any language, requires us to follow a set of rules. These rules are defined by the structure and syntax of the language we are using. To program effectively, we need to know the syntax of the language, and the rules that structure the language.

The simplest way to design a program is simply to create a simple list of things you want it to do. It starts at the beginning and executes linearly until it gets to the end. In other words, each command is executed in turn until there are no more commands left. This works but is very inefficient.

Program languages today are structured and allow you to build them as a set of independently executable procedures or subroutines. These subroutines are then called from a main program as and when they are required. The main program, therefore, controls the flow of control and executes anything that may not be available as a subroutine.

Programs are smaller and more manageable when they are created using subroutines. In a linear program concept, we would have probably had to repeat large sections of code several times to have achieved its goal.

Figure 2b illustrates some pseudo-program language to show how such a structured program might look. In the example, program commands are listed in capitals – uppercase letters. Sections of subroutine code are given names – in lowercase – and paradoxically are identified with a full-stop at their start. The entire flow of the program is contained in the six lines starting with '.main' and finishing with 'END'. Admittedly it is short, but it is clear to read, and you can understand just with a glance, what is happening. Each subroutine name is meaningful.

```
.main
      DO getkeyboardinput
      DO displayresult
      DO getkeyboardinput
      DO displayresult
END

.getkeyboardinput
      ; Instructions to read input from keyboard
RETURN
.displayresult
      ; print the result on the screen
RETURN
```

Figure 2b. Pseudo code illustrating a structured approach to programming.

In this example, the main program just calls subroutines. In a perfect world, this would always be our aim because it also makes it easier to test individual subroutines separately before they are included in the main program. This helps to ensure our program works as we put it together.

Error of Your Ways

One big challenge you face when learning any new program is locating errors. This process is known as debugging. I guarantee (and I have proven this many times) you will first write a program that does not work as expected. You will look at it until the cows come home and not see the error of your ways. You will insist you are right, and the computer is the issue. Then like a bolt out of the blue, you will see the error right there staring at you.

By building a subroutine and then testing it separately, ensuring that it works, you will know when you come to use it as part of your larger program that your hair is safe for another day.

Cross Compilers

This is a term you are likely to come across a lot. The GCC compiler can be found on a lot of other computers, even ones that do not use the ARM chip. You can write and compile ARM assembler on a totally different computer! However, you cannot run the assembled machine code. You must first transfer it from the host machine to the target machine (such as Raspberry Pi). GCC is not the only compiler for the Raspberry Pi or that you can use as a cross-compiler; there are many more available. The forums on the Raspberry Pi website are a good source of such information, and I would suggest that you look around on the web for yourself if this is of interest.

The Raspberry Pi ARM Chip(s)

The ARM chip used in the Raspberry Pi Zero, A, B, A+, B+ is (to give it its full title) a Broadcom BCM2835 System-on-Chip multimedia processor. The System-on-Chip (SoC) means that it contains just about everything needed to run your Raspberry Pi in the one structure (and is a reason why the Raspberry Pi can be so small). The BCM2835 uses an ARM11 design, which is built around the ARMv6 instruction set.

On the Raspberry Pi 2 the chip used is a SoC, BCM2836. This retains all the features of BCM2835 but replaces the single 700MHz ARM11 with a 900MHz quad-core ARM Cortex-A7: everything else remains the same. Being faster and containing more memory, it can run more mainstream software such as Windows 10 and the full range of ARM GNU/Linux distributions.

The Raspberry Pi 3 has an ARM v8 at its core, again using a SoC structure and operating even faster still at 1.2GHz. This is based on four high-performance ARM Cortex-A53 processing units working in tandem. This is also a 64-bit processor that can operate in both AArch32 and AArch64 states.

The Raspberry Pi 4 uses the Broadcom 2711 and is faster again at 1.5GHz. The ARMv8 is a quad-core A72. This is also a 64-bit processor that can operate in both AArch32 and AArch64 states. The 8GB version allows the memory for the full 64-bit version to run efficiently and handle applications that make it a fully-fledged PC!

There is a lot of jargon in those few paragraphs. Right now, from a beginner's point of view I wouldn't worry about it too much. As you learn more about the Raspberry Pi these things will start to become second nature. We'll come back to the SoC towards the end of this book and explain it in a bit more detail.

By the way, one MegaHertZ (1MHz) represents a million cycles per second. The speed of microprocessors, called the clock speed, often is measured in MHz. For example, a microprocessor that runs at 700MHz executes 700 million cycles per second. 1.2 GHz (GigaHertZ) is 1.2 billion cycles per second. We will see later how this speed affects the execution of instructions.

The term 'quad-core' is used above. A quad-core has four independent units called 'cores' that read and execute instructions simultaneously. Overall, a quad-core processor is going to perform faster than a dual-core or single-core processor. Each program you open can work 'in' its own core, so if the tasks are shared, the speeds are better. This so-called 'parallel-processing' is a major feature of ARM.

3: First Time Out

In this chapter we'll go step-by-step through creating and running a machine code program, starting from the moment you turn your Raspberry Pi on right through to making changes to the working program. This program will not do anything spectacular. In fact, you won't see anything other than the prompt symbol return, but the process contains every single step you need to know and implement when entering and running the other programs in this book.

Right now I am assuming you have a copy of the Raspberry Pi OS (Raspbian) image on the SD Card inserted in your Raspberry Pi and that you have used it at least once, to run through the initial setup of important things like keyboard and internet. If you haven't done that yet, then do so now before carrying on here.

The Command Line

When you first boot you will automatically be logged in and deposited at the Desktop screen. Go to top right and, using your mouse, double click on the small image (icon of a monitor). This will open a 'Terminal' window and you will be deposited at the command line, and the prompt facing you will look a little like this:

```
pi@raspberrypi $
```

The 'command line' is a line onto which you enter commands to be executed by the OS. The command line starts where you see the cursor flashing. Anything you type in now, which is executed when you press the <Return> key (also referred to as the <Enter> key), is expected to be a command, so the OS will seek to action that command. Try tying this:

```
dir
```

Type it exactly as it is above. When you press the <Return> key you will get a list of any directories or files that are stored in the current directory. (I will omit the <Return> key detail from now on but please take it as read that when I suggest entering something at the keyboard-especially the command line, you should finish by pressing the <Return> key.)

Now type:

```
Dir
```

You will get a response like to this:

```
bash: Dir: command not found
```

This is an *error message*. The command line is case sensitive, thus:

```
dir
```

and:

```
Dir
```

are not identical in OS eyes which are case sensitive. This is also the case with program file names so:

```
program1
```

and:

```
Program1
```

are *not* the same.

Command line convention is always to work in lowercase characters. Commands are case sensitive. File names may have a mixed bag of character cases as long as you are aware of the difference. It's best always to use lowercase characters so as a matter of course you should ensure that the Caps Lock light is always off.

Creating A Source File

To create a machine code program, we need to go through a 'write-assemble-link' process before we can end up with a file that can be executed. The first step is to write the assembly language program. Because this is the source from which everything flows, this file is called the sources file. It is also signified by having an '.s' appended to its name. For example:

```
program1.s
```

The source files can be created in any suitable text editor. There are plenty of excellent ones around to be had at no cost, so it is worth spending time reading reviews and checking the options out for yourself. You may already have one that you like regardless, so the choice may already be made.

Equally Raspberry Pi OS comes with a selection of editors already installed as part of 'Recommended Software' and you can locate these on the main Application menu (the Raspberry on the menu bar of the desktop). They will most likely be in the 'Accessories' drop-down option. This includes (at the time of writing), both VIM and gVIM, and the Geany Programmer's Editor. (I suggest you try each and settle on one that it to your liking.)

If neither VIM or gVIM is installed you can either look to do so via the Recommended Software option, or from a command line by typing:

```
sudo apt-get install vim
```

And then reply to any prompts – one might ask you about adding extra functionality. It should be safe to respond 'Y'. Installation takes a few minutes, and the Vim website has a lot of useful hints and tips.

If you wish to work 'application-style' then you use the GUI version of Vim and install if needed using:

```
sudo apt-get install vim-gtk
```

As you will spend a lot of your programming time developing assembler it makes sense to spend time getting to learn the ins and outs of Vim. Many of the actions and operations used in VIM are performed utilising keypress combinations (especially the Terminal based version). Figure 3a lists some commands you need to know. The table is not exhaustive by any means and you will find a complete set on the Vim website. But this is more than enough to get you started.

When you start Vim, you can also specify the file name you want to create. If the file already exists it will load the file into the editor window, and you can use it as you please. If the file does not exist, then Vim creates a new blank file of that name for you. Open a new Terminal window and at the command line prompt, type:

```
vim prog3a.s
```

Note that there is a space between 'vim' and 'prog3.s' and also note that there is an '.s' at the end of the name 'prog3' to denote a source file. Convention dictates that 's' represents an assembly language source file.

The screen/window will now be largely blank apart from a column of tildes ('~') running down the left-hand edge and the file's name at the bottom – plus words to denote that it is a new file.

Press the 'i' key. Note how the text:

```
-INSERT --
```

has appeared at the bottom left of the screen. This signifies we are in insert mode. Press the <Esc> key. The '-INSERT--' has disappeared. We are now in Vim command mode.

Pressing 'i' and 'Esc' will become second nature to you. When insert mode is enabled it's a simple matter to key in the assembly language program and edit until your heart's content. In command mode, key presses are interpreted as direct commands to Vim, giving it commands to perform.

Cursor Movement Commands
Letter Action
   ←   move left
   ↓   move down
   ↑   move up
   →   move right
   w   jump by to start of words
   W   jump by words (spaces separate words)
   e   jump to end of words
   E   jump to end of words (no punctuation)
   b   jump backward by words
   B   jump backward by words (no punctuation)
   0   (zero) start of line
   ^   first non-blank character of line
   $ end of line
   G   Go To command (ie, 5G goes to line 5)
Note: Prefix a cursor movement command with a number to repeat it. For example, 4j moves down 4 lines.

Insert Mode - Inserting/Appending text
Letter Action
   i   start insert mode at cursor
   I   insert at the beginning of the line
   A   append after the cursor
   a   append at the end of the line
   o   open (append) blank line below current line (no need to press return)
   O   open blank line above current line
   Esc   exit insert mode

Command mode
Letter Action
   :w   write (save) file but do no exit
   :wq   write file (save) and quit Vim
   :Q   quit (fails if anything has changed)
   :Q!   quit and lose any changes made
   :set   number - use line numbering

Figure 3a: Important Vim commands.

The filename for this program, here 'prog3a.s', is not particularly special. I name all the programs in this book by chapter name. So prog3a.s signifies that the program source file is from Chapter 3 in the book. The 'a' would suggest it is also the first in the chapter. A file called 'prog4b.s' would signify the program is from Chapter 4 and listed as Program 4b and it is the second one in the chapter. This is just for your ease of reference. You can use whatever name you want.

Move back into insert mode (i) and note the flashing cursor at the top left of the screen. Anything you type now will appear where the cursor is. Enter the listing given below in Program 3a. You only have to enter the text below that is between the two lines. (A complete list of programs presented in this book can be found at the end of the Contents list.)

Program 3a. A simple source file.

```
        .global    _start
_start:
        MOV R0, #65
        MOV R7, #1
        SWI 0
```

Note that of the five lines of the program, the first and third, fourth and fifth lines are indented. Only the second begins at the start of the line. The amount of indent you add, or even where you place indents doesn't really matter; they are simply to make it easier to read the program and see where the different layers of the program are.

You can create the indent by pressing the <Tab> key. Other keys behave as you would expect them to, such as arrow keys to move around and the <Delete> and <Backspace> keys to move and edit text. However, there is a space between the words 'global' and '_start' and this space is important. We'll look at what the listing all means shortly.

Press <Esc> and then type:

```
:wq
```

This will save your file and in turn also quit Vim. You will now be back at the command prompt. The source file is now complete!

Come to the Execution

The next step is to convert the source file into an executable file of machine code. We do this with two commands entered at the command line. Enter the following two lines, one after the other, at the command line prompt:

```
as -o prog3a.o prog3a.s
ld -o prog3a prog3a.o
```

These two lines first assemble and then link the assembly language program (linking is discussed shortly). On completion the machine code can be executed and the syntax for this is:

```
./<filename>
```

The './' means 'run' and the file to be run is named immediately after the command – no spaces. Thus:

```
./prog3a
```

When the prompt reappears, the machine code program has completed. Easy as that!

So, we have just written, compiled (assembled and linked) and executed a machine code program – all the basic steps needed were involved in the process above. Of course, as the programs get more complex and we seek to make more use of the tools available then the process will itself become more involved, as we shall see.

Assembler Errors

If at any time during the above process you receive an error message – or any message at all, then look carefully at what you have typed. First look carefully at the assembly language program and then the individual lines of code to assembly, link and finally run the program. If there was an error and you found it, congratulations, you have just debugged your first assembly language program.

If you get an error message from the assembler (this will be after you have pressed <Return> at the end of the first line) it will normally provide you with a line number as a guide. Even if you do not know what the message means note the line number and then reload the source file back into Vim. For example:

```
prog3a.s:5: Error bad expression
```

would indicate there is an error in line 5 of the source file.

With a small file such as this you can count down the lines and locate the one containing the error. Vim also has a line numbering ability. When in Vim command mode type:

```
:set number
```

And notice how line numbers appear down the left of the window. These line numbers do not get saved as part of your source file – they are here as a guide only. Figure 3b shows all this in action using gVim. This shows the line numbers, and that Vim is operating in Insert mode. If you use gVim you will also notice how the various items of syntax are highlighted by different colours. This makes it easy to identify the different components of the listing which are described shortly.

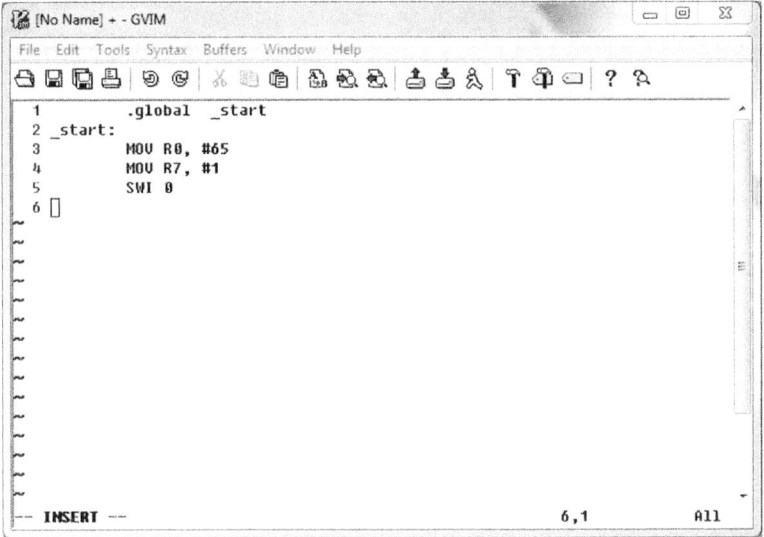

Figure 3b. How line numbers appear in Vim.

You can run gVim from the command line using:

`gvim <filename>`

So, to create or edit Prog3a you might use:

`gvim prog3a.s`

The Components

Let's now look at the above process and understand a bit more the anatomy of the source file and what we did to make it all come together. Look at prog3a.s again. It consists of just five lines.

Each assembler source files point file must have a starting point, and by default in the GCC assembler this is the label:

`_start:`

The first line of this program defines '_start' as a global name and available to the whole program. We'll see later why making it a global name is important. The second line defines where '_start:' is in the program. Note the use of the ':' at the end to define it as a 'label'. We've defined _start as global and now marked where _start is.

The next three lines are assembly language mnemonics, and two of the lines are similar, and use the MOV instruction. When the hash symbol is used in assembly language it is used to denote an immediate value. In other words, the value after the hash is the value to be used. In the first case, the value 65 is to be moved in Register 0. Here 'R' stands for register, which is a special location

41

in the ARM chip, more on which shortly. In the second line, the value 1 is moved into R7 or Register 7.

The final instruction is SWI 0. This is a special instruction that is used to call the Raspberry Pi Operating System itself. In this instance it is being used to exit the machine code program and return control back to the command line prompt (when the program is run of course).

Just a note on the character case used for the assembly language commands in these source files. I am using uppercase letters for mnemonics and registers, I could have just as easily used lower case – inside the source files the character case does not matter, thus:

```
MOV R0, #65
```

and:

```
mov r0, #65
```

are seen as being one and the same thing (note this is different from the Terminal command line which is case-sensitive). I will be using uppercase characters during this book. This makes the commands easier to identify in the text of the book, and makes the commands stand out from labels – which I will continue to place in lower case.

Run the program again:

```
./prog3a
```

At the prompt type:

```
echo $?
```

The following will be printed on the screen:

```
65
```

This was the immediate value loaded into R0. Try editing the 65 to another number, say 49. Now save, reassemble and re-link and run. If you now type:

```
echo $?
```

49 should be printed. The operating system has a limited way of returning information from machine code programs and we'll look at this later.

If you look at prog3a.s again you can see that it consists of two clear sections. At the top (start), are some definitions, and in the lower half, the actual assembly language instructions. Assembly language source files always consist of a sequence of statements, one per line. Each statement has the following format, each part of which is optional:

```
<label:>   <instruction>     @ comment
```

All three of these components can be entered on the same line, or they can be split across lines. It's up to you. However, they must be in the order shown. For example, an instruction cannot come before a label (on the same line).

The 'comment' component is new. When the assembler encounters the '@' it ignores everything after it until the end of the line. This means you can use it to annotate your program. For example, go back and edit prog3a.s by typing:

```
vim prog3a.s
```

The editor window will display your original source file. The cursor will be at the top of the file. Enter insert mode, create a new line, and enter the following:

```
@ prog3a.s - a simple assembler file
```

The comment line, marked by the '@' at the start, is totally ignored by the compiler. Of course, it does make the source file bigger, but this does not affect the executable's performance in any way.

You can also add comments using '/*' and '*/' to enclose the comment at the start and end respectively. For example:

```
/* This comment will be ignored by the assembler */
```

Both methods are acceptable, and it is simply a matter of taste — whichever you prefer.

To convert the source file into an executable file we needed two steps. The first was:

```
as -o prog3a.o prog3a.s
```

The 'as' at the start invokes the assembler program itself which expects several arguments after the command to define the files it will be working with and what it will be doing with them. The first of these is 'o' and this tells the assembler that we want to produce an object file, here called 'prog3a.o' from the source file 'prog3a.s' You can choose another name if you wish; the body of the name does not have to be the same, although keeping it the same makes it easier to keep track of your files. Of course, the suffix is not the same!

The second and final step is to 'link' the file object file and convert it into an executable file using the 'ld' command as follows:

```
ld -o prog3a prog3a.o
```

You can think of linking as the final bit of binding that makes the machine code work. What it produces is an executable file (called an elf file) from the .o (object) file created in the assembly process. It is this ld command that uses the _start: label to define where the program is to be run from. (This may sound crazy, but sometimes the start point of a file may not be at the very front of it, as we shall see!)

Lack of _start

You can learn a lot about the workings of the GCC assembler and linker simply by experimenting. What do you think would happen if we omitted the _start: label from the source file?

Open the prog3a.s file in Vim and delete the line '_start:' thereby erasing the label. Exit Vim and then assemble the program:

```
as -o prog3a.o prog3a.s
```

and now link the program:

```
ld -o prog3a prog3a.o
```

The following error message (or similar) will be produced:

```
ld: warning: cannot find entry symbol _start; defaulting
to 00008054
```

The error message is clear enough. Because it can't find a pointer to where the program starts, the linker is assuming that the program start point is right at the beginning, and the location of this in memory is at the address 00008054. (This address can and probably will vary depending on the individual Raspberry Pi.)

This is a safety net, but not a fail-safe. Always use '_start:' in your files to define the start of execution. This program will run perfectly well — others might not and probably won't!

Linking Files

The letters 'ld' stand for 'link dynamic' and the linking command can combine or daisy-chaining several files together into one long executable program. In such cases only one '_start:' label should be defined across all these files, as there should be only the one start point, and this defines it. This is easy to demonstrate using our sample program.

Create a new file in Vim and call it:

```
part1.s
```

In this file enter the listing shown below as Program 3b:

Program 3b. Part 1 of the source file.

```
/* part1.s file            */
        .global _start

_start:
        MOV R0, #65
        BAL _part2
```

Save the file. Now create a new file called:

```
part2.s
```

and it should contain these lines in the listing below as Program 3c:

Program 3c. Part 2 of the source file.

```
/* part2.s file                 */

        .global _part2
_part2:
        MOV R7, #1
        SWI 0
```

Save and exit this. We have written two source files that we will now compile and link to create a single executable file. At the end of the part1.s we added a new instruction:

```
BAL _part2
```

BAL means branch always, and here branch always to the point in the program marked with the label 'part2:' In the second file we have defined a global variable called 'part2' and marked the point where part2 begins. Because we have used the global labels definition, the location of the address made known by the global definition will be available to all the program parts.

The next step is to compile both new source files:

```
as -o part1.o part1.s
as -o part2.o part2.s
```

Now the labels must be identified and linked using the linker thus:

```
ld -o allparts part1.o part2.o
```

Here the linker will create an executable file called 'allparts' from the files 'part1.o' and 'part2.o'. (You can use a different name for the executable file.) Try running the file with:

```
./allparts
```

The order of 'part1.o' and 'part2.o' could have been swapped — it would not have mattered as the linker resolves such issues. The key here is that each source file is independently written, created but then joined (we might say tethered) together by linking. If you tried to link just one file on its own, you would get an error message because when linking each part references the other. So, in this case the linker is also a safety check.

What this small demonstration shows is that if you start to think carefully about your source files, you can start to develop a library of files that you can dip into each time you need a particular function. If you think back to the last chapter and the concept of a pseudo-program, this could be created using such functions. We'll look at function creation later.

Tidying Up

If you catalogue the root (raspberrypi) directory by typing:

```
dir
```

you will see that amongst other things there are three prog3 files as follows:

```
prog3a.s            the source file
prog3a.o            the object file
prog3a              the executable file
```

(I have added in the description for each file on the right.)

Ultimately you only need the source file as you can create your executable file from this at any time. At the very least you can get rid of the object file using the rm command (rm = remove files):

```
rm prog3a.o
```

To keep things tidy it is worth creating a separate directory for all your assembler files, and you can do this using the 'mkdir' command. To create a directory called aal (arm assembly language) use:

```
mkdir aal
```

Now you can make that directory listing your current directory by typing:

```
cd aal
```

Notice that the command line prompt has been extended to include:

```
/aal $
```

Anything you now create or do will be done so in the aal directory. To move back up to the Raspberry Pi root directory type:

```
cd
```

Note how the prompt on the command line always reflects where you currently 'are' within the hierarchy of the Raspberry Pi filing system.

If when you are looking to load or assemble a file and you get an error message. Check that you are 'in' the correct directory, and the file name is spelt correctly (including use of capital letters). Often that's the issue!

A Comment on Comments

Not everyone will agree, but I think it is imperative you comment your assembly language programs. What you write today will be fresh in your mind, but if you need to upgrade or adapt it later you will almost certainly be struggling to remember exactly what each segment does, and another programmer looking at or trying to improve your work will be completely at sea. To my mind commenting — that is good commenting — is an essential part of writing assembly language programs. All assemblers allow you to place comments in your source file. Comments do not make the final machine code file any longer or any slower in execution. The only overhead is that they affect the size of your source program.

So, comments are a good thing but don't comment for comment's sake. If every line of your assembly language program had a comment it would become ungainly and would detract from the important comments. For example, look at this simple line and comment relative to the ADD instruction:

```
ADD R0, R1, R2          @   R0=R1+R2
```

The comment here is pointless from a program documentation perspective, as we already know — or we should know — from the program line itself what the operation does. What would be relevant here is detailing the significance of the values stored at locations R1 and R2. This might be a better comment then:

```
ADD R0, R1, R2          @ Balance of act1 + act2
```

If you break your assembly program into segments using the format shown in the previous chapter, then for a lot of the time a pertinent comment or two at the start of the section is often also enough. Some things to keep in mind as guidelines:

- Comment all key points in your program.
- Use plain English; don't invent shorthand that someone, (including you) may not understand later.
- If it is worth commenting, then comment properly.
- Make comments neat, readable, and consistent.
- Comment all definitions

If you keep these key points in mind you shouldn't go wrong, and I mention them at the start so you'll hopefully take the point and get into good habits that will last a programming lifetime.

If you are planning to write a lot of machine code, you might want to consider documenting your files externally, creating a database or perhaps a workbook where you keep their details.

Also, beware the multi-file syndrome. As you develop your files you may several versions of them during development., And at the end not be sure which one is which. You can end up with a menagerie of similarly named files. Add a comment at the very start noting why you have moved on from that file. Move the ones you think you don't need into a holding folder. When you have the one you want then add a comment it as such and name it as such.

Geany Programmer's Editor

I mentioned earlier in the chapter that there was a third option when it came to software for creating your source files on the Raspberry Pi Desktop. In the later versions of the Desktop the Raspberry Menu includes a 'Programming' sub menu and in here you are likely to find the 'Geany Programmer's Editor'.

Geany is an IDE or 'integrated development environment' and provides a variety of formatting options for various projects and languages. It also uses tabs which allows you to have multiple source files open. It also provides line numbers automatically.

If you remember to save your file as a text files with a '.s' extension this is a great alternative option. That said it is good to understand how some of the traditional text editors work in the first instance.

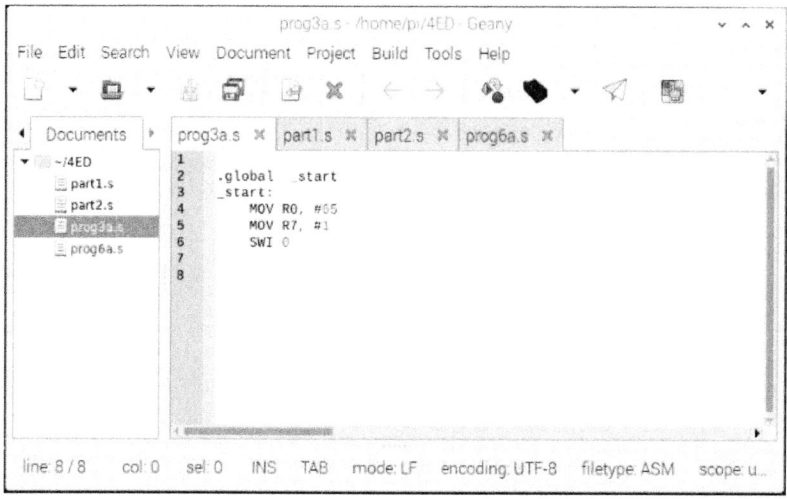

Figure 3c. Geany IDE look and feel.

Figure 3c also shows that line numbering is automatic, and a plethora of additional information is provided around the perimeter of the Geany window.

4: Bits of a RISC Machine

There are 10 types of people in the world — those that understand binary notation and those that don't.

If that statement leaves you confused, don't worry. After reading this section of the book you'll 'get' the joke. If you have already had a smile at it then you're well on your way to racing through this section. What I will say at the onset though is that a thorough understanding of the way binary notation is presented and how it can be manipulated is fundamental to effective, efficient machine code programming.

When you create machine code programs you are working at the most basic level of the computer. There is nothing below it. In the opening chapters we touched on binary and hexadecimal numbers. Hex numbers are a compact way of writing numbers which in binary would be long strings of 1s and 0s. Because of its design as a reduced instruction set computer, the Raspberry Pi can do many different things using a base set of instructions and does so by getting the absolute maximum meaning out of every single one of these 1s and 0s. To understand fully how a RISC machine works we need to understand how binary and hex are constructed and how they are utilised by the ARM chip.

To recap from the opening chapters: The instructions the ARM CPU operates with consist of sequences of numbers. Each number represents either an instruction (opcode) or data (operand) for the machine code to execute or manipulate. Internally these numbers are represented as binary numbers. A binary number is simply a number constructed of 1s or 0s. Binary is important as internally these 1s and 0s are represented as 'on' or 'off' conditions (electronically usually +5V or 0V) within the microprocessor, and as an assembly language programmer we will often want to know the condition of individual binary digits or bits.

Opcodes and operands are built by combining sets of eight bits, which are collectively termed a byte. Convention dictates the bits in these bytes are numbered as illustrated in Figure 4a.

| 7 | 6 | 5 | 4 | 3 | 2 | 1 | 0 |

Figure 4a. Numbering of the bits in a byte.

The number of the bit increases from right to left, (not left to right) but this is not as odd as it may first seem.

Consider the decimal number 2934, we read this as two thousand, nine hundred and thirty-four. The highest numerical value, two thousand is on the left, while the lowest, four, is on the right. We can see from this that the position of the digit in the number is especially important as it will affect its 'weight'.

The second row of Figure 4b introduces a new numerical representation. Each base value is suffixed with a small number or power, which corresponds to its overall position in the number. Thus, 103 is 10 x 10 x 10 = 1000. The number in our example consists of two thousands plus nine hundreds plus three tens and four units.

Value	1000s	100s	10s	1s
Representation	10^3	10^2	10^1	10^0
Digit	2	9	3	4

Figure 4b. Decimal weights of ordinary numbers.

In binary representation, the weight of each bit is calculated by raising the base value, two, to the bit position (see table below). For example, bit number 7 (b7) has a notional representation of 2^7 which expands to: 2 x 2 x 2 x 2 x 2 x 2 x 2= 128. The *weight* or *value* of each bit is shown in Figure 4c.

Bit Number	b7	b6	b5	b4	b3	b2	b1	b0
Representation	2^7	2^6	2^5	2^4	2^3	2^2	2^1	2^0
Weight	128	64	32	16	8	4	2	1

Figure 4c. The binary weights of numbers.

Binary to Decimal

As it is possible to calculate the weight of individual bits, it is a simple matter to convert binary to decimal numbers into decimal. The two rules for conversion are:
1. If the bit is set ('1'), add its weight
2. If the bit is clear ('0'), ignore its weight

Raspberry Pi OS Assembly Language

Let's try an example and convert the binary number 10101010 into its equivalent decimal value.

Bit	Weight	Value
1	128	128
0	64	0
1	32	32
0	16	0
1	8	8
0	4	0
1	2	2
0	1	0

Figure 4d. Converting binary numbers to decimal numbers.

In Figure 4d, we add the value column to get 170. Therefore, 10101010 binary is 170 decimal (128+0+32+0+8+0+2+0). Similarly, the binary value 11101110 represents 238 in decimal as shown in Figure 4e.

Bit	Weight	Value
1	128	128
1	64	64
1	32	32
0	16	0
1	8	8
1	4	4
1	2	2
0	1	0

Figure 4e. Converting binary numbers to decimal numbers.

Decimal to Binary

To convert a decimal number into a binary number, the procedure is reversed — each binary weight is, in turn, subtracted. If the subtraction is possible, a 1 is placed into the binary column, and the remainder carried down to the next row. If the subtraction is not possible, a 0 is placed in the binary column, and the number moved down to the next row. For example, the decimal number 141 is converted into binary as shown in Figure 4f.

51

Decimal	Weight	Remainder	Binary
141	128	13	1
13	64	13	0
13	32	13	0
13	16	13	0
13	8	5	1
5	4	1	1
1	2	1	0
1	1	0	1

Figure 4f. Converting a decimal number to its binary equivalent.

Therefore, 141 decimal is 10001101 binary.

Binary to Hex

Although binary notation is probably as close as we can come to representing the way numbers are stored within the Raspberry Pi, they are rather unwieldy to deal with. And row after row of 1s and 0s simply get lost as your eyes start to rebel and make funny patterns. When dealing with binary numbers we more commonly use an alternative form to represent them – hexadecimal or 'hex' for short. Hexadecimal numbers are numbers to the base of 16. This is not as awkward as first seems and presents many advantages.

Decimal	Hex	Binary
0	0	0000
1	1	0001
2	2	0010
3	3	0011
4	4	0100
5	5	0101
6	6	0110
7	7	0111
8	8	1000
9	9	1001
10	A	1010
11	B	1011
12	C	1100
13	D	1101
14	E	1110
15	F	1111

Figure 4g. Decimal, hexadecimal and binary numbers.

Base 16 requires sixteen different characters to represent all possible digits in a hex number. To produce them, the numbers 0 to 9 are retained and then we use the letters A, B, C, D, E, F to represent values from ten to 15. The binary and decimal values for each hex number are shown in Figure 4g. If you have followed the previous section on binary numbers something interesting may stand out when you look at Figure 4g.

Notice how four bits of a binary number can be represented in one hex number. Thus, a full byte (8 binary bits) can be depicted with just two hex characters. Using decimal notation, a byte would require three characters. Hex is a very compact and easy way of representing binary.

To convert a binary number into hex, the byte must be separated into two sets of four bits, termed nibbles, and the corresponding hex value of each nibble extracted from the table above:

Convert 01101001 to hex:

```
0110 = 6
1001 = 9
```

The answer is 69. Because it is not always apparent whether a number is hex or decimal (69 could be decimal), hex numbers are usually preceded by a unique symbol such as 0x (which is the notation used in this book):

```
0x69
```

By reversing the process hex numbers can be converted into binary.

Hex to Decimal and Back

To transform a hex number into decimal, the decimal weight of each digit should be summed. Convert 0x31A to decimal:

3 has a value of $3 \times 16^2 = 3 \times 16 \times 16 = 768$

1 has a value of $1 \times 16^1 = 1 \times 16 \quad = 16$

A has a value of $1 \times 16^0 = 10 \times 1 \quad = 10$

Add these together to give 794 decimal.

Converting decimal to hex is a bit more involved and requires the number to be repeatedly divided by 16 until a value less than 16 is obtained. This hex value is noted, and the remainder carried forward for further division. This process is continued until the remainder itself is less than 16.

Example: convert 4072 to hex:

4072/16/16 =15	= F	Remainder: 4072-(15*16*16)=232
232/16	=14 = E	Remainder: 232-(14*16)=8
Remainder =8	= 8	

Therefore, 4072 decimal is 0xFE8.

Both conversions are a little long winded, and you can probably see why it is so much easier to work in hex and forget about decimal equivalents. In truth, this is what you will get used to doing. Although it may seem alien at present, it will become second nature as you develop your assembly language expertise. (Besides, if you want to convert hex to decimal, you can use the Pi!)

Binary Addition

It is easy to add and subtract binary numbers. In fact if you can count to two you will have no problems whatsoever. Although it is not vital to be able to add and subtract 1s and 0s 'by hand', this chapter introduces several concepts which are important, and will help you in your understanding of the next chapters and ultimately in programming the ARM.

There are just four simple straightforward rules when it comes to adding binary numbers. They are:

    0+0=0   [nought plus nought equals nought]
    1+0=1   [one plus nought equals one]
    0+1=1   [nought plus one equals one]
    1+1=0(1)   [one plus one equals nought, carry one]

Note in the last rule, one plus one equals nought, carry one. The '1' in brackets is called a *carry bit*, and its function is to denote an overflow from one column to another, remember, 10 binary is 2 decimal (and thus the opening line of the Chapter!). The binary carry bit is like the carry that may occur when adding two decimal numbers together whose result is greater than 9. For example, adding together 9+1 we obtain a result of 10 (ten), this was obtained by placing a zero in the unit column and carrying the 'overflow' across to the next column to give: 9+1=10. Similarly, in binary addition when the result is greater than 1, we take the carry bit across to add to the next column (the twos column). Let's try to apply these principles to add the two 4-bit binary numbers, 0101 and 0100.

            0101   0x5
    +   0100   0x4
    =   1001   0x9

Going from right to left we have:

    1+0   =1
    0+0   =0
    1+1   =0(1)
    0+0+(1)   =1

In the example, a carry bit was generated in the third column, and this is carried to the fourth column where it is added to two noughts. Adding 8-bit numbers is accomplished in a similar manner:

```
        01010101              0x55
  +     01110010              0x72
  =     11000111              0xC7
```

If the eighth bit, also called the *most significant bit,* creates a carry then this can be carried over into a second byte. However, within the CPU of most chips there is another way to handle this using something called a *Carry flag.*

Subtraction

So far, we have dealt exclusively with positive numbers, however, in the subtraction of binary numbers we need to be able to represent negative numbers as well. In binary subtraction though, a slightly different technique from everyday subtraction is used, in fact we don't really perform a subtraction at all – we add the negative value of the number to be subtracted. For example, instead of executing 4-3 (four minus three) we execute 4 + (-3) (four, plus minus three).

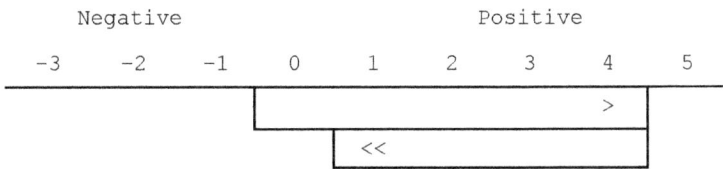

Figure 4h. Subtracting numbers.

We can use the scale in Figure 4h to perform the example 4+(-3). The starting point is zero. First move to point 4 (four points in a positive direction) signified by the '>' and add to this -3 (move three points in a negative direction). We are now positioned at point 1 which is indicated by '<<'. Try using this method to subtract 8 from 12, to get the principle clear in your mind.

To do this in binary we must first have a way of representing a negative number. We use a system known as signed binary. In signed binary, bit 7 is used to denote the sign of the number. Traditionally a '0' in bit 7 denotes a positive number and a '1' a negative number.

Sign Bit	Bits 0-6 give value						
1	0	0	0	0	0	0	1

Figure 4i. Signed binary representation of -1

Figure 4i shows how a signed binary number is constructed. Here, bits 0-6 give the value, in this case '1'. The sign bit is set so denoting a negative value, so the value represented in signed binary is -1.

Sign Bit	Bits 0-6 give value
0	1	1	1	1	1	1	1

Figure 4j. Signed binary representation of 127.

The value 01111111 would represent 127 in signed binary. Bits 0-6 give 127, and the sign bit is clear. This is illustrated in Figure 4j.

Twos Complement Numbers

Just adjusting the value of bit 7 in this way is not an accurate way of representing negative numbers. Adding -1+1 should equal 0, but ordinary addition gives the result of 2 or -2 unless the operation takes special notice of the sign bit and performs a subtraction instead. Twos complement representation provides a means to encode negative numbers in ordinary binary, such that addition still works, without having to take the additional sign adjusting step.

To convert a number into its negative counterpart, we must obtain its twos complement value. This is done by inverting each bit and then adding one. To represent -3 in binary, first write the binary for 3:

```
00000011
```

Now invert each bit by flipping its value so that 0s become 1s and 1s become 0s. This is known as its **ones complement** value:

```
11111100
```

Now add 1:

```
  11111100
+ 00000001
= 11111101
```

Thus, the twos complement value of 3 = 1111101. Now apply this to the original sum 4+(-3):

```
      00000100    4
      11111101   -3
= (1) 00000001    1
```

We can see that the result is 1 as we would expect, but we have also generated a carry due to an overflow from bit 7 (this is the value in brackets above). This carry bit can be ignored for our purposes at present, though it does have a certain importance as we shall see later when performing subtraction in assembly language.

Here's another example that performs 32-16, or: 32+(-16).

32 in binary is:
> `00100000`

16 in binary is:
> `00010000`

The twos complement of 16 is:
> `11110000`

Now add 32 and -16 together:

```
      00100000    32
  +   11110000   -16
= (1) 00010000    16
```

Ignoring the carry, we have the result, 16.

We can see from these examples that, using the rules of binary addition, it is possible to add or subtract signed numbers. If the carry is ignored, the result including the sign is correct. Thus, it is also possible to add two negative values together and still obtain a correct (negative) result. Using twos complement signed binary let's perform -2+-2

2 in binary is:
> `00000010`

The twos complement value of 2 is:
> `11111110`

We can add this value twice to perform the addition:

```
      11111110    -2
  +   11111110    -2
= (1) 11111100    -4
```

Ignoring the carry, the result is -4. You might like to confirm this by obtaining the twos complement value of -4 in the usual manner.

Understanding twos complement isn't strictly necessary for most applications, but it can come in handy as you can discover the value of every bit in a number whether it is positive or negative.

When Twos Don't Add Up

There are a couple of occasions when twos complement doesn't add up and interestingly, they are based around representing 0 and -0.

The first is when dealing with 0 (zero). Working with 8-bits for simplicity, the twos complement of 00000000 is 10000000. When you drop the most significant bit, you get 00000000, which is what you started with. This works as it means that you can't really have -0 and that you can only have one value of 0 in twos complement.

The second situation arises with 10000000 because it can have no negative value. The inverse of 10000000 is 01111111, and now add one to obtain its twos complement and you get 10000000, which is what you started with.

Because the most significant bit in 10000000 is 1, the value is negative. When you invert it and add 1, you get 10000000 which is the binary representation of 128 so the original value must, therefore represent -128.

This anomaly is the reason why integer and long value variables in many forms of BASIC are asymmetrical. In 8-bits, the values range from -128 to +127 and in 32-bits (four-bytes) values range from -2,147,483,648 to +2,147,483,647.

Desktop Calculator

Depending on the Desktop settings you have when you installed your Raspberry Pi Operating System on your Pi, you should find that the Accessories menu has a 'Calculator' included. This will run on the desktop and can be used to do many of the number exercises that we have discussed, and other operations that we will cover during the course of the book, when used in Scientific mode. I'll leave you to explore those possibilities. Converting numbers between bases such as binary, hex and decimal is certainly possible along with other number bases such as Octal (8).

5: ARM Arrangements

The ARM has a specific and special design. This is known as its architecture because it refers to how it is constructed and how it looks from the user's point of view. Understanding this architecture is an important aspect of learning to program the chip. You need to appreciate how it all fits together and how the various elements interact. In fact, the purpose of much of the machine code we will be creating is to gain access and manipulate the various parts in the ARM itself.

Because of its design as a reduced instruction set computer it can do many different things using a small set of instructions. The way it operates is determined by the mode. This means that once you have understood the basic layout of the ARM chip you only then have to understand what its different operational modes are. That said, for almost all situations that you encounter when learning to program the ARM you will be operating in User Mode.

Word Lengths

In the binary examples we looked at in the previous chapters we have used single byte values. Indeed, all the early popular computers worked at this level with machine code. The design of these circuit boards reflected this in that they had the eight data lines. In broad terms, these lines were directly related to the bits in the CPU byte. Thus, the CPU could move data around the board by toggling the logical condition on each line by making it a 1 or 0. It did this by changing the voltage on the line between 5V and 0V.

An ARM chip is more sophisticated and can operate much faster by manipulating larger amounts of information. It does this by being designed as a 32-bit or 64-bit CPU. In the case of 32-bit this equates to four-bytes of information. So instead of manipulating eight lines of information there are 32 lines. Collectively these four-bytes are called a word. The ARM word length is said to be four-bytes. However, it is more than capable of working with single byte lengths, and it does this just as effectively. Keep in mind that other computer systems may define their word length as something different, but on the Raspberry Pi a word is four-bytes or 32-bits in length.

The most significant bit (msb) in an ARM word is located at bit 31 (b31), and the carry bit in an operation is generated if there is an overflow out of bit 31. If a carry occurred from bit 7 it would be carried into bit 8, or from the first byte in the second byte.

Byte and Word Accessed Memory

As a computer or smart phone user you will be familiar the role that memory plays in operation. The more you have the more you can store. Each memory address has a unique location. Generally, as the number of bits increases then so does the amount of memory that can be directly addressed. The early ARM chips only used 26-bits of the 32-bits for addressing memory. This placed certain restrictions on the processor – and of course, the amount of memory it could directly address – so later ARM chips had full 32-bit addressing. The lowest address in this range is accessed by placing 0s on all the lines, and the highest by placing 1s on all the lines. The first is addressed as 0x0000 and the highest as 0xFFFFFFFF (or 0x3FFFFFF on old pre-Raspberry Pi 26-bit address bus ARMs).

Memory control devices for the ARM allowed for 32-bit addressing. Figure 5a illustrates schematically how this memory is arranged as word length blocks composed of four-bytes a piece, so the minimum and maximum memory addresses are extended to 0x00000000 and 0xFFFFFFFF – this is the case on the Pi.

	bit31			bit 00
(Word 0)	b03	b02	b01	b00
(Word 1)	b07	b06	b05	b04
(Word 2)	b0B	b0A	b09	b08
(Word 3)	b0F	b0E	b0D	b0C

Figure 5a. Memory word blocks on the ARM.

The ARM 'sees' memory in these word blocks but can also address the individual bytes within each word. From an operation point of view, all memory is arranged as word-aligned blocks. As illustrated in Figure 5a above the word-aligned blocks corresponded with Word 00, Word 01, Word 02, and Word 03. Note how Word 00 has the byte numbers b00, b01, b02 and b03 within it. Word 01 has bytes b04, b05, b06 and b07 in it, and so on. Word blocks are aligned in this fashion and cannot be changed. You cannot have a word-aligned block that consists of the bytes, b02, b03, b04 and b05. (Note that 'b' here relates to byte and not bit, as used in some previous examples.)

ARM saw the need 64-bit processors and started working new designs long before announcing its new ARMv8 architecture, the first ARM architecture to include a 64-bit instruction set. ARM also learnt from the mistakes and successes of other chip designers who moved to 64-bits. ARM's new 64-bit architecture is fully compatible with its 32-bit architecture. This means that if the processor is running on a 64-bit enabled operating system, the processor can run unmodified ARMv7 32-bit code (or binaries).

The Raspberry Pi 2B v1.2 was the first of the series to have ARMv8 architecture and this was carried into the Raspberry Pi 3 and 4. Both operate in 32-bit mode but can be run in 64-bit mode. But this is getting ahead of ourselves and we will return to it later in the book, and for the most part now you will notice no difference.

Locations in memory are addressed by a unique hexadecimal number. A memory address that corresponds to the start of a word is called a word boundary and is said to be 'word-aligned'. A memory address is word-aligned if it is directly divisible by four. The following addresses are all word-aligned:

```
0x00009030
0x00009034
0x00009038
0x0000903C
```

Word-aligned addresses are especially significant to the ARM as they are fundamental to the way the ARM chip fetches and executes machine code. For example, the address 0x00009032 is not word-aligned. You cannot store an ARM machine code instruction on a non-word-aligned address.

The GCC assembler provides a few tools to help ensure word boundaries are correctly managed. At the very least trying to assemble something that is not correctly addressed will generate an error message to that effect. For the most part, this is transparent and, as a 'Beginner' it will not raise its head anytime soon.

Registers

The ARM has several internal areas where it stores, tracks and processes information. This speeds things up and makes operations quicker as there is no external memory access required. These internal areas are called registers. In User Mode (the standard operating configuration) there are 16 registers available and each can hold a word (four-bytes) of information. You can think of these registers as single word locations within the ARM. Figure 5b shows how this comes together and includes an extra register – the Status Register.

As you can see from this programmer's model, registers R0-R12 are available for use at any time. R13-R15 have defined uses, however R13 and R14 are only used occasionally and are manipulated by just a few instructions. You as the programmer will be controlling these operations, so can also use them if required. Only R15 should not be used. I don't say cannot because it can be used, but you should be very clear what you are doing with it, and the complications it can bring if you do. ARM instructions can access R0 to R14 directly while most instructions can access R15.

As each register is one word wide, this means that each register can hold an address location in a single register. In other words, a register can hold a number which points to a location anywhere in the memory map of the Raspberry Pi. A key function of registers is to hold such addresses.

The GCC Assembler allows us to use the labels listed above to refer to these registers, for example, R0 and R10.

Register Bank	
R0	Available
R1	Available
R2	Available
R3	Available
R4	Available
R5	Available
R6	Available
R7	Available
R8	Available
R9	Available
R10	Available
R11	Available
R12	Available
R13	Stack Pointer
R14	Link Register
R15	Program Counter
Current Program Status Register	

Figure 5b. The ARM User Mode register bank.

The LDR and STR instructions are used to LoaD a Register and STore a Register from and to memory in a variety of ways. Here are a couple of examples:

```
LDR R1,[R5] @ Load R1 with contents of loc given in R5
STR R1,[R6] @ Store R1 contents at address given in R6
```

In both examples, one register is expected to have a memory address in it. The registers are enclosed in square brackets in these examples, and this tells the assembler that they contain addresses. This type of specification is called an addressing mode and the ARM have several addressing modes. We'll examine these in later chapters.

R15 - Program Counter

The Program Counter R15 is important. If you don't treat it with respect, your whole program can crash. Its function is simple — to keep track of where your program is in its execution of machine code. In fact, the PC holds the address of next instruction to be fetched. We will look at this register in more detail later in the book, Chapter 13 is dedicated to it.

The GCC Assembler allows you to use PC as well as R15 when referring to the Program Counter. For example:

```
MOV PC, R0 @ Move R0 into R15, Program Counter
```

The PC in the instruction will resolve correctly as if you had used R15.

Current Program Status Register

The CPSR— or just plain Status Register — is used to store significant information about the current program and the results of operations it is carrying out and has carried out. Specific bits within the register are used to denote pre-assigned conditions and whether they have occurred or not. So how does the information get flagged inside the one register? It does this by manipulating the values of individual bits within the register. Figure 5c illustrates how this is configured.

31	30	29	28	27...8	7	6	5	4	3	2	1	0
N	Z	C	V		I	F	T	MODE				

Figure 5c. The Status Register configuration.

The four most significant bits hold what are known as flags, called as such as they are designed to flag a certain condition when it happens. These flags are:

N = Negative flag

Z = Zero flag

C = Carry flag

V = Overflow flag

When an instruction executes, if it has been requested to, the ARM updates the Status Register. If the condition under test occurred, then a 1 is placed in the relative flag bit: it is set. If the condition has not occurred, then the flag bit is cleared: a 0 is placed in it.

Bits and Flags

If you followed the previous sections on binary arithmetic, then some of the concepts here will be familiar to you. We have discussed negative numbers, and the Negative flag is used to signify a potential negative number. The Carry flag represents the Carry bit — we discussed this in 8-bit operations, but the addition of 32-bit numbers works the same. The Zero flag is straightforward; it's set if the result is zero. Finally, the Overflow flag is new, but simply sets if the operation caused a carry from bit 30 into the top bit at bit 31. If this occurred using signed numbers, it could indicate a negative result, even if a negative number was not generated. (Remember, bits start numbering at zero so, the 32nd bit is, in fact, numbered bit 31, or b31.)

For example, if the result of an operation gave 0, the Zero flag would be set. This is the Z bit in Figure 5c. If an addition instruction generated a carry bit, then the Carry flag would be set to 1. If a carry were not generated, then the Carry flag would be clear (C=0).

Assembly language has mnemonics that allow us to test these Status Register flags and act based on their condition. Here are a couple of examples:

```
BEQ zeroset          @ jump to zeroset if Z=1
BNE zeroclear        @ jump to zeroclear if Z=0
```

BEQ is Branch if EQual and this instruction will cause a 'jump' to a named label if the Zero flag is set. BNE is Branch if Not Equal and this instruction will cause a jump to the named label if the Zero flag is clear.

There are instructions to test the other flags in a like manner. The BNE instruction is often used to make sections of program repeat or loop a predetermined number of times until a counter decrements to 0 at which point the Zero flag will be set.

In Figure 5c, the I and F bits are called interrupt disable bits and discussed in Chapter 26. The T bit is to do with processor states. At this point we'll assume that it is always set to 0 to signify ARM State (we will come back to this in Chapter 24). The final five bits are used to signify the processor mode — we will be largely using User Mode (but this will be touched on again in Chapter 26 as well).

Interestingly there is no one single instruction that you can use to gain access to the Status Register. You can only manipulate its contents at bit level by carrying out an associated action.

Setting Flags

There are two instructions that have a direct effect on the Status Register flags, they are CMP (CoMPare) and CMN (CoMPare Negative). Of these the first is the more common in use and it takes the form:

```
CMP <Operand1> <Operand2>
```

CMP performs a notational subtraction, taking Operand2 away from Operand1. The physical result of the subtraction is ignored, but it updates the Status Register flags according to the outcome of the subtraction, which will be positive, zero or negative (there can never be a carry). If the result of the subtraction were 0 the Zero flag would be set.

Operand1 is always a register, but Operand2 can be a register or a specific or immediate value. For example:
```
CMP R0, R1    @ Compare R0 with R1. R0 minus R1
CMP R0, #1    @ Compare R0 with 1.  R0 minus 1
```
The CMP instruction is often used in combination with the BEQ instruction, to create a branch or jump to a new part of the program:
```
CMP R0, R1
BEQ zeroflagset
```
Here control will be transferred to the part of the program marked by the label 'zeroflagset' if the comparison between R0 and R1 is zero. If the branch does not take place then it would show that the result of the CMP was not zero – there would be no need to perform a BNE function. The code following could handle that situation.

CMP and CMN are the only instructions that directly affect the condition of the Status Register. By default, the rest of the ARM instruction set does not update the Status Register. For example, if R0 and R1 both contained 1 and we performed:
```
SUB R0, R0, R1
```
The result would be 0. But none of the flags in the Status Register would be altered in any way. They would retain the status they had before the instruction was performed.

S Suffix

However, the ARM does provide a method of allowing an operation such as SUB to update the Status Register. This is done by using the Set suffix. All we do is append an 'S' to the end of the mnemonic we want to use to modify the flags:
```
SUBS R0, R0, R1
```
This subtracts the contents of R1 from R0, leaving the result in R0 and at the same time updating the flags in the Status Register.

This S suffix effectively allows you as the programmer to use one less set of instructions. Without it we might use:
```
SUB R0, R0, R1
CMP R0, #0
BEQ iszero
```
But with it we can remove the CMP line thus:
```
SUBS R0, R0, R1
BEQ iszero
```

The GCC Assembler recognises the use of the S suffix. It is also tolerant of spaces between the instruction and the S, so these two examples will assemble perfectly:

```
SUBS R0, R0, R1
SUB  S R0, R0, R1
```

The Set suffix is one of many that exist, and we'll have a look at more of these in Chapter 9. This example shows one of the many ways the reduced instruction set was developed.

R14: The Link Register

The BEQ and BNE instructions illustrated above are examples of conditional branch instructions. These are absolute in that they offer a definitive change of direction — branch if equal or branch if negative. There is a second style of branch instructions known as Branch and Branch with Link (BL). The BL implements a subroutine operation; effectively it jumps to somewhere else in the program and allows you to come back to the point right after the BL instruction in the program.

When the BL instruction has executed, this return address (the address of the next instruction) is loaded into R14, the Link Register (LR). When the subroutine has completed, the Link Register is copied into the Program Counter, R15, and the program continues operating where it left off before the call was made.

One way of copying the Link Register into the Program Counter would be thus:

```
MOV R15, R14
```

The following is also accepted by the assembler:

```
MOV PC, LR
```

If you are familiar with any form of BASIC, you can think of BEQ and BNE as being the equivalent of GOTO commands and BL as being a GOSUB command.

R13: Stack Pointer

The Stack Pointer contains an address that points to an area of memory which we can use to save information. This area of memory is called the 'stack' and it has some special properties that we will look at in Chapter 17. It is worth noting at this point that there is only one ARM implemented stack, but you can create as many stacks as you like, which must also be manged by you.

6: Data Processing

In this chapter we'll look at some of the data processing instructions. This is the largest group of instructions, 18 in all, which manipulate information. They can be divided further into sub-groups as follows:

ADD, ADC, SUB, SBC, RSB, RSC

MOV, MVN, CMP, CMN

AND, ORR, EOR

BIC, TST, TEQ

MUL, MLA

The AND, ORR, EOR, BIC, TST and TEQ instructions are examined in Chapter 8.

Each of the remaining instructions expect information to be supplied to them in the following configuration:

        <Instruction> <Dest>, <Operand1>, <Operand2>

Let's look at each field in more detail.

<Instruction>
This is the assembly language mnemonic to be assembled. It can be used in its raw form as listed above, or with the additions of suffixes, such as S.

<Dest>
This is the destination where the result is to be stored, and the destination is always an ARM Register, in the range R0-R15.

<Operand 1>
This is the first item of information to be manipulated and, again, will always be an ARM Register in the range R0-R15. Operand1 may be the same as the Destination register.

<Operand 2>
Operand2 has more flexibility than Operand1 in that it can be specified in three different ways. As with Operand1, it may be an ARM Register in the range R0-R15. It may also be a specified value or constant — a number for example. For a constant, the exact number to be used is quoted in the assembler listing. The hash, '#', is used to signify an immediate constant.

Operand2 may also be what is called a shifted operand and we will look at this instance in Chapter 11 when we have looked at the arithmetic shifting of numbers.

Here are some examples of data processing instructions in use:

```
ADD R0, R1, R2          @ R0=R1+R2
ADDS R2, R3, #1         @ R2=R3+1 and set flags
MOV R7, #128            @ R7=128
```

Some instructions do not require both operands. For instance, the MOV instruction does not use Operand1; it only requires Operand2. The reason for Operand2 rather than Operand1 is that it can use a Register definition or a constant value (or shifted, as we shall see).

Addition Instructions

In this section we'll look at the ADD and SUB commands in a little more detail, and we'll also start looking at what is happening in the registers themselves, including the Status Register and its flags.

There are two instructions that handle addition. They are ADD and ADC. The latter is ADd with Carry. They both take a similar form:

```
ADD (<suffix>) <dest>, <Operand1>, <Operand2>
ADC (<suffix>) <dest>, <Operand1>, <Operand2>
```

Here's some code that uses the ADDS instruction. This program clears R0, places 1 in R1 and sets all 32-bits of R2. This is the largest number we can store in a four-byte register. What will happen if we were to run this program?

```
MOV R0, #0
MOV R1, #1
MOV R2, #0xFFFFFFFF
ADDS R0, R1, R2
```

On completion the registers will show:

```
R1:   0x00000001
R2:   0xFFFFFFFF
R0:   0x00000000
```

Nothing seems to have happened! The values have all been loaded, but no addition seems to have taken place as R0 still has 0 in it. In fact, it has, but by adding the 1, we created a carry bit (remember the binary additions we did in the earlier chapters?). So, if we were to look at the Status Register, we would see:

```
NZCV
0110
```

If we had run this program using only ADD and not ADDS then the Carry flag would not have been updated and would merely reflect the condition they were in when they were last updated via an appropriate instruction. Of course, the Carry flag may have been set by a previous instruction, so we might have received a correct answer, but only by good fortune. The good fortune method is not an efficient way to program in any language. It pays to double check.

Program 6a shows how simply two numbers can be added together in machine code. Enter this in Vim or Geany using the filename:

```
prog6a.s
```

Program 6a. Simple 32-bit addition.

```
/* Perform R0=R1+R2          */

        .global  _start
_start:
        MOV R1, #50             @ Get 50 into R1
        MOV R2, #60             @ Get 60 into R2
        ADDS R0, R1, R2         @ Add the two, result in R0

        MOV R7, #1              @ exit through syscall
        SWI 0
```

You can assemble, link, and run this using the following:

```
as -o prog6a.o prog6a.s
ld -o prog6a prog6a.o
./prog6a
```

Now print the result with:

```
echo $?
```

The result will be 110.

(Remember, to be able to print a result from the machine code using bash, we need to ensure that the result is held in R0 and that the operating system exit is used.)

Whenever we add two values, unless we are 100% sure that there will have been no carry, or the significance of that fact is not important to us, a check for the carry should always be made.

Program 6b below adds two 64-bit numbers. This relates to two-words, so two registers are needed to hold the number, with one holding the low four-bytes and the other the high four-bytes. Because we have a potential carry situation from low-word to high-word when we add the two it is imperative, we take the Carry flag into consideration. For this we need to use the ADC instruction.

Raspberry Pi OS Assembly Language

The code assumes that the first number is in R2 and R3 and the second is in R4 and R5. The result is placed in R0 and R1. By convention, the lower register always holds the lower half of the number:

Program 6b. 64-bit addition.

```
/* Add two 64-bit numbers together      */

        .global   _start
_start:

        MOV R2, #0xFFFFFFFF        @ low half number 1
        MOV R3, #0x1               @ hi half number 1
        MOV R4, #0xFFFFFFFF        @ low half number 2
        MOV R5, #0xFF              @ hi half number 2
        ADDS  R0, R2, R4           @ add low and set flags
        ADCS  R1, R3, R5           @ add hi with carry

        MOV R7, #1                 @ exit through syscall
        SWI 0
```

You can assemble, link, and run this using the following:
```
as -o prog6b.o prog6b.s
ld -o prog6b prog6b.o
./prog6b
```

Now print the result with:
```
echo $?
```

The result will be 254. Why?

On completion, registers R0 and R1 will contain 0xFFFFFFFE and 0x101, respectively. The result was therefore:
```
0x101FFFFFFFE
```

In the first ADDS instruction, the addition caused the Carry flag to be set, and this was picked up in the ADCS operation. If we substitute the ADCS with another ADDS the result is:
```
0x100FFFFFFFE
```

In decimal terms the result is starker, out by 4,294,967,296!

You may be wondering why the ADCS instruction was not used in both parts of the addition. Generally, if you set out doing any addition you would want to ensure the Carry flag is clear before starting. If not and you used ADCS and it was set from a previous operation you would get an erroneous result. Use of ADDS ensures that the carry is ignored but gets updated at the end of the addition.

In answer to the question earlier about why the echo command returned 254, this is 0xFE in hex, which is the least significant byte of the value stored in R0. The echo command does not return what is stored in R0 but what is in the least significant byte of R0.

How would you modify this segment to add two three-word values? The temptation might be to repeat the ADDS and ADCS sequence. This would be wrong. You should continue using the ADCS instruction until all the words have been added. You only use ADDS on the first word to define the Carry condition in the first instance. From then on it is ADCS.

If you are writing a program that does not produce the correct result and the values it is returning are wildly out, it is always worth checking that you have used the correct sequence of addition instructions. Chances are that is where the 'bug' sits.

If the three-word numbers were held in R4, R5, R6 and R7, R8, R9 we could sum the result in R1, R2, R3 as follows:

```
ADDS R1, R4, R7 @ Add low-words & check for carry
ADCS R2, R5, R8 @ Add middle words with carry
ADCS R3, R6, R9 @ Add high-words with carry
```

It should go without saying that you need to check to see if the Carry flag is set as it is the most significant bit in your result.

Subtraction

While there are two instructions that deal with addition, there are four for subtraction.

```
SUB (<suffix>) <dest>, <Operand1>, <Operand2>
SBC (<suffix>) <dest>, <Operand1>, <Operand2>
RSB (<suffix>) <dest>, <Operand1>, <Operand2>
RSC (<suffix>) <dest>, <Operand1>, <Operand2>
```

You can see that there are complementary instructions to addition: a straightforward subtraction that ignores the flags and then one that considers the Carry flag (SBC). The second set of subtraction instructions works in an identical fashion but uses the operands in the reverse order. For example:

```
SUB R0, R1, R2
```

subtracts the contents of R2 from R1 and puts the result in R0. However,

```
RSB R0, R1, R2
```

subtracts the contents of R1 from R2 and puts the result in R0. As with the previous examples the S suffix can be used with the instructions:

```
SUBS R0, R1, R2
```

If R0=0, R1=0xFF and R2=0xFE, the SUBS instruction is performing:

0xFF-0xFE

which is:

255-254

The result should be 1, and this is indeed so. However, on investigation the Status Register would show that the Carry flag has been set. Why?

If we change SUBS to RSB so that:

RSBS R0, R1, R2

Then by loading the same values into the registers the result in R0 is 0xFFFFFFFF and the Carry flag is clear! In subtraction, the Carry flag is used the 'wrong' way round so that if a borrow is required the flag is unset or clear. It acts like a NOT Carry flag! This is useful when dealing with numbers over 32-bits and ensures the correct result. The result in this last instance also sets the Negative flag as 0xFFFFFFFF represents a negative value in signed numbers. The above example illustrates this perfectly and is because of the use of twos complement numbers.

When a section of code is not giving you the result you expect it always makes good sense to check the condition of the Status Register flags. They may not behave as you expect.

The two rules here to remember then are:

- If a borrow is generated, then the Carry flag is clear, C=0
- If a borrow is not generated, then the Carry flag is set, C=1

When we perform a multi-word subtraction, borrowing from one word means we need to subtract an extra one from the next word. However, as we have seen, a borrow results in the Carry flag being zero, not one as we would have liked. To compensate for this, the ARM inverts the Carry flag before using it in the SBC operation. This system can be extended to subtract operands which require any number of words to represent them — simply repeat the SBC instruction as many times as required.

You may be wondering why the ARM instruction set has reverse subtract instructions. Again, this ties in with the overall philosophy of speed. By being able to specify which operand is subtracted from which, we effectively remove the necessity of having to go through a data swapping process to get the operands in the right order.

Multiplication

The ARM has a couple of instructions that will perform 32-bit multiplication. The first of these, MUL provides a direct multiplication and takes the form:

```
MUL (<suffix>) <dest>, <Operand1>, <Operand2>
```

MUL is a bit different to instructions such as ADD and SUB in that it has certain restrictions on how its operands can be specified. The rules are:

Dest: Must be a register and cannot be the same as Operand1. R15 may not be used as the destination of a result.

Operand1: Must be a register and cannot be the destination register.

Operand2: Must be a register and cannot be an immediate constant or shifted operation.

In summary, you can only use registers with MUL, cannot use R15 as the destination, and the destination register cannot be used as an operand. Here's an example:

```
MUL S R0,R4,R5    ; R0=R4*R5 and set status
```

Program 6c demonstrates MUL in action. Two numbers are placed in R1 and R2 and the multiplied result into R0.

Program 6c. 32-bit multiplication.

```
/* multiply two numbers R0=R1*R2      */

        .global  _start
_start:

        MOV R1, #20         @ R1=20
        MOV R2, #5          @ R2=5
        MUL R0, R1, R2      @ R0=R1*R2

        MOV R7, #1          @ exit through syscall
        SWI 0
```

You can assemble, link, and run this using the following:

```
as -o prog6c.o prog6c.s
ld -o prog6c prog6c.o
./prog6c
```

Now print the result with:

```
echo $?
```

Raspberry Pi OS Assembly Language

MLA is MuLtiply with Accumulate. It differs from MUL in that it allows you to add the results of a multiplication to a total. In other words, you can accumulate values. The format of the command is:

```
MLA (<suffix>) <dest>, <Op1>, <Op2>, <sum>
```

The rules stipulated at the start of this section still apply here. There is an extra operand, <sum>, which must be specified as a register. For example:

```
MLA R0, R1, R2, R3   @ R0=(R1 * R2) + R3
```

The register specified by <sum> may be the same as the <dest> register, in which case the result of the multiplication will be accumulated in the destination register, thus:

```
MLA R0, R1, R2, R0 @ R0=(R1 * R2) + R0
```

is possible.

Let's adapt Program 6c to use it, creating Program 6d, as listed below:

Program 6d. Using MLA - Multiply with Accumulate.

```
/* Multiply two numbers with accumulate R0=(R1*R2)+R3    */

        .global  _start
_start:

        MOV R1, #20         @ R1=20
        MOV R2, #5          @ R2=5
        MOV R3, #10         @ R3=10
        MLA R0, R1, R2, R3  @ R0=(R1*R2)+R3

        MOV R7, #1          @ exit through syscall
        SWI 0
```

You can assemble, link, and run this using the following:

```
as -o prog6d.o prog6d.s
ld -o prog6d prog6d.o
./prog6d
```

Now print the result with:

```
echo $?
```

The result returned will always be 10 more than the product of the two values in R1 and R2. This is because the value 10 was seeded into R3.

Note that the <dest> register cannot be used as <op1> nor <op2>. So:

```
        MLA R0, R0, R2, R3   @ R0=(R0 * R2) + R3
```
Would fail to assemble and generate an error message.

Divide Arrives

The ARM processor used on the Raspberry Pi 1 and Raspberry Pi Zero did not provide a division instruction, so dividing two numbers either required some ingenuity or performed using a count-subtraction methodology.

With the Raspberry Pi 2, and subsequent releases, the SDIV and UDIV instructions were available for use, signed and unsigned division, respectively. The instructions, which have no effect on the status register flags, operate directly on registers, and take the form:

```
SDIV <dest>, <numerator>, <denominator>
UDIV <dest>, <numerator>, <denominator>
```

Here <dest> is the destination register which contains the quotient on completion. The remainder must be calculated separately. If <dest> is omitted, then the result is in <numerator>. Program 6e below shows an example of use.

Program 6e. Signed Division with SDIV.

```
/* Signed Division Example RPi 2 and Greater */

        .global _start
_start:

    MOV R3, #20        @ Numerator
    MOV R4, #5         @ Denominator
    SDIV R0, R3, R4    @ R0=R3/R4
                       @ Do not use SP or PC,
                       @ SR flags not altered
                       @ div by 0 returns 0
    MOV R7, #1         @ exit through syscall
    SWI 0
```

The result can be printed out by typing:

```
echo $?
```

Which will return '4' based on the listing.

Chapter 12 shows how division can be performed without these instructions. It also shows how the remainder can be calculated, as this is invariably required also.

The Raspberry Pi 2 included a new SoC and this utilised the BCM2836 and associated FPU with saw the division infrastructure implemented. This has continued since with subsequent releases of the SoC (System on Chip).

Move Instructions

There are two data move related instructions. MOV and MVN are used to load data into a register from another register or to load register with a specific value. The instructions do not have an Operand1 and take the form:

```
MOV (<suffix>) <dest>, <Operand2>
MVN (<suffix>) <dest>, <Operand2>
```

Here are a couple of examples:

```
MOV R0, R1          @ Copy contents of R1 to R0
MOV R5, #0xFF       @ Place 255 in R5
```

If you look at the comment in the first example above, although the instruction is MOVe it is important to realise that the contents of the source register are unchanged. A copy is being made. Also, unless the S Flag is used the Status Register is not changed either. This instruction:

```
MOVS R0, #0
```

would place zero into R0 and set the Zero flag at the same time.

MVN is MoVe Negative (or MoVe Not). The value being moved is negated in the process. This means that 1s become 0s and 0s become 1s or the one's complement form of the number is taken.:

```
        MVN R0, #9     @ Move -9 into R0
9:      0x00000009     00000000 00000000 00000000 00001001
MNV     0xFFFFFFF6     11111111 11111111 11111111 11110110
```

Here are some examples of the instruction:

```
MVN R0, #0          @ set R0 to -1
MVN R1, #1          @ set R1 to -2
```

We will learn in Chapter 11 that there are restrictions on the value of contents being loaded into registers as immediate values. Put simply, there are some numbers you just can't use directly, and it is not because they are too big, for instance. This can also be an issue when dealing with addresses in memory. We'll examine why, and how to circumvent the problem in due course.

Compare Instructions

We encountered these instructions when we looked at the Status Register and flags in the previous chapter. They are two comparison instructions, and they have the format:

```
CMP <Operand1>, <Operand2>  @ Set flags of <Op1>-<Op2>
CMN <Operand1>, <Operand2>  @ Set flags of <Op1>+<Op2>
```

These instructions do not move information or change the contents of any of the registers. What they do is update the Status Register flags. Since the purpose of CMP and CMN is to directly affect the Status Register flags there is no reason to use the S suffix. CMP works by subtracting Operand2 from Operand1 and discarding the result.

```
CMP R3, #0
```

The example above would only set the Zero flag if R3 itself contained 0, otherwise the Zero flag would be clear.

```
CMP R3, #128
```

Here, the Zero flag would be set if R3 contained 128. If R3 held anything less than 128 the Negative flag would be set. What would cause the Overflow flag to be set? If you are ever in any doubt what the result would be, then simply check it out longhand by doing the binary arithmetic!

CMN is the negative version of compare. This is good if you want to control a loop decrements past zero. In such case you could use:

```
CMN R0, #1              @ Compare R0 with -1
```

The idea is the same behind the reason of the MVN instruction. It allows comparisons to be made with small negative immediate constants which could not be represented otherwise.

An important point to be wary of is that, in MVN, the logical NOT of Operand2 is taken. In CMN it is the negative of the operand that is used. Thus, to compare R0 with minus 3 we would write:

```
CMN R0, #3
```

The ARM will automatically form the negative of Operand2 and then make the comparison.

As with CMP, the purpose of CMN is to affect the Status Register flags and the S suffix is not applicable.

Ordering Numbers

The order that information is stored in memory is of some considerable significance. Consider the hexadecimal number below:

```
0xFF00AA99
```

If this is stored in four consecutive bytes of memory how are they ordered? Thus:

```
0xFF, 0x00, 0xAA, 0x99
```

or:

```
0x99, 0xAA, 0x00, 0xFF
```

These two methods are called **big-endian** and **little-endian**, respectively. As you can see the bytes are stored in the reverse order to each other depending on the method used.

ARM chips are **bi-endian**, and can use either method, which is defined by a specific bit in the CPSR which defines which 'endianness' to use. By default, Raspberry Pi OS uses the little-endian methodology. For the most part the order of the bytes will be transparent in use as the assembler takes care of this for us.

7: ROS Ins and Outs

When we use computers and operating systems such as Raspberry Pi OS, we take an awful lot for granted. We type commands at the keyboard, these get 'actioned' and more often than not, provide output in the form of information or results by way of what is displayed on the screen. There's a lot going on.

Consider a couple of what would seem relatively simple tasks, typing a command at the keyboard and then getting a response on the screen. These are things we do every time we interact with the Raspberry Pi OS command line. The question is then, how do we get input from the keyboard and write information to the screen in our machine code programs?

In the strictest sense you do it yourself. But this involves a good deal of knowledge about the various hardware components of the Raspberry Pi, because to write a message to the screen for instance, we have to know exactly where the hardware that drives the screen is located within the computer's memory and, in turn how to write the information to it. Equally, to read input from the keyboard we need to understand how the keyboard is mapped and how to read that matrix to identify which keys are being pressed.

Reading and writing to the hardware to do this is often termed bare metal programming, because you are 'talking' to the computer hardware directly. Whilst this is potentially exciting, it is rather an advanced topic and not necessarily the domain of a beginner's book such as this. Equally though unless you are specifically bare metal programming as an exercise there is absolutely no need for you to do it. Instead we can access the operating systems own routines to do this.

SWI and SVC Commands

The SWI instruction allows you as the programmer to gain access to predefined routines or libraries of operating systems functions. SWI stands for SoftWare Interrupt because when it is encountered it causes the flow of your program to be paused and handed over to the appropriate routine. Once the SWI instruction has been completed, control is handed back to the calling program which can continue on its way. The SWI command is also often referred to as SVC or SuperVisor Call as this is a mode of operation that is invoked in the ARM chip when called.

You will probably recall that we have used a SWI command in all our assembler programs so far. We used it to exit the code back to the command line prompt. This use took the form:

```
MOV R7, #1
SWI 0
```

All SWI calls are executed with SWI 0 (or SVC 0 can be used instead). The actual function to be performed is determined by the number held in register R7. This is called the Operating System Call or 'Syscall' for short, number. In addition, other registers may also have to be seeded with information, so a call to SWI 0 often requires some setting up before being executed. For example, to write a string of characters to the screen three other items of information must be placed in specific registers.

To use these SWI calls effectively then, we need to know what they do, what information must be passed and into what registers. Information may be passed back by the SWI call and in such cases, we need to know what information and in what registers.

Appendix B contains a list of the Syscalls available in the Raspberry Pi OS. A detailed description of all the SWI calls is not provided, but the more common and useful ones are described at various points in this book. No official list of Syscalls exist but there are various sources on independent websites.

Let's look at what are arguably the two most important Syscalls at this stage in our learning —printing to the screen and reading from the keyboard. These are important as we will use them a lot in the program examples in the rest of this book. In using them we will need to look at a few more features of the GCC assembler and use a few assembly language techniques that we won't learn about in detail until later.

Writing to the Screen

To write a sequence or string of ASCII characters to the screen we need to use the 'write' function. This is Syscall 4. The parameters required by Syscall 4 are as follows:

```
R0= determines output stream, 1 for the monitor
R1= the address of the string of characters
R2= the number of characters to be written
R7= the number of the Syscall, so R7=4
```

(Incidentally, ASCII stands for American Standard Code for Information Interchange, and an ASCII code is a simple number used to represent the character. Appendix A contains the ASCII character table, and this is universal in acceptance as a standard.)

The GCC assembler provides us with a facility to store an ASCII string of characters within the body of our machine code file. Program 7a illustrates the setup for this. The key here is to note the GCC assembler directive '.ascii' on the last line. This directive informs the assembler that an ASCII string of characters follows the string that is enclosed by quotes. You will also notice '\n' at the end of the character string, but within the quotes. The backslash character signifies that the next character is a 'control-character' and as such has an action. Here '\n' means generate a new line. A label is used to mark the start of the location of the string — in this case I have been original and called it 'string'.

Program 7a. Syscall 4 to write a string to the screen.

```
/* How to use Syscall 4 to write a string */

    .global  _start
_start:

    MOV R7, #4              @ Syscall number
    MOV R0, #1              @ Stdout is monitor
    MOV R2, #19             @ string is 19 chars long
    LDR R1,=string          @ string located at string:
    SWI 0

_exit:
                            @ exit syscall
    MOV R7, #1
    SWI 0

.data
string:
.ascii "Hello World String\n"
```

Create, assemble, and link the program and try it out for yourself. The instruction:

```
    LDR R1,=string
```

Can be read as:

```
    LoaD Register R1 with the address of the label string:
```

When Syscall 4 is made it identifies the output stream, the 1 passed in R0 defines the standard output device, the monitor. It then extracts the length of the string from R2 and prints that number of characters out starting at the address held in R1. The number of characters held in R2 includes spaces and any punctuation. The final '\n' character is regarded as one character. Try altering the value loaded into R2 and see if you can predict the result. For example, try:

```
            MOV R2, #11
```

You will also note that there is an extra directive in the program:

```
            .data
```

This informs the assembler that what follows should be treated as a subsection containing data, as opposed to assembly language code.

The data subsection could have been placed at the start of the source file had we desired. We would then have needed to signify the start of the assembly language subsection by using a directive thus:

```
            .text
```

How you structure your files is entirely a matter of which way you wish to work. I tend to prefer placing data and data areas at the end of programs to avoid any alignment problems. You may recall from Chapter 5 that ARM machine code must be assembled on four-byte word boundaries, in other words start at an address that is directly divisible by four. This may not be the case if a string of 10 characters was used, for example. This can be corrected by using an align directive, something discussed later.

Reading from the Keyboard

To read a sequence (or string) of ASCII letters from the keyboard we need to use the 'read' function. This is Syscall 3. The parameters required by Syscall 3 are similar to Syscall 4 and are as follows:

```
            R0=  input stream, this is 0 for the keyboard
            R1=  the address of the buffer for the string of
                 read characters to be placed
            R2=  the number of characters to be read
            R7=  the number of the Syscall, so R7=3
```

You can use Program 7a as a basis for the new program. You can make a copy of it at the command line by using the cp command as follows:

```
            cp prog7a.s prog7b.s
```

Now edit the source file to contain the new _read routine. The entire program is given below.

Program 7b. Syscall 3 to read from the keyboard.

```
/* How to use Syscall 3 to read from keyboard */

        .global _start
_start:
_read:
                                @ read syscall
        MOV R7, #3              @ Syscall number
```

```
        MOV R0, #0              @ Stdin is keyboard
        MOV R2, #5              @ read first 5 characters
        LDR R1,=string          @ string placed at string:
        SWI 0

_write:
                                @ write syscall
        MOV R7, #4              @ Syscall number
        MOV R0, #1              @ Stdout is monitor
        MOV R2, #19             @ string is 19 chars long
        LDR R1,=string          @ string located at string:
        SWI 0

_exit:
        @ exit syscall
        MOV R7, #1
        SWI 0

.data
string:
.ascii "Hello World String\n"
```

Here we still need to define the ASCII string. I have purposely left the original text in place so that you can see what results from using the function. The label string: points to what is effectively a buffer or place for the input read from the keyboard to be placed. We could have just defined an empty string, for example:

```
.ascii "                              "
```

(There are other ways to reserve empty spaces in memory in programs and these will be discussed later.)

R2 is now used to hold the number of characters we want from the read process. It is important to remember that this is not the number of characters that can be typed. When _read: is executed it accepts all input at the keyboard until the Return key is pressed. Only at that stage does it extract the first x characters as defined by the value in R2. Thus typing:

```
123456789
```

At the keyboard would see 12345 (the first five characters) placed into the string buffer. The rest would then be dealt with as though a Bash command had been entered and therefore generates an error message. (Bash being the name given to the Raspberry Pi OS command line shell you have been working within.) The '_write:' routine would print out the newly created string which in this instance would be:

```
12345 World String
```

12345 having overwritten 'Hello'.

Run the program again and just type in:

```
12
```

Now the string printed is:

```
12
lo World String
```

Note here that a newline has been generated. This is because the <Return> was inserted into the string buffer as well. We will come back to Syscalls in Chapter 18.

eax and Others

Much of the Syscall documentation you come across with have been written with non-ARM machines in mind and specifically i386 processor systems. As such you will find yourself dealing with an alien set of register references. Figure 7a lists these registers and their ARM equivalents which should assist you in breaking down what needs to go where.

i386	ARM	Function
eax	R7	Syscall Number
ebx	R0	Argument 1
ecx	R1	Argument 2
edx	R2	Argument 3
esi	R3	Argument 4
edi	R4	Argument 5
eax (on Return)	R0	Return value or error number

Figure 7a. 386 v ARM registers for Syscalls.

Makefile

So far as we have developed new source files and we have assembled and linked the files by typing the commands at the command line. This is repetitive but made easier by the Terminal history feature. By using the up and down arrow keys while in Terminal you can scroll through previously entered commands, which in turn can be edited.

GNU also provide a very clever piece of software called 'Make'. This is a tool that allows programmers to control the generation of executable files from a single controlling file. When you see a piece of software installing on your computer then chances are that the whole process is bring controlled by a Make file. Make is a very sophisticated tool and you can find out more about it in detail from the GNU website.

Program 7c is a source file (although you save it without the '.s' suffix) that will automate the whole assemble and link process for you. It is extremely flexible and can deal with most possibilities. (Note the '#' characters are equivalent of the '@' in assembler files. They allow comments to follow.)

Program 7c. Automate assembly and linking with Make.

```
PROGRAMS = prog7a prog7b

# If we've supplied a goal on the command line
# then set it as the list of programs we already know about.
ifneq ($(MAKECMDGOALS),)
     ifneq ($(MAKECMDGOALS),clean)
          PROGRAMS = $(MAKECMDGOALS)
     endif
endif

# The default rule if none specified on the command line
all: $(PROGRAMS)

# Make knows how to compile .s files, so all
# we need to do is link them.
$(PROGRAMS): % : %.o
        ld -o $@ $<

clean:
        rm -f *.o $(PROGRAMS)
```

Create the above file and call it 'makefile' - there is no need to append an '.s' to the filename, just plain 'makefile'. Ensure this file is aved in the same directory as your source file. Also, note that the two lines:

```
ld -o $@ $<
```
and
```
rm -f *.o $(PROGRAMS)
```
must be indented by a *single tab character* for Make to work.

Run the makefile by typing, at the command line prompt:

```
make
```

The variable PROGRAMS (first line in makefile) is being used to hold the names of the source files to be assembled and linked. You can enter one or as many names as you like here, with each being separated by a space. And effectively that is all you need to do. The rest of the program will assemble each of the files, create the object files and then link them.

In the listing above this would mean the source files called prog7a and prog7b. Note the '.s' suffix is implied, and you do not need to include it.

```
PROGRAMS = prog7a prog7b
```

This also implies the makefile exists in the same directory as your source code files. If the source files have previously been assembled and linked they will be overwritten provided the target files are older than their associated source files. If the files do not exist, then make will complain with an error message. You can 'force' the re-make by using:

```
make -B
```

If you want to assemble and link a specific file or files, you can enter the file name after the commands thus:

```
make prog7a
```

This would assemble and link the source file called 'prog6a' provided it existed. This would be in preference to any filenames listed on that first makefile line.

At the command line, typing:

```
make clean
```

Will delete the '.o' files from the directory based on initial definition for PROGRAMS.

It makes good sense to include a makefile in each and any directory where you create and save your source files that need to be assembled and linked.

The 'make' utility is very versatile is and can be utilised in several ways. If you wish to study 'make' in more detail the GNU website has plenty of manuals and examples at:

```
www.gnu.org/software/make/
```

Some further 'makefile' examples are provided at further points in the book, and the source files that can be downloaded as previously mentioned include relevant makefile examples in the respective directory, where appropriate.

If you downloaded the program files from my website, you would find that a makefile (or similar) is included for each of the programs if appropriate.

8: Logical Operations

In computer terms, logic can be defined as the non-arithmetic operations performed that involve yes/no decisions. The ARM has three different logical operators: AND, OR and EOR. In each case, the logical operation is performed between the corresponding bits of two separate numbers. As such there can only ever be two possibilities: yes or no. In binary these are represented as 1 and 0. These instructions are useful when it comes to identifying or forcing the state of individual bits in sets of data.

Each operation has the four distinct set of rules.

Logical AND

The four rules for AND are:

    0 AND 0 = 0   [Nought and nought is nought]

    1 AND 0 = 0   [One and nought is nought]

    0 AND 1 = 0   [Nought and one is nought]

    1 AND 1 = 1   [One and one are one]

The AND operation will only generate a 1 if both corresponding bits being tested are 1. If a 0 exists in either of the corresponding bits being ANDed, the resulting bit will always be 0. Example:

```
        1010
        0011
   AND= 0010
```

In the result only bit 1 is set; the other bits are all clear because in each case one of the corresponding bits being tested contains a 0. It is important to remember in these logical operations that there is no carry bit. The tests are done on the individual bits, and we are not adding or subtracting numbers here.

The main use of the AND operation is to 'mask' bits or 'preserve' bits. For example, to preserve the low nibble (bits 0 to 3) of a byte and completely clear the high nibble (bits 4 to 7) so that the byte is set to all zeros we use the AND operator, masking the original with the value 00001111. If the byte we wished to preserve was the low nibble of say, 10101100, we would logically AND it thus:

```
       10101100
       00001111
AND=   00001100
```

Here, the top four bits are cleared, and the lower four bits have had their condition preserved.

Logical OR

The four rules for OR are:

    0 OR 0 = 0 [Nought or nought is nought]

    1 OR 0 = 1 [One or nought is one]

    0 OR 1 = 1 [Nought or one is one]

    1 OR 1 = 1 [One or one are one]

Here the OR operation will result in a 1 if either or both the bits contain a 1. A 0 will only occur if neither of the bits contains a 1. Example:

```
      1010
      0011
OR=   1011
```

Here, only bit 2 of the result is clear, the other bits are all set as each pair of tested bits contains at least one 1.

One common use of the OR operation is to ensure that a certain bit (or bits) is set — this is sometimes called 'forcing bits'. For example, if you wish to force bit 0 and bit 7 you would need to OR the byte with 10000001.

```
      00110110
      10000001
OR=   10110111
```

The initial bits are preserved, but bit 0 and bit 7 are 'forced' to 1. These two bits were originally clear. The other bits remain unaffected.

Logical EOR

The Exclusive OR operation has the four rules:

    0 EOR 0 = 0   [Nought exclusive or nought is nought]

    1 EOR 0 = 1   [One exclusive or is one]

    0 EOR 1 = 1   [Nought exclusive or one is one]

    1 EOR 1 = 0   [One exclusive or one is nought]

This operation sets the bit if it is Exclusive to the OR operation. If both bits being tested are identical, 0 and 0 or 1 and 1 then the result is 0. A 1 will only result if both bits being tested are not alike.

```
        0101
        1110
EOR=    1011
```

This instruction is often used to complement, or invert, a number. This is done by performing an exclusive or with 11111111.

```
        00110110
        11111111
EOR=    11001001
```

Compare the result with the first byte — they are completely opposite: 1s where 0s were and 0s where 1s were.

The MVN instruction introduced in the last chapter effectively performs an EOR on Operand2 to obtain its result.

Logical Instructions

The process remains the same no matter how wide the data is. The examples above are one byte wide. The operation is the same in four-bytes (or as many bytes as you need). The operation takes place on the directly associated bits, and no Status Register flags are involved or considered, and there is no Carry involved at any point.

AND, ORR and EOR are the instructions used to perform the three main logical operations. The form is the same as previous commands:

```
AND (<suffix>) <dest>, <Operand1>, <Operand2>
ORR (<suffix>) <dest>, <Operand1>, <Operand2>
EOR (<suffix>) <dest>, <Operand1>, <Operand2>
```

In these cases, Operand1 is a register, while Operand2 can be a register or immediate value. The operations themselves do not set the Status Register flags but can be forced to do so with the suffix.

Here are a few examples of these instructions in use:

```
AND R0, R0, #1      @ preserve state of b0 in R0
ORR R1, R1, #2      @ ensure bit 1 in R1 is set
EOR R2, R2, #255    @ invert bits in low byte R2
```

Here's a short segment of code to look at:

```
MOV R0, #129
AND R0, R0, #1
ORR R0, R0, #2
EOR R0, R0, #255
```

The result is 0xFC and here's how we arrived at it (dealing with just the low byte of the word):

```
Load 129          10000001
AND with 1        00000001
Result            00000001
OR with 2         00000010
Result            00000011
EOR with 255      11111111
Result            11111100
```

Here are some practical examples of the ORR and EOR commands in use, with a typical application of each of them.

ORR to Convert Character Case

Program 8a illustrates how the ORR instruction converts a character from upper case to lower case. For example, it will take 'A' and convert it to 'a'. The ASCII value of the letter 'A' is 0x41 (65) and the ASCII character for 'a' is 0x61 (97). By comparing the hex numbers, we can see that the difference between 'A' and 'a' is 0x20.

ASCII	Value	Binary
A	0x41	0100 0001
a	0x61	0110 0001
Difference	0x20	0010 0000

Figure 8a. Binary difference between ASCII 'A' and 'a'.

As both these characters mark the start of their section of the alphabet, it follows that the difference between an uppercase and lowercase value would always be the same. Figure 8a shows how this pans out in 8 bits of binary.

I hope you can see that we can achieve this difference by using the ORR instruction with the binary value 0010 0000 or 0x20 (32).

Program 8a. Converting character case.

```
/* Using ORR to toggle a character case */

        .global _start
_start:
_read:                    @ read syscall
        MOV R7, #3        @ Syscall number
        MOV R0, #0        @ Stdin is keyboard
        MOV R2, #1        @ read one character only
        LDR R1,=string    @ string at string:
        SWI 0
```

```
_togglecase:
    LDR R1, =string        @ address of char
    LDR R0, [R1]           @ load it into R0
    ORR R0, R0, #0x20      @ change case
    STR R0, [R1]           @ write char back

_write:                    @ write syscall
    MOV R7, #4             @ Syscall number
    MOV R0, #1             @ Stdout is monitor
    MOV R2, #1             @ string is 1 char long
    LDR R1,=string         @ string at start:
    SWI 0

_exit:
    @ exit syscall
    MOV R7, #1
    SWI 0

.data
string:     .ascii " "
```

Program 8a above does this in the section called 'togglecase'. The routine starts by reading a character at the keyboard (press a capital letter and press Return) which it then stores at 'string'. The togglecase routine then places the address of the stored character into R1 and uses a technique called indirect addressing to load the character into R0. (This form of addressing is discussed in Chapter 15.) The value in R0 is then masked with 0x20 and the indirect addressing technique used to store the modified contents of R0 back at the address held in R1.

Note that no check is made here to ensure that the character entered is in the range A-Z. How would you adjust the program to convert a lowercase character into an uppercase one?

Bit Clear with BIC

The BIC instruction sets or clears individual bits in registers or memory locations. Its format is:

    BIC (<suffix>) <dest>, <Operand1>, <Operand2>

The Bit Clear instruction forces individual bits in a value to zero.

    BIC R0, R0, #%1111   @ clear low 4 bits of R0.

If R0 held 0xFFFFFFFF then the example above would clear the lowest four bits to leave 0xFFFFFFF0.

```
R0:         11111111 11111111 11111111 11111111
BIC #0xF    00000000 00000000 00000000 00001111
Result is:  11111111 11111111 11111111 11110000
```

The BIC command performs an AND NOT operation on Operand1 with Operand2.

Flag Tests

There are two instructions whose sole purpose is to test the status of bits within a word. Like CMP there is no destination for the result, which is reflected directly in the Status Register (therefore the S suffix is not required). The two instructions are TeSt BiTs (TST) and Test EQuivalence (TEQ). The formats are:

```
TST <Operand1>, <Operand2>
TEQ <Operand1>, <Operand2>
```

TST is a test bits instruction, and Operand2 contains a mask to test on Operand1. It performs the equivalent of a logical AND with the outcome updating the Zero flag:

```
TST R0, #128 @ Test if b7 of R0 is set
```

TEQ is test equivalence and uses an EOR process. It is a handy way of seeing if particular bits in registers are the same.

```
TEQ R0, R1 @ Test if R0 & R1 are same
```

You can use suffixes with both the TST and TEQ instructions so that you can test for other conditions as well as that of the Zero flag (detailed in the next chapter).

Program 8b uses the TST instruction to convert a number held in R6 into a binary number, which is then displayed on the screen. The number to be printed is placed in R6. There are a few things of interest in this program which we have not encountered yet and they will be explained in detail in the following chapters. Note how the program is broken into clearly named sections.

Program 8b. Printing a number as a binary string.

```
/* Convert number to binary for printing */
    .global _start

_start:
    MOV R6, #251            @ Number to print in R6
    MOV R10, #1             @ set up mask
    MOV R9, R10, LSL #31
```

```
        LDR R1, = string        @ Point R1 to string
_bits:
        TST R6, R9              @ TST no, mask
        BEQ _print0
        MOV R8, R6              @ MOV preserve, no
        MOV R0, #49             @ ASCII '1'
        STR R0, [R1]            @ store 1 in string
        BL _write               @ write to screen
        MOV R6, R8              @ MOV no, preserve
        BAL _noprint1

_print0:
        MOV R8, R6              @ MOV preserve, no
        MOV R0, #48             @ ASCII '0'
        STR R0, [R1]            @ store 0 in string
        BL _write
        MOV R6, R8              @ MOV no, preserve
_noprint1:
        MOVS R9, R9, LSR #1     @ shuffle mask bits
        BNE _bits
_exit:
        MOV R7, #1
        SWI 0

_write:
        MOV R0, #1
        MOV R2, #1
        MOV R7, #4
        SWI 0
        MOV PC, LR

.data
string:    .ascii " "
```

The mnemonic LSL is used in a couple of places. This stands for logical shift left and is used to shuffle the bits in a word along — left in this case. In the program it is used as follows:

```
MOV R10, #1
MOV R9, R10, LSL #31
```

Here #1 is being placed into R10, via R9, and shifted 31 times to the left, so that only the most significant bit in the register is set. This is because we cannot load the value we require directly into the register due to constraints that are imposed on use of immediate values (more on this shortly).

So, the line does this:

```
MOV R10, #1:    00000000 00000000 00000000 00000001
LSL #31         10000000 00000000 00000000 00000000
                <<  shift left by 31 places   <<
```

We now enter the 'bits' loop:

```
_bits:
    TST R6, R9              @ TST no, mask
    BEQ _print0
    MOV R8, R6              @ MOV preserve, no
    MOV R0, #49             @ ASCII '1'
    STR R0, [R1]            @ store 1 in string
    BL _write               @ write to screen
    MOV R6, R8              @ MOV no, preserve
    BAL _noprint1
_print0:
    MOV R8, R6              @ MOV preserve, no
    MOV R0, #48             @ ASCII '0'
    STR R0, [R1]            @ store 0 in string
    BL _write
    MOV R6, R8              @ MOV no, preserve
```

R6 holds the number ('no'). We know that the most significant bit of the mask is set (b31) and TST tests to see if it is in 'number' too. If it is, then the following BEQ will occur and a 1 will be printed. If not a 0 will be printed. Note that in each case we preserve the value in R6 as this is our number to be tested, and we need to use R0 to print the 1 or 0 in the _write routine. The ASCII value for '1' (49) or '0' (48) is placed in R0 and stored in string: in either case. (This should be familiar to you now as we have used this technique a few times in previous programs.)

In either case we now use the _write routine as a subroutine, this means that we only need to assemble it once in the program. The program uses:

```
    BL _write
```

to jump to the routine. BL stands for Branch with Link. When this occurs the address of the next instruction is saved, and the program jumps to the named label. If you look at the end of the _write routine, it ends with:

```
    MOV PC, LR
```

This effectively puts the saved address (in the Link Register) back into the Program Counter (PC) thereby causing program flow to restart after the original BL instruction. These concepts are dealt with in some detail in Chapter 10, so all will become clearer.

In the _noprint1 section we use a logical shift right to shift the mask bit along one place to the right, making sure that we update the Status Register flags using the S suffix. The program continues to loop, and print 1s and 0s as required, until all 32-bits have been tested.

```
_noprint1:
    MOVS R9, R9, LSR #1 @shuffle mask bits
    BNE _bits
```

This program is a great visual aid to see how bit patterns develop. When you run it, work your way up through the numbers from '1' to see the output. You should recognise the binary very clearly now.

You could have a go at improving this program by requesting a number to be entered at the keyboard and then displaying its value in binary. To do that though you would need to be able to convert an ASCII value into hex so you can store it in a register. A technique to do this is given later in the book.

In Program 9a there are a few instances where the ASCII value of 1 or 0 has been required. In these cases we have used the ASCII number as an immediate value, thus:

```
    MOV R0, #49
```

It is also possible to do this using the character itself:

```
    MOV R0, #'1'
```

Here the ASCII character is enclosed in single quotes. This is certainly more readable and also means that you don't have to go looking for the number representation.

System Call Registers

One of the downsides of using operating system calls is that you need thing carefully about register usage. Most Syscalls need information passed to them via registers for them to complete their function. So, if you plan to use Syscalls, plan your register usage from the start. It could save a lot of editing later.

9: Conditional Execution

The concept of the suffix was introduced in an earlier chapter to illustrate how S can be appended onto instructions to force the Status Register flags to be updated. For example:

```
ADDS R0, R1, R2          @ R0=R1+R2 & set flags
```

Without the S, using the instruction in its basic form, ADD has no effect on the Status flags. S is just one of many suffixes that exist and can be used in a similar way to expand the functionality of just about every operation in the ARM's instruction set.

Almost all ARM instructions can have a suffix applied to them that will only allow the command to be executed if the condition under test is true. If the condition is not met, then the instruction will be ignored. The suffix CS denotes Carry Set, so the instruction it is appended to will only be executed if the Carry flag is set at the time the ARM reaches the instruction. In programming terms, it gives you the ability to make every instruction a conditional operation.

The list of condition codes is extensive and is given in Figure 9a.

The GCC Assembler understands these conditional codes, and you can append them for use in your programs by adding the letters onto the end of the mnemonic. You can leave spaces between the mnemonic and the condition code as well if this aids readability. These two examples are both acceptable:

```
MOVCS R0, R1
MOV CS R0, R1
```

In these examples:

```
MOV CS R0, R1
```

the contents of R1 will only be moved into R0 if the Carry flag is set. Likewise:

```
MOV CC   R0,R1
```

will only move the contents of R1 into R0 if the Carry flag is clear.

Some suffixes alter more than one flag and in such instances these operations might require certain combinations of flags to be at a combination of set or clear. Thus, we can conveniently group the condition codes into two sets:

those that are performed on the result of a single Status Register flag and those that are executed based on the result in two or more flags.

Suffix	Meaning
EQ	Equal
NE	Not Equal
VS	Overflow Set
VC	Overflow Clear
AL	Always
NV	Never
HI	Higher
LS	Lower than or Same
PL	Plus clear
MI	Minus set
CS/HS	Carry Set
CC/LO	Carry Clear
GE	Greater than or Equal
LT	Less Than
GT	Greater Than
LE	Less than or Equal

Figure 9a. ARM assembly language condition codes.

Condition codes act on the status of the flags; they do not set the Status Register flags in the first instance. You will need to use a compare instruction or an associated S suffix instruction to do that. A good understanding of binary and arithmetic operations will aid your understanding of how instructions are affected by these condition flags.

There are examples of the use of conditional execution throughout the programs in this book. Indeed, Chapter 10 also includes a perfect illustration of how the use of conditional codes can greatly reduce the size of your program.

This chapter contains an awful lot of information. Even for the experienced programmer it can be quiet daunting, so don't be too concerned it if you don't fully understand it at this staged. Note its contents and refer to it when you need to. Use Figure 9a as your reference point.

Single Flag Condition Codes

Falling into this group are the suffixes:

```
EQ, NE, VS, VC, MI, PL, CC, AL, NV
```

These conditional flags are provided in complementary pairs. In the first set below, EQ and NE, they both act on the condition of the Zero flag — one when it is set, and the other when it is clear. If you are testing one condition and it is false then you do not have to test for the alternative condition as, by definition, it must be true as it can only be one of two states.

EQ: Equal

Z=1: Instructions that use the EQ suffix will only be executed if the Zero flag is set. This will be the case if the previous operation resulted in zero. Subtracting two numbers of the same value will result in zero and accordingly set the Zero flag. A compare operation would set the Zero flag if the two values being compared were the same. If the result of any operation is not zero, then the Zero flag is clear (Z=0).

Example:
```
MOVS  R0, R1    @ Move R1 into R0 and set flags
MOVEQ R0, #1    @ If 0, load R0 with 1
```

Here, the Zero flag will be set if 0 is moved into R0 from R1. If this is the case then the next instruction will be executed, and 1 will be written into R0. The instruction will not be executed if the Zero flag is clear, thereby proving that the value in R0 was non-zero.

NE: Not Equal

Z=0: Instructions that use the NE suffix will only be executed if the Zero flag is clear. This will be the case if the previous operation did not result in zero. Subtracting two unlike numbers will clear the Zero flag. A compare operation would set the Zero flag if the two values being compared were the same. If the result of any operation is not zero, then the Zero flag is clear (Z=0).

Example:
```
CMP   R5, R6       @ Compare R6 with R5 & set flags
ADDNE R5, R5, R6   @ If not zero R5+R6 and put in R5
```

Here, the CMP instruction is used to compare contents of R5 and R6. If they are not the same (so that the Zero flag will be clear, Z=0) then R5 and R6 are summed and the result placed in R5.

VS: Overflow Set

V=1: Instructions that use the VS suffix will only be executed if the Overflow flag is set. This flag is set because of an arithmetic operation producing a result which cannot be represented in the 32-bit destination register, creating a potential overflow situation. In cases like this, data placed in the destination register may not have value and thus require corrective action by the programmer. Examples of this can be found in Chapter 5.

VC: Overflow Clear

V=0: Instructions that use the VC suffix will only be executed if the Overflow flag is clear. This flag is set because of an arithmetic operation producing a result which cannot be represented in the 32-bit destination register. That is, an overflow situation. If the flag is clear, then no such overflow has occurred. This condition tests for the no overflow condition.

MI: Minus Set

N=1: Instructions that use the MI suffix will only be executed if the Negative flag is set. This flag is set because of an arithmetic operation producing a result which is less than zero. This would occur if a large number is subtracted from a smaller one. Logical operations may also set the Negative flag if they cause bit-31 of the destination register to be set.

Example:
```
SUBS R1, R1, #1      @   Subtract 1 from R1 & set flags
ADDMI R0,R0, #15     @   If negative add 0x0F to R0
```

Here, the SUB instruction takes 1 from the contents of R1, and the S suffix is used to update the flags as the result is stored into R1. The ADD in the next line only takes place if the N flag is set and if so 15 is added to R0.

PL: Plus Clear

N=0: Instructions that use the PL suffix will only be executed if the Negative flag is clear. This flag is cleared if the result of an arithmetic operation is positive, one that is greater than or equal to zero. Note that the EQ suffix will test for zero only, the PL instruction tests for a plus or non-negative result. It is important to note the subtle difference here.

Example:
```
SUBS  R1, R1, #1      @ Sub 1 from R1 & set flags
ADDMI R0, R0, #15     @ If neg add 0x0F to R0
ADDPL R0, R0, #255    @ If pos add 0xFF to R0
```

This example illustrates how compilations of conditional instructions act on alternative results. This builds on the MI example above: if the result was a positive number then 255 is added to the contents of R0 and stored there. As you can see, only one of these instructions can take place and both act on the result of the SUBS instruction. Because neither of the following ADD instructions has used the S suffix, the status flags will not have changed since the CMP instruction.

CS: Carry Set (HS: Higher or Same)

C=1: Instructions that use the CS or HS suffix will only be executed if the Carry flag is set. This flag is set if an arithmetic operation creates a result bigger than 32-bits. The Carry flag can be thought of as the 33rd bit. The Carry flag can also be set by using an ARM shift operation which is examined in Chapter 11.

Example:
```
ADDS R0,R0,#255  @ Add 0xFF to R0 and save in R0
ADDCS R1,R1,#15  @ Carry set add 0x0F to R1 save in R1
```

CC: Carry Clear (LO: Lower)

C=0: Instructions that use the CC or LO suffix will only be executed if the Carry flag is clear. This flag is clear if an arithmetic operation creates a result that fits inside 32-bits. The Carry flag is also affected by using any ARM shift operation which are examined in Chapter 11.

Example:
```
ADDS R0,R0,#255  @ Add 0xFF to R0 and save in R0.
ADDCS R1,R1,#15  @ If Carry=1 add 0x0F to R1 save in R1
ADDCC R1,R1,#128 @ If Carry=0 add 0xF0 to R1 save in R1
```

As with the PL example, this has a definitive action that is controlled by the status of the Carry flag.

AL: Always

Instructions that use the AL suffix are always executed and do not rely on the setting of any of the Status Register flags. Given that instructions will always execute if there are no conditional suffixes, the AL suffix is the default setting for all appropriate instructions.

Example:
```
ADDAL, R0,R1,R2    @  Add R1 and R2 and save in R0
ADD R0,R1,R2       @  Add R1 and R2 and save in R0
```

These two instructions have the same result.

A common use of the AL suffix is with the Branch instruction to provide a three-letter mnemonic and greater clarity:
```
    B start         @ Branch to start
    BAL start       @ Branch to start
```

NV: Never

Instructions that use the NV suffix are never executed and do not rely on the setting of any of the status flags. This suffix is included for completeness. It can be used as a way of making space within a program as the instruction will be assembled. This space might be used to store data or modify the program itself at some point, and in more advanced cases, allow for pipelining effects (Chapter 12).

Example:

```
ADDNV R0, R1, R2       @ Never perform the addition.
```

Multiple Flag Condition Code

Falling into this group are six suffixes:

```
HI, LS, GE, LT, GT, LE.
```

These condition codes are executed based on the condition of two or more Status Register flags. They are most often used after a CMP or CMN instruction. This set of condition codes is further divided into two groups: those that operate on unsigned numbers (HI and LS) and those that operate on signed numbers (GE, LT, GT and LE).

HI: Higher (Unsigned)

C=1 AND Z=0: Instructions that use the HI suffix will only be executed if the Carry flag is set and the Zero flag is clear. This happens in a comparison if Operand1 is greater than Operand2.

Example:

```
CMP R10, R5        @ Compare Registers R10 and R5
MOVHI R10,#0       @ If R10 > R5 then set R10 to zero
```

It is important to remember that this condition assumes the two values being compared are unsigned and that negative values are not being used in a twos complement format.

LS: Lower Than or Same (Unsigned)

C=0 OR Z=1: Instructions that use the LS suffix will only be executed if the Carry flag is clear and the Zero flag is set. This happens in a comparison if Operand1 is less than Operand2. Again, it is important to remember that the condition assumes that the two numbers being compared are unsigned.

Example:

```
CMP   R10, R5        @ Compare Registers R10 and R5
ADDLS R10,R10,#1     @ If R10<=R5 add 1 & save in R10
```

GE: Greater or Equal (Signed)

(N=1,V=1) OR (N=0,V=0): This instruction will execute if both the Negative flag and Overflow flag are the same. This happens when two values are being compared: Operand1 was greater than or equal to, Operand2.

Example:
```
CMP   R5, R6         @ Compare contents of R5 and R6
ADDGE R5,R5,#255     @ If R5 >= R6 then add 0xFF to R5
```

It is important to remember that this condition assumes the two values being compared are signed quantities.

LT: Less Than (Signed)

(N=1, V=0) OR (N=0, V=1): This instruction will execute if the Negative and Overflow flags are different. This happens if Operand1 is less than Operand2. Again, the condition assumes that the two values being compared are signed quantities.

Example:
```
CMP   R5, #255       @ Compare contents of R5 with 0xFF
SUBLT R5,R5,R6       @ If R5<0xFF subtract R6 from R5,
                     @ save result in R5
```

GT: Greater Than (Signed)

(N=1, V=1) OR (N=0, V=0) AND Z-0: This instruction will execute if the result is a positive number and not zero. Here, Operand1 is greater than Operand2 and the assumption is that signed numbers are used. So, both the Negative flag and Overflow flag must be the same, and the Zero flag clear.

Example:
```
CMP   R5, R6              @ Compare R5 with R6
ADDGT R0,R1,R2            @ If R5>R6 add R1+R2 & put in R0
```

LE: Less Than or Equal To (Signed)

(N=1, V=0) OR (N=0,V=1) OR Z=1: This instruction will execute if the result between two values, Operand1 is less than or equal to Operand2. The assumption is that signed numbers are used. To achieve this both Negative flag and Overflow flag must be different, or the Zero flag must be set.

Example:
```
CMP   R5, #10        @    Does R5 contain 0x0A?
SUBLE R0,R1,R2       @    If R5<=0x0A subtract R2 from R1
                          and put result in R0
```

Mixing the S Suffix

The S suffix can be mixed with conditional suffixes. This ensures that the result of whatever action taking place will also update the Status Register flags. We saw in a couple of earlier examples how preserving the status of flags after an action means that it is possible to act on the outcome of a conditional execution for both results. This assumes that the Status Register flags are not updated. If you want the Status Register flags to be updated by the conditional operation, then the S suffix should be added after the conditions suffix thus:

```
ADDCSS R0, R1, R2      @ Add R2 to R1 if Carry=1,
                         Update Status flags as well
```

It is important to place the S suffix after the condition code otherwise the assembler will miss it if it is placed before.

Trying to assemble:

```
ADDSCS R0, R1, R2
```

gives an error.

10: Branch and Compare

This chapter has a more detailed look at the use of the compare instructions and the most economical ways of using them.

Branch Instructions

A machine code program will run linearly executing each action, one after the other. A branch instruction allows the program flow to be transferred to a different point in the program, where the linear execution recommences until another branch is encountered. The two common variants of the branch instruction have the format:

```
B (<suffix>) <label>
BL (<suffix>) <label>
```

In effect, combined with conditional flags, there is a branch for every occasion. Although it' is perfectly possible to use the B instruction on its own, it is preferable to use the AL suffix so as not to lose the 'B' in a bigger program:

```
BAL start
```

But this is also perfectly acceptable:

```
B start
```

The <label> is a marked position in the assembly language program. There is a physical limit to the distance a branch can occur. This is plus or minus 32 Mb, as this is the largest address that can be represented in the space allocated for the label position. The named label is not stored in the machine code, nor is the absolute address of the label.; what is stored is the offset from the current position. When the ARM encounters the branch instruction it treats the value following as a positive (forward) or negative (backward) adjustment to the PC from the current position.

Chapter 13 looks at Register 15 in more detail and discusses how branches are calculated.

The Link Register

The Branch with Link instruction, BL, allows you to pass control to another part of your program – a subroutine – and then return on completion. BL works like the normal branch instruction in that it takes its destination as an address, normally specified by a label in an assembly language program. However, before it branches it copies the contents of the Program Counter (R15) into the Link Register (R14).

```
BLEQ subroutine   @ Branch & save PC if Z flag set
```

Once the subroutine has completed the contents of the Link Register, can be transferred into the Program Counter to return control to the calling segment of code:

```
MOV R15, R14
```

This is arguably the least elegant instruction implementation on the ARM chip. It is effective and does the job; however, other CPUs have specific subroutine call and return instructions. For example, on the 6502 chip the mnemonics JSR <label> and RTS are used to jump and return to and from subroutines.

A MOV instruction is used to move the return address from R14 back into the Program Counter. This will have no effect on the Status Register flags, and therefore, flags are preserved from whatever was going on before the return.

It is important to remember that each time a BL instruction is executed the contents of R15 are copied into R14. This means that if the program is already in a subroutine and another is called, the original link address will be overwritten with the new link address.

If your program is going to nest BL calls inside one another, the Link Register must be preserved on each occasion. The Link Register can then be re-seeded with the return address each time the subroutine is completed. In such cases, housekeeping is important. Re-seeding the wrong address back into the Program Counter will most likely crash your program.

A common way to store these nested addresses is to utilise the stack as a store. This is described in Chapter 17.

Using Compare Instructions

Your machine code will regularly need to check the result of an operation and then, depending on that result, take a course of action. There are a range of instructions that allow you to do this and a couple also that jump, or 'branch' to another part of the program. These comparisons instructions directly affect the Status Register flags at which point you can act on what you find. The following segment will count from 1 to 50 and uses compare and branch instructions to control the loop to do so:

```
        MOV R0,#1              @Initialise count
loop:
        ADD R0,R0,#1           @ Increment count
        CMP R0,#50             @ Compare with limit
        BLE loop
```

This program continues to add 1 to the value in R0, which was initially set at 1. R0 is compared to 50, and a BLE occurs if Less than or Equal to is the result. So, the loop control continues until R0=50. Then the loop continues until R0=51, because R0 would have been incremented to 51 in the instruction before the CMP, which is the point when the BLE instruction fails to loop back to 'loop'.

This segment of code is perfectly acceptable, but we can reduce its length, by making the loop count down thus:

```
        MOV R0,#50             @ Initialise count
loop:
        SUBS R0,R0,#1          @ Decrement count
        BNE loop               @ Loop if not Zero
```

Here, we use SUBS to decrement and set the flags and can therefore, get away with excluding the CMP instruction. If you are counting a sequence of iterations and do not need the count value for anything, it is better and more efficient to count down. This means fewer instructions and a faster execution.

Compare Forward Thinking

Because the only effect of the comparison instructions is to test the condition of Status Register flags, by thinking about what you require, you can get away without using them. Let's look at an example. The segment below is a loop that will cycle until R0 and R1 are the same. If R0 is greater than R1 it will subtract R1 from R0 and place the result in R0. If on the other hand R0 is less than R1, it will subtract R0 from R1 and place the result in R1. When they are the same, the program will finish.

```
        MOV R0, #100           @ arbitrary values in R0 & R1
        MOV R1, #20
loop:
        CMP R0, R1             @ Are they the same: Z=1?
        BEQ stop               @ if so stop
        BLT less               @ if R0 < than R1 go to less
        SUB R0,R0,R1           @ otherwise sub R1 from R0
        BAL loop               @ branch always back to start
less:
        SUB  R1,R1,R0          @ subtract R0 from R1
        BAL loop               @ branch always to the start
stop:
```

While this code is perfectly acceptable and does the job, we can reduce it by taking full advantage of conditional execution of instructions:

```
        MOV R0, #100        @ arbitrary values in R0 & R1
        MOV R1, #20
loop:
        CMP R0, R1          @ Are they the same: Z=1?
        SUBGT R0,R0,R1      @ sub R1 from R0 if Great Than
        SUBLT R1,R1,R0      @ else sub R0 from R1 as Less
        BNE loop            @ branch is not equal
```

As we are testing for greater than and less than conditions, we can make direct use of the GT and LT suffixes respectively and tag them onto the end of the SUB subtraction instruction.

Using Conditionals Effectively

In Chapter 8, we saw how to use the TST instruction to print out a binary number. There, Program 8b used the section of code below to select whether a '1' or '0' will be used for printing:

```
_bits:
        TST R6, R9          @ TST no, mask
        BEQ _print0
        MOV R8, R6          @ MOV preserve, no
        MOV R0, #49         @ ASCII '1'
        STR R0, [R1]        @ store 1 in string
        BL _write           @ write to screen
        MOV R6, R8          @ MOV no, preserve
        BAL _noprint1

_print0:
        MOV R8, R6          @ MOV preserve, no
        MOV R0, #48         @ ASCII '0'
        STR R0, [R1]        @ store 0 in string
        BL _write
        MOV R6, R8          @ MOV no, preserve
```

On the face of things, this is a perfectly acceptable way to archive the result of printing either a 1 or 0 to the screen dependent on the result of a test. Indeed, it is, but that is without a full understanding of the ARM instruction set. Now consider the listing for Program 10a and the new section of code from _bits down which, using conditional instructions, is half the size of the original segment. Now, dependent on the result of the TST instruction one of the MOV commands – and only one – will get executed, dependent on the condition of the Zero flag. This is much more elegant and easier to follow.

Program 10a. Conditional execution to improve program size.

```
/* Convert to binary for printing */

        .global _start
_start:
    MOV R6, #251            @ Number to print in R6
    MOV R10, #1             @ set up mask
    MOV R9, R10, LSL #31
    LDR R1, = string        @ Point R1 to string
_bits:
    TST R6, R9              @ TST no, mask
    MOVEQ R0, #48           @ ASCII '0'
    MOVNE R0, #49           @ ASCII '1'
    STR R0, [R1]            @ store 1 in string
    MOV R8, R6              @ MOV preserve, no
    BL _write               @ write to screen
    MOV R6, R8              @ MOV no, preserve

    MOVS R9, R9, LSR #1     @ shuffle mask bits
    BNE _bits

_exit:
    MOV R7, #1
    SWI 0

_write:
    MOV R0, #1
    MOV R2, #1
    MOV R7, #4
    SWI 0
    BX LR                   @ Branch eXchange

    .data
string:     .ascii " "
```

Branch Exchange

The Branch Exchange (BX) and Branch with Link (BLX) offer a third way of branching within a program. However, it should be said they are most commonly used to effect an entry into Thumb code – a subset of ARM – a subject addressed in Chapter 27, and as such should be avoided until that point and when you are familiar with their added implications. How would you rewrite the routine so that there is no need to use the BX instruction?

11: Shifts and Rotates

The ARM has an internal mechanism called the 'barrel shifter' which can shuffle the bits in a word left or right. Most microprocessors have standalone instructions that allow you to perform this directly. However, the ARM only allows these movements as part of other instructions. It is a significant process because moving bits left or right can be a simple way of multiplying or dividing numbers quickly.

Three types of shifts that can be performed. They are logical, arithmetic and rotate. Rotate is the only one that does not have an arithmetic function—it is included purely to move bits. Figure 11a lists the six types of bit moves available for use.

Mnemonic	Meaning
LSL	Logical Shift Left
LSR	Logical Shift Right
ASL	Arithmetic Shift Left
ASR	Arithmetic Shift Right
ROR	Rotate Right
RRX	Rotate Right with eXtend

Figure 11a. Shift instructions available for use.

Although the barrel shifter is in operation during shifts and rotates, practically, its operation is transparent to the user.

Logical Shifts

Logically shifting a number left or right by one position has the effect of doubling it or halving it. By increasing the number of logical shifts, you can multiply and divide numbers accordingly.

Figure 11b shows how a single Logical Shift Left (LSL) moves the bits on a full word of data. In an LSL, the most significant bit (b31) drops out and into the Carry flag and the hole made by b0 shifting along into b1 is filled with a 0.

LSL	C	Word									
Before	x	b31	b30	b29	b28	b27	...	b3	b2	b1	b0
After	b31	b30	b29	b28	b27	b26	<<	b2	b1	b0	0

Figure 11b. Logically shifting bits left.

Consider the single byte binary value 00010001. In decimal this is 17. If we perform a logical shift on this number by one place to the left (LSL #1) we get: 00100010 which is 34. We have effectively doubled, or multiplied the number, by two. This assumes that we drop off the top digit and insert a 0 at the least significant bit. This is illustrated in Figure 11c.

	b7	b6	b5	b4	b3	b2	b1	b0		
Before	0	0	0	1	0	0	0	1		#17
After	0	0	1	0	0	0	1	0	<0	#34

Figure 11c. Doubling a number with a single LSL.

This is a single byte example. The ARM uses four-bytes, so the whole word is shifted to the left in this fashion. The bit that was in b7 gets moved across into the next byte and into what is effectively b8, and so on. The bit that gets shifted out at the very top, bit 31, gets moved into the Carry flag. The Carry flag can be tested to see if there is an overflow in the number multiplication.

As mentioned, the ARM does not have any standalone shift instructions, but it does implement them as an add-on to Operand2 to use within instructions and they affect the whole 32-bits of the register specified. Using the example illustrated above, we might code it thus:

```
MOV R1, #17
MOVS R0, R1, LSL#1
```

Note the structure of the syntax for this. Operand1 is the destination for the result (R0), and the LSL is performed on Operand2 (R1). Here, the logical shift is given as an immediate value, but it could also have been specified in a register, which makes it available for alteration. A value from 0 to 31 can be used in a shift command. Using:

```
LSL #5
```

would multiply a value by two, five times =32 (2 x 2 x 2 x 2 x 2). It would perform LSL five times. Here, the new spaces would be filled with 0s and the Carry flag would reflect the value of the last bit 'falling out' from b31. All the other bits moved out are 'lost'. This means that the multiplication only remains true provided we do not lose any significant bits through the Carry flag. Therefore, for large numbers care must be taken that significance is retained. In other words, the result must fit inside 32-bits. This multiplication rule breaks down if we were using twos complement numbers.

Logical Shift Right

Figure 11d shows how a Logical Shift Right (LSR) affects the bits in a word of data. The most significant bit (b31) goes right with a 0 taking its place. The least significant bit, b0 drops into the Carry flag.

LSR	C	Word								
Before	x	b31	b30	b29	b28	b27	...	b3	b2	b1	b0
After	b0	0	b31	b30	b29	b28	>>	b4	b3	b2	b1

Figure 11d. Logically shifting bits right.

The effect of LSR is to divide the number by two. Figure 11e shows this using our previous example. We start with 34 and perform an LSR #1 to arrive back at our original value of 17. Here a 0 is drawn in at the top end (b31) and any value falling out on the right (b0) is taken into the Carry flag. As with LSL the Carry flag is used to capture what is falling out so it can be tested if required.

	b7	b6	b5	b4	b3	b2	b1	b0		
Before	0	0	1	0	0	0	1	0		#34
After	0	0	0	1	0	0	0	1	>0	#17

Figure 11e. Dividing a number by two with a single LSR.

Arithmetic Shift Right

In an arithmetical shift the sign bit is preserved. Here b31 is saved; everything else is shifted one place to the right with b0 dropping into the Carry flag. These examples are shifted by one place only, but the principle is the same for multiple shifts with b31, the sign bit being preserved, and the last bit moved out of b0 is dropped into the Carry flag. This is illustrated in Figure 11f:

ASR	C	Word									
Before	x	b31	b30	b29	b28	b27	...	b3	b2	b1	b0
After	b0	b31	b31	b30	b29	b28	>>	b4	b3	b2	b1

Figure 11f. Arithmetic shift right preserving sign bit.

The advantage of ASR is that the shift considers the sign of the data and so a twos complement number may be represented. It extends the original sign of the number from b31 to b30 and ensures the division is performed correctly for both positive and negative numbers.

```
    MOV R1, #255
    MOV R2, #1
    MOVS R0, R1, ASR R2
```

When we execute the segment above it would leave a value of 0x7F (128) in R0 with R1 and R2 unchanged, but the Carry flag set.

The conditional tests can also be used as with a normal MOV instruction. This following line would only be executed if the Carry flag is set:

```
MOV CS S R0, R1, ASR R2
```

An arithmetic shift left (ASL) is identical in operation to LSL, and there is no difference between them in the result. As a matter of course, you should always use LSL instead of ASL as some assemblers may not compile it and issue an error message. Others may just give a warning.

Rotations

There are two instructions that allow you to rotate bits to the right and in conjunction with the Carry flag. Rotate Right (ROR) moves the bits out from the low end and feeds them straight back in the high end. The last bit rotated out is also copied into the Carry flag as well as being rotated around. Figure 11g illustrates how the bits move. The Rotate instructions have no arithmetic action of significance and are included to shift bit patterns.

ROR>	C	Word									
Before	x	b31	b30	b29	b28	b27	...	b3	b2	b1	b0
After	b0	b0	b31	b30	b29	b28	>>	b4	b3	b2	b1

Figure 11g. The Rotate Right instruction.

The following segment:

```
MOV R1, #0xF000000F
MOVS R0, R1, ROR #4
```

would give a result of 0xFF000000 with the Negative and Carry flags set. The ROR #4 shuffles the bits four places to the right.

The top bytes, 0xF000 move to the right by four giving 0x0F00; The low bytes 0x000F move to the right by four to give 0x0000; The 0xF, which has dropped out of the lower byte, is rotated to the top four bits of the high byte to give 0xFF00. Of course, the bits in the middle would all be shuffled along as well, but as they are 0s this is not noticeable. Finally, a copy is made of the last bit out, which was originally in the position bit 4, and placed in the Carry flag.

Extended Rotate

There is also an extended version or Rotate Right called RRX:

```
MOV R0, R1, RRX
```

This RRX operation is unique in that you cannot specify the number of movements it makes as you are only allowed one. RRX always and only rotates data right by one position. The Carry flag value is dropped into b31, and the value in b0 is moved into the Carry flag. Figure 11h shows how the bits are moved.

All bits are preserved albeit in a different order. RRX uses the Carry flag as a 33rd bit and so everything is preserved.

RRX>	C	Word									
Before	x	b31	b30	b29	b28	b27	...	b3	b2	b1	b0
After	b0	x	b31	b30	b29	b28	>>	b4	b3	b2	b1

Figure 11h. Rotate Right with Extend.

Uses of Shifts and Rotates

The shifts and rotate commands can be used with any of the following data processing instructions:

```
ADC, ADD, AND,
BIC,
CMN, CMP,
EOR,
MOV, MVN,
ORR,
RSB,
SBC, SUB,
TEQ, TST
```

They can also be used to manipulate the index value of LDR and STR operations as described in Chapter 13/15. This also illustrates some handy uses for this group of modifiers. Chapter 12 also illustrates use of some of the logical instructions.

Immediate Constant Range

We have seen the use of immediate constants in instructions:

```
SUB R0, R1, #3
```

Here the immediate constant is specified as Operand2, '3' in this case. However, there is a limit to the size of the number that can be specified in this constant, and more particularly, some numbers just can't be used — 257, for example.

The reason for this is in the way ARM instructions are encoded. There are only 12-bits available for storing an immediate value as the operand. The encoding of ARM instructions is beyond the scope of this book. However, accepting that 12-bits are available, this is how the ARM uses these bits: The 12-bit-field is split into two, one part of 8-bits and one of 4-bits. The 8-bit-field is used to represent a numeric constant and the 4-bit-field one of 16 different positions (each themselves then shifted by two) which the 8-bit value may be rotated to through an even number of positions.

Figure 11i summarises this scheme showing the position of the 8-bit value afforded within the 32-bits as defined by the position bits, 0-15. The '+' is used in the diagram to represent 0s, in the hope it makes it easier to read. The ROR column shows the value to be used in the shift.

A couple of examples should make this clearer. Suppose we wanted to use 173 as immediate constant. In binary this is:

```
00000000 00000000 00000000 10101101
```

This value can be presented in 8-bits, so no shift is required, and the position bits will be set to 0.

Let's now examine the number 19,968. In binary across 32-bits this is:

```
00000000 00000000 01001110 00000000
```

If we compare this to the patterns in Figure 11i, we can see this has the value placed at position 12. To create this number as an immediate operand we would use 78 (01001110) and rotate it right by 24.

This provides us with the second way that an immediate operand can be specified as a shifted operand, and this takes the format shown in the following line:

```
Instruction (<Suffix>) <Op1>, <Op2>, <Op3> <Shift>
```

Here's an example:

```
MOV R1, #78
MOV R0, R1, ROR #24
```

Here, R1 is loaded with 78, then rotated right 24 places and the result placed in R0. The result generated would be 19,968. Of course, we can use all these values directly as immediate constants as the assembler will resolve them directly for us, so we can use:

```
MOV R0, #19968
```

and the assembler works it out. It is the values that cannot be calculated in this way through Figure 11i that are the issue.

```
Bit31                                    bit0    Psn   ROR
++++++++++++++++++++++++76543210          0     0
10++++++++++++++++++++++++765432          1     2
3210++++++++++++++++++++++++7654          2     4
543210++++++++++++++++++++++++76          3     6
76543210++++++++++++++++++++++++          4     8
++76543210++++++++++++++++++++++          5     10
++++76543210++++++++++++++++++++          6     12
++++++76543210++++++++++++++++++          7     14
++++++++76543210++++++++++++++++          8     16
++++++++++76543210++++++++++++++          9     18
++++++++++++76543210++++++++++++         10     20
++++++++++++++76543210++++++++++         11     22
++++++++++++++++76543210++++++++         12     24
++++++++++++++++++76543210++++++         13     26
++++++++++++++++++++76543210++++         14     28
++++++++++++++++++++++76543210++         15     30
```

Figure 11i. Immediate operands calculation.

Although 257 cannot be used as an immediate constant, it can be seeded by storing it in a register and then using the register to specify the value.

```
ADD R0, R1, #257
```

would cause an error, along the lines of:

```
Invalid constant
```

but the following would achieve the same result:

```
MOV R2, #256        @ Load R2 with 256
ADD R2, R2, #1      @ Add one to make 257
ADD R0, R1, R2      @ Add 257 to R1 and save in R0.
```

If we are using MOV instructions, then the assembler allows us the omit this and use the logical instruction directly to the same effect:

```
LSL R0, R1, #1
LSR R0, R1, #2
LSR R0, R1, #3
ROR R0, R1, #4
RRX R0, R1
```

Top Move

The MOVT instruction assists in loading values into registers, that might now be possible using other methods. More particularly it can load a two-word value into the top bytes of a specified register without disturbing the lower two words. For example, we can use it to assist in the loading of an address into a register:

```
MOV R1, #0x0008
MOVT R1, #0x3F20
```

R1 would now contain, 0x3F200008.

Generally, the MOVT instruction it is used to load a value that could not otherwise be done using an immediate value. So, if the assembler throws out an error message along the lines:

```
Error: invalid constant (xxxxxxxx) after fixtup.
```

Here 'xxxxxxxx' is the value you specified. The 'fixup' refers to the assembler trying to resolve the issue but couldn't and thus the error message! Thus, you will need to use the MOV/MOVT combination.

12: Smarter Numbers

In Chapter 6 we introduced the two basic multiplication instructions MUL and MLA. These were the original multiplication instructions wired into the ARM. Since v3 of the ARM additional instructions have been added to deal with signed and unsigned numbers up to 64-bits long. We'll look at some of the more useful ones here. Several have specific uses and are aimed at more complex tasks such as digital processing.

Long Multiplication

The SMULL and UMULL instructions offer signed and unsigned multiplication using two registers containing 32-bit operands to produce a 64-bit result, which is split across two destination registers. The format of the instruction is:

```
SMULL (<suffix>) <destlLo>, <destHi>, <Op1>, <Op2>
UMULL (<suffix>) <destlLo>, <destHi>, <Op1>, <Op2>
```

For signed multiplication, the values passed through Operand1 and Operand2 are assumed to be in twos complement form. You cannot use the PC in these instructions and the SP should be avoided as it is not supported in some later ARM chips, although it can be used on the Raspberry Pi. It should go without saying that the two destination registers should be different.

The following example will produce the full 64-bits from the product of two unsigned 32-bit numbers, assuming the two unsigned numbers are in R1 and R2. On exit R3 and R4 hold the result with the low-word of the product in R3 and R4 the high-word.

```
UMULL R3, R4, R1, R2
```

To give you an idea of how code-saving these newer instructions are, the listing presented as Program 12a will perform the same operation using the original MUL instruction. As with the above example the routine assumes that the two unsigned numbers are in R1 and R2 and on exit R3 and R4 hold the result, with the low-word of the product in R3 and R4 the high-word. On exit, both R1 and R2 are non-defined. R5, an extra register, is also used.

Raspberry Pi OS Assembly Language

Program 12a. Long multiplication 'the hard way'

```
/* Multiply without use of UMULL          */
/* mult: routine can be replaced with one instruction! */

@ R1=Unsigned 32-bit number 1 (low)
@ R2=Unisgned 32-bit number 2 (high)

@ On Exit:
@ R3=Result (low-word product)
@ R4=Result (high-word product)
@ R1= Undefined, R2= Undefined, R5= Undefined

        .global  _start
_start:
        MOV R1, #0xF0000002     @ Going to do...
        MOV R2, #0x2            @ [R3,R4]=R1*R2

mult:
        MOVS R4, R1, LSR #16    @ R4 is ms 16-bits of R1
        BIC R1, R1, R4, LSL #16 @ R1 is ls 16-bits of R1
        MOV R5, R2, LSR #16     @ R5 is ms 16-bits of R2
        BIC R2, R2, R5, LSL #16 @ R2 is ls 16-bits of R2

        MUL R3, R1, R2          @ Low partial product
        MUL R2, R4, R2          @ First mid-partial product
        MUL R1, R5, R1          @ Second mid-partial product
        MULNE R4, R5, R4        @ High partial product

        ADDS R1, R1, R2         @ Add mid-partial
        ADDCS R4, R4, #0x10000  @ Add Carry to high partial
        ADDS R3, R3, R1, LSL #16 @ Add middle partial product
        ADC R4, R4, R1, LSR #16 @ Sum into low & high-words

        MOV R7, #1              @ Exit Syscall
        SWI 0
```

The ADDS following the MULNE test is used in preference to MLA here as we need to preserve the Carry flag for the ADDCS that follows.

120

If you do not follow this example, try writing it out longhand, or work through it using GDB, after you have read Chapter 14, so that you can view register contents during a step-through process.

Long Accumulation

SMLAL and UMALA are the signed and unsigned equivalents of MLA. As with the previous instructions the signed or unsigned values acting at Operand1 and Operand2 are multiplied together, but in this instance the result is added to any value already in destLo and destHi.

```
SMLALS R1, R2, R5, R6
```

There are also a couple of interesting variants of the command which are only applicable with signed multiplication.

SMLAxy permits multiplication with accumulate using 16-bit operands with a 32-bit accumulator. This is interesting and the full syntax is:

```
SMLA<x><y> (<suffix>)><dest>, <Op1>, <Op2>, <Op3>
```

Here <x> and <y> can be either B or T which stand for Bottom and Top, referring to the bottom or top two bytes of Operand1 and Operand2, respectively. Operand3 contains the value to be added to the result of the multiplication of the bytes identified in Operand1 and Operand2.

For example:

```
SMLABTCC R0, R1, R2, R3
```

Here if the Carry is clear (CC) then the low half-word of R1 will be multiplied with the top half-word of R2. The result will be added to the value in R3 and the result stored in R0.

The SMLAWy instruction (Signed Multiply Wide) is similar but in this circumstance either the top two or bottom two bytes of Operand2 are utilised to multiply with Operand1. The upper 32-bits of the result (which may be 48-bits long) are placed in the destination register. This is therefore a 16-bit by 32-bit multiplication with accumulation. The full syntax is:

```
SMLAW<y> <dest>, <Operand1>, <Operand2>, <Operand3>
```

For example:

```
SMLAWB R0, R5, R6, R7
```

Here the bottom half-word of R6 is multiplied with the full word in R5 and the value in R7 is added to the result, which is dropped into R0.

SMUAD and SMUSD work on 16-bit values and offer Signed Multiply with Addition and Signed Multiply with Subtraction, with the twist of allowing optional exchange of operand halves. The syntax for the commands is:

```
SMUAD<X> (<suffix>) <dest>, <Operand1>, <Operand2>
SMUSD<X> (<suffix>) <dest>, <Operand1>, <Operand2>
```

If 'X' is included in the instruction, then the most and least significant half-words of Operand2 are exchanged. If 'X' is omitted, then no exchange takes place. The instruction then multiplies the contents of the two lower half-words of Operand1 and Operand2 and saves the result, and then multiplies the contents of the two upper half-words of the operands and saves the result.

For SMUAD (Dual Signed 16-Bit Multiply with Addition) the two partial products are then added, and the result placed in the destination register. For SMUSD (Dual Signed 16-Bit Multiply with Subtraction) the second partial product (the upper half-word) is subtracted from the first partial product.

Examples:
```
SMUADXEQ    R5, R6, R7
SMUSD       R5, R7, R9
```

Division and Remainder

In Chapter 6 we saw that the early versions of the Raspberry Pi, namely the original A and B along with the Zero, did not support an instruction to undertake division. The ARM chips used in the subsequent versions, had SDIV and UDIV introduced. Program 12b shows how you can carry out a division using two 32-bit values without division specific instructions.

It assumes that the dividend is in R1, and the divisor is in R2. On exit R3 holds the quotient, R1 the remainder and R2 the original divisor. No check is made to see if the divisor is zero, which will fail — but this is a simple check to add. You will recall that the SDIV and UDIV instructions do not calculate the remainder, so this routine might be useful if you require that value as well.

On completion R0 contains the quotient so, typing:

    echo $?

Will print '5'. The remainder of the division ('11') is in R1.

Program 12b. Division the long way.

```
/* Long Divide using no specific Divide instruction */
/* Provides Quotient and Remainder as result        */
@ On Entry: R1=Dividend,  R2=Divisor
@ On Exit: R3=Quotient, R1=Remainder, R2 Original Divisor

        .global  _start
_start:
        MOV R1, #111        @ Going to do 111/20
        MOV R2, #20
        MOV R4, R2          @ Preserve Divisor
        CMP R4, R1, LSR #1
```

```
Div1:   MOVLS R4, R4, LSL #1      @ Double Divisor until
        CMP R4, R1, LSR #1        @ 2xR4>divisor
        BLS Div1
        MOV R3, #0                @ Initialise quotient

Div2:   CMP R1, R4                @ Can we subtract R4?
        SUBCS R1, R1, R4          @ Do so if possible
        ADC R3, R3, R3            @ Double quotient, add new
bit
        MOV R4, R4, LSR #1        @ Halve R4
        CMP R4, R2                @ Loop until gone past...
        BHS Div2                  @ ..original divisor
        MOV R0, R3                @ Move quotient into R0

        MOV R7, #1                @ Exit Syscall
        SWI 0
```

Smarter Simple Multiplication

We had a look at simple multiplication in an earlier chapter. Now armed with the knowledge of shifts and bit operators, we can look at easier ways to achieve multiplication results. In the examples that follow R0 is used as the main register, However, any register may be used.

If you want to multiply by a factor of two then you should use LSL directly:

```
        MOV R0, R0, LSL #n
```

Where 'n' is the constant. Replacing n above by, say 4, would produce:

```
        R0=R0 x 2 x 2 x 2 x 2
```

This is, in effect, 2^n.

To multiply by $(2^n)+1$, examples being 3, 5, 9, 17 etc., use:

```
        ADD R0, R0, R0, LSL #n
```

again, where n is the value.

Conversely to multiply by $(2^n)-1$, examples being 3, 7, 15 etc., use:

```
        RSB R0, R0, R0, LSL #n
```

where n is the value.

To multiply a number by 6 first multiply by three and then by two:

```
        ADD R0, R0, R0, LSL #1
        MOV R0, R0, LSL #1
```

Much More Inside

I have only touched on some of the more advanced arithmetical instructions available on the ARM chip inside the Raspberry Pi. There are many, many more along with several variations on the ones I have covered here. The best way to examine these is simply to set up seed programs, that is programs which load numbers into registers before executing a particular command, and then step-through the executing program using GDB, examining the registers along the way as you do so.

13: Program Counter R15

Register 15 is the Program Counter, and it is important. If you don't treat it with respect your program can crash. If this happens your Raspberry Pi will most likely 'freeze' and will not recognise anything you do until you turn the power switch off and re-boot. Time-consuming, annoying, and frustrating. It will happen occasionally, but it's good for the soul to keep those occasions to a minimum!

R15 performs a simple function. It keeps track of where your program is in an executing machine code program. It holds the 32-bit addresses of a physical memory location. In fact, the PC holds the address of the next instruction to be fetched. So, if you happen to load it with a number which relates to your step count for the day, you will understand why the program might crash.

The PC can be used within instructions in a variety of ways. R15 can be used in data processing instructions, which means that it can be used as either Operand1 or Operand2. Example:

```
ADD R0, R15, #8
```

This is an example of R15 acting as Operand1. This line would add 8 to the value (address) in R15 and save the result in R0.

```
SUB R0, R9, R15
```

Here, as Operand2, the value in R15 is subtracted from R9 and the result stored in R0.

R15 can also be used as the destination register in an instruction. In such instances, it should expect to be loaded with an appropriate value for the Program Counter as it will seek to fetch the next instruction from it.

```
MOV R15, R14
```

places the value held in R14 into R15. As R14 is the Link Register, this is an effective way of returning from a previously called routine. Generally, it (or a variation of it) will be used to hand control back to the point from where the machine code was called.

Pipelining

It is important to understand how the ARM goes about fetching, decoding, and executing instructions. The instruction pipeline is a design feature of the ARM that is fundamental to its execution speed. This is because when it comes to executing machine code the ARM is doing three things almost simultaneously: fetching, decoding, and executing. As these operations cannot be performed on the same instruction at the same time, the ARM has three instructions on the go at once. It is executing one, decoding a second and fetching a third. When an instruction is executed everything gets shuffled along one place as a new instruction is fetched. The instruction that was previously fetched is then being decoded, and the one that was being decoded is now being executed. There is a continuous stream running through the pipeline as illustrated in Figure 13a.

	Fetched	Decoded	Executed
Cycle 1	Op1	empty	empty
Cycle 2	Op2	Op1	empty
Cycle 3	Op3	Op2	Op1
Cycle 4	Op4	Op3	Op2

Figure 13a. The Fetch, Decode and Execute cycle of the ARM.

It takes three cycles for the ARM to fill the pipeline when it starts operating. Once an instruction has been executed it is discarded as the next instruction overwrites it. It is because of this multi-tasking process that the ARM can achieve great processing speeds. During the process of decoding, the ARM is identifying what registers are to be used in the instruction when it is executed.

In Figure 13a, on Cycle 4, the PC holds the address of Op4 — the next one to be fetched. Figure 13b shows where each cycle of the pipeline is relative to the PC.

Contents	Action
PC	Next instruction to fetch
PC-4	Being decoded
PC-8	Currently executing
PC-12	Previously executed

Figure 13b. The PC relative to instruction processing.

This three-stage pipeline was the original design of the ARM chip. In fact, today's ARM processors are even more sophisticated and the ARM chip in your Raspberry Pi has a pipeline that is no less than eight operations long. But for this book and the concepts we are evaluating the original model remains sound for evaluating the pipeline effect (although we'll come back to the subject in Chapter 27). The effect of pipelining must always be considered. Otherwise in certain circumstances your program may not function as you might expect. Consider this instruction:

```
MOV R15,R15
```

If you place this in your program it will cause the next instruction to be skipped. This is because the address accessed from the PC is two-words (eight bytes) more than the address of the MOV instruction. When written back into the PC by the operation, execution resumes a couple of words (instructions) further on, thereby skipping the instruction in between.

Remember that the address held in the PC is always eight bytes more than the address of the instruction being executed.

Calculating Branches

We looked at branches in Chapter 10. Let's examine how they are handled by the Program Counter.

A branch typically takes this format:

```
BAL label
```

Here 'label' is taken to be a label or a marked position in the assembly language program. Remember there is a physical limit to the distance a branch can occur; it is plus or minus 32 Mb as this is the largest address that can be represented in the space allocated for the label position. An absolute address is not stored. What is stored is the offset from the current position. When the ARM encounters the Branch instruction it treats the value following as a positive (forward) or negative (backward) adjustment to the PC from the current position.

Because of the way instructions are encoded, the branch value is a 24-bit signed offset in twos complement form. The word offset is shifted left by two places (bits) to form a byte offset. This offset is added to the PC. Look at the following example shown in Figure 13c:

```
Address  Label     Instruction
0x0100             BEQ    zero
         ...
         ...
0x0120             BL     notzero

0x1C30   zero:     <instructions>
         ...
         ...
0x2C30   notzero:  <instructions>
```

Figure 13c. Calculating branches.

The first column is the address of the instruction. Here we have two labels whose addresses are 0x1C30 and 0x2C30. The first instruction:

```
BEQ zero
```

is located at 0x0100, and the second instruction:

```
BL notzero
```

is located at 0x0120.

Because of pipelining when the BEQ zero instruction is executing, the instruction that is being fetched will be two instructions later, which is eight bytes later. So, the byte offset for the BEQ instruction will be:

```
0x1C30 - 0x0100 - 8 = 0x1B28
```

So, the word offset for the BEQ zero instruction is:

```
0x1B28 / 4 = 0x6CA
```

For the 'BL notzero' instruction the calculation is:

```
0x23C0 - 0x0120 - 8 = 0x2B08
0x2B08 / 4 = 0xAC2
```

Backward branches work in a similar way but must have the pipeline affected added to the calculation.

By using relative or offset values as branch destinations, it becomes possible to write machine code programs that are totally relocatable. In other words, they can be loaded and run into any part of memory. As soon as you hard code the actual definitive address into place it ties the machine code into one location.

14: Debugging with GDB

The Raspberry Pi OS comes with a complete debugging tool, GDB, which you will find useful when the time comes to unravel your programs and are trying to understand why something doesn't work the way you expected. It is also a great way to learn about the operation of your programs.

One of two things generally happens when your machine code program doesn't work correctly. The first is that the result returned is not the one expected. The second is that no result is returned, and the system freezes requiring a hard reset. Of course, both situations can occur together as well!

For a wrong result, the likelihood is that a constant or address are out-of-kilter. The positive side is that your routine seems to be functioning, and there are no logical or branch errors. Here, it is a matter of trying to track down where the 'error' is occurring. The type of result being returned might give you a clue, and you will need to examine this and make some deductions of your own. For example, if you are getting a result that is one more than you were expecting (and 'one' in this case might not be a number) then perhaps a loop is being executed more times than it should. The loop counter might need adjusting, or your conditional branch instruction might need changing. Being able to see what a loop counter value is at this point would be useful. It may also be that values in registers have been mixed or not referenced correctly in your assembler — for instance, you might have used R1 when you should have used R3, or you may have wished to code an immediate value but didn't specify it as such.

Frozen Cases

For a frozen Pi, things can be a bit more involved. Perhaps a routine is trapped in a continuous loop. The loop counter may not be decremented and so will continue to process while power is applied. It might also be that you have mismanaged a stack or corrupted the Program Counter.

Trapping all these types of errors will become an everyday programming task for you. It is part and parcel of programming. That is why it is useful to develop your programs in small sections or functions. Each has a purpose, and each can be tested independently.

If you find that a program crashes or hangs, one key issue is to locate at what point this happens. The best way to do this is to get some visual feedback on how far the machine code gets before being upset. This allows you to at least narrow down your search. For example, if you are getting screen output from your code then you will have some idea that most likely you ignore everything that went before the last item displayed.

If you are having issues with your code and cannot narrow down the segment creating the issue then you can populate your code with an instruction to print out a marker on the screen, to show you where you are, and therefore have a good idea exactly where the issue lies.

Let's say a machine code program has five areas of operation. We could place an appropriate call to a '_write' style routine at the start of each one as illustrated in Figure 14a.

```
.area1
BL  _write      @ Print A
...
.area2
BL  _write      @ Print B
...
.area3
BL  _write      @ Print C
...
.area4
BL  _write      @ Print D
...
.area5
BL  _write      @ Print E
...
```

Figure 14a. Locating issues by use of a _write style function.

Now when the program is run, as each area is reached, a letter will be printed to the screen. Let's say we had the following result:

ABC

before the program froze. This would show that the program had seized somewhere in area3, because 'D' was never printed. Now you can concentrate your efforts in this area. You might add in additional calls to print out more letters or numbers inside area3. This will then narrow your search and allow you to concentrate your debugging efforts in the right area. Once you have narrowed the area down you can look more closely at the segment.

Assembling for GDB

GDB is the GNU project debugger. It is supplied with Raspberry Pi OS and is run from the command line. It provides a wide range of tools that will allow you to interrogate your machine code programs in many ways from within an enclosed environment. GDB can operate on many, many levels and it would be fair to say that it has a command for almost every occasion. It is customisable as well. As with most GNU software it has extensive documentation available online. In this chapter we'll look at some practical examples, and we'll use Program 10a as the centrepiece of the demonstration.

Before you can use GDB the core program has to be assembled using an additional directive so that it generates additional information that can be used by GDB:

```
as -g -o prog10a.o prog10a.s
ld -o prog10a prog10a.o
```

The -g option generates the additional data for the debugger. From your point of view nothing different has happened. You can start GDB as follows:

```
gdb <filename>
```

where <filename> is the name of the assembled file to be interrogated. So:

```
gdb prog10a
```

will launch the debugger and load the information relating to prog10a. If you forget to specify a filename then you can use the 'file' command at the gdb prompt:

```
file prog10a
```

Now typing:

```
list
```

will produce the output shown in Figure 14b. (You may need to press the <Return> key to continue the listing. - This is where you see the '(gdb)' lines.) The numbers at the start are simply line numbers. They relate to what you would see if you had line numbers enabled when editing your source code. However, within GDB you can utilise these numbers with many of the commands that are at your disposal.

Important: The line numbers you have may differ from those shown here, equally the memory addresses given here may also be different on your system. This doesn't make the listing wrong: you just need to relate to the changes in your listing.

```
$ gdb prog10a
GNU gdb (Raspbian 8.2.1-2) 8.2.1
Copyright (C) 2018 Free Software Foundation, Inc.
License GPLv3+: GNU GPL version 3 or later <http://gnu.org/licenses/gpl.html>
This is free software: you are free to change and redistribute it.
There is NO WARRANTY, to the extent permitted by law.
Type "show copying" and "show warranty" for details.
This GDB was configured as "arm-linux-gnueabihf".
Type "show configuration" for configuration details.
For bug reporting instructions, please see:
<http://www.gnu.org/software/gdb/bugs/>.
Find the GDB manual and other documentation resources online at:
    <http://www.gnu.org/software/gdb/documentation/>.

For help, type "help".
Type "apropos word" to search for commands related to "word"...
Reading symbols from prog10a...done.
(gdb) list
1               /**** Convert number to binary for printing   */
2               /*                                             */
3               /* Registers: R6=number, R8=preserve, R9=mask  */
4               /* R7 needed for syscall, R1 points to string  */
5
6                       .global _start
7
8               _start:
9                       MOV R6, #251            @ Number to print in R6
10                      MOV R10, #1             @ set up mask
(gdb)
11                      MOV R9, R10, LSL #31
12                      LDR R1, = string        @ Point R1 to string
13
14              _bits:
15                      TST R6, R9              @ TST no, mask
16                      MOVEQ R0, #48           @ ASCII '0'
17                      MOVNE R0, #49           @ ASCII '1'
18                      STR R0, [R1]            @ store 1 in string
19                      MOV R8, R6              @ MOV preserve, no
20                      BL _write               @ write to screen
(gdb)
21                      MOV R6, R8              @ MOV no, preserve
22                      MOVS R9, R9, LSR #1     @ shuffle mask bits
23                      BNE _bits
24
25              _exit:
26                      MOV R7, #1
27                      SWI 0
28
29              _write:
30                      MOV R0, #1
(gdb)
31                      MOV R2, #1
32                      MOV R7, #4
33                      SWI 0
34                      BX LR
35
36              .data
37              string: .ascii " "
(gdb)
Line number 38 out of range; prog10a.s has 37 lines.
(gdb)
```

Figure 14b. Listing a loaded file in GDB.

The Disassembler

A disassembler does the opposite to an assembler. It takes the values stored in memory and converts them back into an assembly language listing. For example, at the GDB prompt enter:

```
disassemble _start
```

You should get output that looks something like that shown in Figure 14c.

One thing the -g option did when it assembled the source code was to create a list of the labels or functions defined in the original source code, which allows us to refer to these directly when using GDB. The first column in the listing generated is the address in memory where the code is assembled. (This address may differ on your output.) The second column inside the chevrons shows the number of bytes from the start of the function.

```
Dump of assembler code for function _start:
   0x00010074 <+0>:    mov    r6, #251       ;0xfb
   0x00010078 <+4>:    mov    r10, #1
   0x0001007c <+8>:    lsl    r9, r10, #31
   0x00010080 <+12>:   ldr    r1, [pc, #60]  ;0x100c4 <_write+20>
End of assembler dump.
(gdb)
```

Figure 14c. Disassembling a function in GDB.

Notice the last line in this listing has disassembled to something a little different than was in our original source. It has converted the original:

```
LDR R1, = string
```

into an absolute address. In this case:

```
ldr    r1, [pc, #60]
```

This means load R1 with the address which is 60 ahead of the current PC address (R1=PC+60). So here pipelining is taken into account. The actual address is 0x100c4 and is given after the semi colon at the end of the line, as is the label it is referring to!

You can also disassemble an area of memory by specifying a start and end address. By using the '/r' switch at the start it is also possible to include the hexadecimal opcodes and operands.. For example:

```
disassemble /r _bits
```

will give the output shown in Figure 14d:

```
Dump of assembler code for function _bits:
0x00010084 <+0>:     09 00 16 e1   tst     r6, r9
0x00010088 <+4>:     30 00 a0 03   moveq   r0, #48
0x0001008c <+8>:     31 00 a0 13   movne   r0, #49
0x00010090 <+12>:    00 00 81 e5   str     r0, [r1]
0x00010094 <+16>:    06 80 a0 e1   mov     r8, r6
0x00010098 <+20>:    04 00 00 eb   bl      0x100b0 <_write>
0x0001009c <+24>:    08 60 a0 e1   mov     r6, r8
0x000100a0 <+28>:    a9 90 b0 e1   lsrs    r9, r9, #1
0x000100a4 <+32>:    f6 ff ff 1a   bne     0x10084 <_bits>
End of assembler dump.
(gdb)
```

Figure 14d. Using the /r switch when disassembling.

The third set of figures listed are the opcodes and operands for each of the instructions. If you look at the address line starting 0x00010098 you can see that the offset for the BL instruction has been calculated (0xb0). If the program is 'running' (discussed below) the current position of the PC is shown by a '\=>' on the left of one of the addresses.

Figure 14e provides a summary of some of the more common disassembly options in GDB.

Command	Description
disas <function>	Disassemble the named function. Example: disas _start
disas <addr1>, <addr2>	Disassemble from address <addr1> to <addr2>. Example: disas 0x8084, 0x08A4
disas <line>	Disassemble around the line number. Example: disas 19
/r	Include hex opcodes in output. Example: disas /r _start
/m	Include information in output. Example: disas /m _write
b <line>	Set breakpoint at line number. Line number can also be a <label>
r	Run
s	Step to next command
c	continue running program
q	quit and exit gdb
i r	Print contents of all registers
i b	Print list of all breakpoints
delete <number>	Delete breakpoint <number>
x/Nfu <expression>	Print contents of memory as per expression. N=Number; f= format (x = hex, d = decimal, t = binary. u = unit size (b = bytes, h = halfwords, w for words)
CTRL-C	Interrupt running program

Figure 14e. Common disassembly commands.

Breakpoints

The major debugging facility at your disposal is without a doubt the use of breakpoints, and the ability to step-through commands one-by-one, single-stepping, and allow you to watch your program in action.

Breakpoints are temporary halt signs in a machine code program, which GDB allows you to place where and when you want, so when you run your program from within GDB the program will be halted each time a breakpoint is reached, at the same point, preserving all registers. By inserting one or more breakpoints in a machine code program, it is possible to 'stop and look at register and flag contents at any chosen point. This can come in very handy when a program is not working as it should. By examining the contents of registers and the setting of flags you should be able to narrow down and kill the culprit causing the problem. As you might imagine it is also a great way to learn the operation of each instruction.

Breakpoints can be set using labels or line numbers using the 'b' command at the GDB prompt thus:

```
b _bits
```

In the first case the breakpoint is set at the address where '_bits' is assembled. This will be confirmed visually thus:

```
Breakpoint 1 at 0x10084: file prog10a.s, line 15
```

Let's set a second breakpoint immediately after the two conditional MOV statements. From the file listing we can see this is at line 18:

```
b 18
```

Which returns: `Breakpoint 2 at 0x10090: file prog10a.s, line 18`

Typing: `info b`

will print a listing of any breakpoints set so far, as shown in Figure 14f:

```
1 breakpoint    keep y    0x00010084 prog10a.s:15
2 breakpoint    keep y    0x00010090 prog10a.s:18
```

Figure 14f. Breakpoint listings.

This shows the two breakpoints set. Deleting breakpoints is just as easy:

```
delete 2
```

would delete breakpoint 2.

We can execute programs and get them to stop at defined breakpoints. If the above two breakpoints are in place, typing:

```
run
```

at the GDB prompt would produce:

```
Breakpoint 1, _bits () at prog10a.s:15
   15    TST R6, R9        @ TST no, mask
```

The program has run but has stopped *before* executing the command on line 15. We can now get a dump of all the register contents by typing:

```
info r
```

This would give a listing like that shown in Figure 14g:

```
(gdb) info r
r0              0x0                 0
r1              0x200c8             131272
r2              0x0                 0
r3              0x0                 0
r4              0x0                 0
r5              0x0                 0
r6              0xfb                251
r7              0x0                 0
r8              0x0                 0
r9              0x800000000         2147483648
r10             0x1                 0
r11             0x0                 0
r12             0x0                 0
sp              0x7efff3a0          0x7efff3a0
lr              0x0                 0
pc              0x10084             0x10084 <_bits>
cpsr            0x10                0
fpscr           0x0                 16
(gdb)
```

Figure 14g. Register dump after breakpoint 1 has halted the program.

At this point in the program the code listed through to line 14 will have been executed and this is reflected in the contents of the registers. To continue to the next breakpoint type:

```
continue
```

and then list the register contents again. These are shown in Figure 14h.

```
Breakpoint 2, _bits () at prog10a.s:18
18              STR R0, [R1]        @ Store 1 in string
(gdb) info r
r0              0x30                48
r1              0x200c8             131272
r2              0x0                 0
r3              0x0                 0
r4              0x0                 0
r5              0x0                 0
r6              0xfb                251
r7              0x0                 0
r8              0x0                 0
r9              0x800000000         2147483648
r10             0x1                 1
r11             0x0                 0
r12             0x0                 0
sp              0x7efff3a0          0x7efff3a0
lr              0x0                 0
pc              0x10090             0x10090 <_bits+12>
cpsr            0x40000010          1073741840
fpscr           0x0                 0
(gdb)
```

Figure 14h. Register dump after breakpoint 2 has halted the program.

Here we can see that the ASCII code for '0' has been placed into R0 so the MOVEQ command was the one that was executed. This is reflected in the CPSR where the Zero flag is set. Note how the PC reflects where we are in the execution cycle.

Try setting a third breakpoint at line 25 (this can be done while the program is 'running') and continue to the breakpoint. Listing the register contents will show output as depicted in Figure 14i.

R9 has been updated with the new mask value and note now how the link register has an address in it. Compare the source listing so you can see where these new values have come from.

You can execute your program in GDB a line at a time by simply pressing the 's' key. This is called 'single stepping'. You should try this and watch the program cycle through the _write function as well. You can also print the register contents at any point. GDB is totally interactive and Figure 14j lists some of the more popular commands to experiment with.

```
Breakpoint 3, _bits () at prog10a.s:23
23              BNE _bits
(gdb) info r
r0              0x1                 1
r1              0x200c8             131272
r2              0x0                 0
r3              0x0                 0
r4              0x0                 0
r5              0x0                 0
r6              0xfb                251
r7              0x4                 4
r8              0xfb                251
r9              0x400000000         1073741824
r10             0x1                 1
r11             0x0                 0
r12             0x0                 0
sp              0x7efff3a0          0x7efff3a0
lr              0x1009c             65692
pc              0x100a4             0x100a4 <_bits+32>
cpsr            0x10                16
fpscr           0x0                 0
(gdb)
```

Figure 14i. Register dump after breakpoint 3 has halted the program.

Breakpoint Labels

Rather than worrying about program line numbers for setting breakpoints, you can always devise a system of predefined labels to use within your source files. Typically, this might be after data has been loaded from memory or a register, so you can examine to see if it is loaded correctly; after a round of processing; and equally on completion.

Command	Action
break <function>	Set a breakpoint at the named function. Example: b _start
break <lineno>	Set a breakpoint at the file line number given. Example: b 23
break <offset>	Set a breakpoint at specified lines forward/backwards from current position. Example: b +5
break *<addr>	Set a breakpoint at specified address. Example b *0x8074
info break	List and provide information about all set breakpoints
delete (<no>)	Delete the specified breakpoint(s). If no number delete all. Example: delete 2

Figure 14j. Common breakpoint commands.

Memory Dump

You can look at sections of memory, including your code and data areas. The latter is useful to see how data is changed in response to your program's operation. If you know that you have cleared memory or filled a section with 0s before running your program, you can be sure that what is there after you have.

The 'x' (for examine) command produces output in a variety of formats. To get a hex dump of memory of the program itself type the following at the GDB prompt:

```
x/22xw _start
```

This will produce a listing like that shown in Figure 14k.

```
(gdb) x/22xw _start
0x10074 <_start>:     0xe3a060fb   0xe3a0a001   0xe1a09f8a   0xe59f103c
0x10084 <_bits>:      0xe1160009   0x03a00030   0x13a00031   0xe5810000
0x10094 <_bits+16>:   0xe1a8006    0xeb000004   0xe1a06008   0xe1b090a9
0x100a4 <_bits+32>:   0x1afffff6   0xe3a07001   0xef000000   0xe3a00001
0x100b4 <_write+4>:   0xe3a02001   0xe3a07004   0xef000000   0xe12fff1e
0x100c4 <_write+20>:  0x000200c8   0x00154120
```

Figure 14k. A hex dump of memory in GDB.

The command format is as follows:

```
x/nfu <addr>
```

Here the '/' is used to signify a change in the defaults; f being format which is hexadecimal by default; and u the unit size. <addr> is the start address from which this is to happen. In the example above 'w' specifies word or four-byte wide units and to show 22 of them, starting at 0x08. Other unit sizes that are available are: b=bytes, h=halfwords (bytes), g=giant words (eighth bytes).

When you specify a unit for x then that becomes the default value until it is changed again. When GDB is started the default value is 1.

The 'i' command in combination with 'x' can be used as an alternate way to produce a disassembly listing. Here:

```
x /13i 0x10084
```

will disassemble the _bits function, as shown in Figure 14l.

The combinations are almost endless, and it is a good investment of time to print a copy of the GDB Manual out and keep it bound and close to hand. GDB is really one of those tools that you will always be looking to get more from, and a printed copy is a good place to make notes and keep track of your favourite formats.

```
(gdb) x/13i 0x10084
   0x10084 <_bits>:       tst     r6, r9
   0x10088 <_bits+4>:     moveq   r0, #48        ; 0x30
   0x1008c <_bits+8>:     movne   r0, #49        ; 0x31
   0x10090 <_bits+12>:    str     r0, [r1]
   0x10094 <_bits+16>:    mov     r8, r9
   0x10098 <_bits+20>:    bl      0x100b0 <_write>
   0x1009c <_bits+24>:    mov     r8, r9
   0x100a0 <_bits+28>:    lsrs    r9, r9, #1
=> 0x100a4 <_bits+32>:    bne     0x10084 <_bits>
   0x100a8 <-exit>:       mov     r1, #1
   0x100ac <_exit+4>:     svc     0x00000000
   0x100b0 <_write>:      mov     r0,#1
   0x100b4 <_write+4>:    mov     r2, #1
```

Figure 14l. Disassembling combinations.

Finally, if you are wondering, typing 'quit' will exit GDB and return you to the Raspberry Pi OS command line.

Shortcuts

Most of the GDB commands can be limited to their starting letters:

```
info registers    >>    i r
continue          >>    c
step              >>    s
quit              >>    q
```

GDB Make Options

You should consider working through the long multiplication example provided as 'prog12a' using GDB. Stepping through the code line-by-line and printing the register contents out is highly informative. It should also get you used to the ways of workings with the debugging tool.

Of course, your use of makefile will arguably change as well. Now there is the debug assembled code it is a good option therefore to use Make to assemble in this manner utilising the '-g' option. The program listed as Program 14a provides an updated makefile that allows this to happen. The format here is a bit different.

Program 14a. Flexible makefile for debugging code.

```
OBJX = prog10a
OBJS = prog10a.o

ifdef GFLAG
        STATUS = -g
else
        STATUS =
endif

%.o : %.s
        as $(STATUS) $< -o $@

debugfile: $(OBJS)
        ld -o $(OBJX) $(OBJS)

gdbdebug: $(OBJX)
                gdb $(OBJX)
clean:
        rm -f *.o $(OBJS)
        rm -f *.o $(OBJX)
```

You will need to save this as 'makefile' as well—be careful not to overwrite any previous makefile you may have modified. Ultimately you will arrive at a way of working that suits you.

As previously adjust the names of the source make file accordingly in the first two lines. You can now assemble and link this with or without the -g option. The key to doing this is remembering the 'force option' using the -B flag. Use either:

```
make GFLAG=1 -B
```

To include the debug details, or:

```
make GFLAG= -B
```

In either case you can see from the resultant output in each case how the file is being assembled and linked. You can also jump straight into gdb if you wish after with:

```
make gdbdebug
```

You can delete all files other than the source files with:

```
make clean
```

15: Data Transfer

In most of the examples we have used so far, all data instructions have come from either the contents of a register or an immediate constant, a specified value:
```
ADD R0, R1, R2
SUB R0, R1, #7
```
There is only so much information that can be held in a set of registers, and registers generally must be kept clear to perform operations on data. In general, data is created and then held at known memory locations. In such cases, we need to manage these memory blocks. To load and store data in memory we must know two things. First, the actual address of the data, and second, its ultimate destination – where it's coming from or going to. Registers are used in both circumstances, and the method of doing so depends on the addressing mode used. There are three addressing modes offered by the ARM:

- Indirect Addressing
- Pre-Indexed Addressing
- Post-Indexed Addressing

These methods load or store the contents of a specified register, but in each case the data source or destination is different.

ADR Directive

In Chapter 6 we examined the use of immediate constants and saw that although the MOV and MVN instructions can be used to load constants into a register, not all constant values are accessible in this way. The knock-on of this is that they cannot be used to generate every available memory address for the same reason. Therefore, the GCC Assembler provides a method that will load any 32-bit address. In its simplest form it looks like this:
```
ADR <Register>, <Label>
```
An example would be:
```
ADR R0, datastart
```

Despite its appearance, the ADR is a directive and not an ARM instruction. It is part of the assembler. What it does is take the hard work out of calculating the right number for you. When the assembler encounters this directive, it does the following:

- Notes the address of where the instruction is being assembled.
- Notes the address of the specified label.
- Calculates the offset between the two memory positions.

It will then use this information as part of an appropriate instruction, normally ADD or SUB, to reconstruct the location of the address or label containing the information.

It's worth looking at what we write in an example program and what gets assembled to illustrate the point. Look at the listing given in Program 15a:

Program 15a. Use of the ADR directive.

```
/**** Using the ADR directive ****/

     .global _start
_start:
     ADR R0, value
     MOV R1, #15

_exit:
     MOV R7, #1
     SWI 0

value:
     .word 255
```

Program 15a does nothing really, other than point ADR at the data label and show R0 as the destination register. When this is assembled using the -g option, it will produce something like what is shown in Figure 15a, if you use GDB and enter:

    x/5i _start

the ADR directive has not assembled an address. It has assembled a relative address that will be used as an offset for the Program Counter. Here the ADD instruction is used to add 8 to the PC, the address of value which comes right after the last instruction.

```
0x10054 <_start>:       add     r0, pc, #8
0x10058 <_start+4>:     mov     r1, #15
0x1005c <_exit>:        mov     r7, #1
0x10060 <_exit+4>:      svc     0x00000000
0x10064 <value>:        ;<undefined> instruction:    0x000000ff
```

Figure 15a. Disassembly of Program 15a

Note also that the instruction:

```
SWI 0
```

Has been disassembled to:

```
SVC 0x00000000
```

Showing the mnemonics are interchangeable. The preferred method is probably SVC these days, but I am still old hat and use SWI. The final line in the listing is where the value 255 is stored. GDB tried to interpret this but didn't recognise it thus the message.

In GDB type:

```
x/5w _start
```

The output will be similar to that shown in Figure 15b:

```
(gdb) x/5w _start
0x10054 <_start>:     0xe28f0008  0xe3a0a100f 0xe3a07001  0xef00000
0x10064 <value>:      0x000000ff
```

Figure 15b. Hex dump of Program 15a.

Here the 255 (0xFF or 0x000000ff) stored at the label marked by 'value:' can clearly be seen. This illustrates another new feature of the assembler. In an earlier chapter we used the directive called '.string' to load an ASCII character string into memory. Here the '.word' directive allows us to store a word — or four-bytes — into memory. The format of this is shown clearly in Program 15a and it can be referred to by using a named label. (We'll look at '.word' and other directives in Chapter 18.)

This also illustrates another particularly important aspect of the ADR pseudo-instruction. The values it references must always be within the '.text' or executable section of the code. You will recall that use of the .string directive, which was being accessed by the LDR instruction, was placed in the .data section of the code. If you try and use ADR to access information in a data area you will get an error message.

Indirect Addressing

The ARM is constructed with a 'load and store' architecture, but you cannot access memory locations directly. You can only access them indirectly via a register. The beauty of indirect addressing is that it enables the whole of the ARMs memory map to be reached through a single register.

There are two instructions that read and write memory data:

```
LDR        LoaD Register from memory
STR        STore Register to memory
```

Indirect addressing provides an easy method to read or write to a memory location. The address of the location is held in a register. So, the address location is accessed indirectly. The advantage of this method is that you can change the source or destination location simply by changing the contents of the register. This makes it a handy way to dip into tables of data. Rather than writing a separate routine for each, a general purpose one can be developed, with the address operand being 'seeded' on each occasion the routine is called.

In its simplest form indirect addressing takes the format:

```
LDR (<suffix>) <Operand1> [<Operand2>]
STR (<suffix>) <Operand1> [<Operand2>]
```

For example:

```
LDR R0,[R1]   @ Load R0 with contents of location in R1
STR R0,[R2]   @ Store R0 at memory location in R2
```

Executing the above two instructions would effectively transfer a word of data from one point in memory to another. Figure 15c illustrates this and is based on the instruction:

```
LDR R0, [R1]
```

At the onset R1 holds the memory address, here 0x9308, and that memory address contains the value 0xF80A. This value is loaded into R0. So, on completion of the instruction R0 will contain 0xF80A. The value in R1 is unaltered.

All the addressing modes allow use of suffixes to effect conditional execution. So, for example:

```
LDREQ R0, [R1]
```

Here, the load operation into R0 from the address in R1 will only take place if the Zero flag is set.

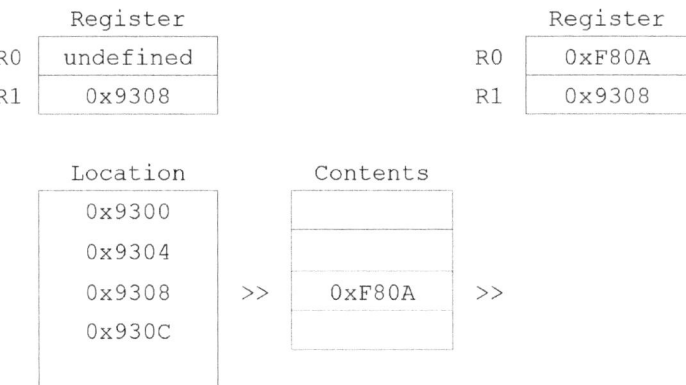

Figure 15c. Indirect addressing of memory using LDR R0, [R1].

ADR and LDR

In previous examples we have seen that LDR can be used in a pseudo-instruction manner to load the address of a label directly into a register. For example:

```
LDR R0, =string
```

would load R0 directly with the address of the label called string. The advantage of LDR used in this way is that it can access memory across the board and is the preferred method if you are using data sections specifically to hold information. Labels accessed by ADR must be within .text sections of code and within the executable code area.

Pre-Indexed Addressing

Pre-indexed addressing provides the ability to add an offset to the base address to give the final address. The offset can be an immediate constant or a value in a register, or indeed, the shifted contents of a register. The format of the instruction is:

```
LDR  (<suffix>) <destination>, [(<base>,(<offset>)]
STR  (<suffix>) <destination>, [(<base>,(<offset>)]
```

The modifying constant or register is simply placed as part of Operand2, separated by a comma, within the square brackets. For example:

```
LDR R0, [R1, #8]
```

Here, 0x08 is added to the address in R1 and the four-byte value at that address (R1+8) is placed in R0. The value of R1 is not changed or adjusted by the constant. This is depicted in Figure 15d. R1 contains the memory address 0x9300. This is added to the specified constant value 8, to give a final source address of 0x9308. The contents of this location, 0xFB0A are loaded into R0.

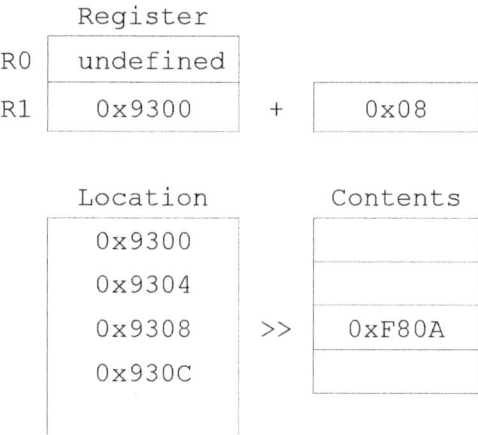

Figure 15d. Pre-Indexed Addressing.

You can use two registers inside the square brackets too:
```
STR R0, [R1, R2]
```
This instruction, when executed, would store the value in R0 at the address given by adding the contents of registers R1 and R2 together. R1 and R2 are not adjusted in any way.

You can also subtract the offset as well, simply by using a minus sign:
```
LDR R0, [R1, #-8]
STR R0, [R1, -R2]
```
Finally, the offset operand may be rotated using one of the shift operations thus:
```
LDR R0, [R1, R2, LSR#4]
```
The value in R2 is shifted right by two bits and added to R1. This gives the address of the data to be loaded into R0. This final construction is useful when it comes to moving through data held in memory, given that it is located in four-byte blocks (viz, 32-bits and the size of a register) and that an LSL #2 operation (which is 2 x 2 = 4) moves you elegantly to the next word boundary.

The following segment replaces the third item in a four-byte wide list with the second item in the list, with the address of the start of the list held in R1, in this example held as 0x9300:
```
MOV R2, #4              @ four-byte offset
LDR R4, [R1, R2]        @ load R4 from (0x9300+4)
STR R4, [R1, R2, LSL #1] @ store R4 at(0x9300+8)
```
Here, 4 is given as the offset, tfor the first LSR. Then the LSL #1 shifts the bits along by four places. The #4 in R2 becomes #8 which is added to the address in R1. The value in R2 does not change itself. If you wanted to locate the next

item in this list, you would need to increment either R1 or R2 by four. But there is a far more elegant way as we shall see.

Accessing Memory Bytes

Program 15b illustrates the use of pre-indexed indirect addressing, using an offset to extract characters from a string located at a base address. It also uses the instruction, LDRB to load a register with a single byte, and STRB to store a single byte.

ASCII characters are represented in single bytes, so LDRB will allow us to load single bytes of memory, rather than a word, at the specified location. To start with, R1 is loaded with the address of the string, and 26 as an offset into R2. The STRB instruction is complementary to LDRB in that it writes a single byte of information into memory. Program 15b uses both commands to overwrite one string with another:

Program 15b. Use of pre-indexed indirect addressing.

```
/* Use of pre-indexed addr to move characters */
        .global _start
_start:
        LDR R1, =string      @ Get 1st string location
        LDR R3, =numbers     @ Get 2nd string location
        MOV R2, #26          @ chars in alphabet
_loop:
        LDRB R0, [R1, R2]    @ get byte at R1+R2
        STRB R0, [R3, R2]    @ save byte to R3+R2
        SUBS R2, R2, #1      @ decrement and flag set
        BPL _loop            @ and loop while positive
_write:
        MOV R0, #1
        LDR R1, =numbers
        MOV R2, #26
        MOV R7, #4
        SWI 0
_exit:
        MOV R7, #1
        SWI 0
.data
string:
        .ascii "ABCDEFGHIJKLMNOPQRSTUVWXYZ"
numbers:
        .ascii "01234567891011121314151617"
```

At entry, _start sets up R1 and R3 with the address of the two strings. R2 is used to hold the counter which is initialised at 26 — the number of letters in the alphabet.

The LDRB instruction loads the byte at R1+R2 into R0 and this is then stored at R3+R2. So, first time around the last character in string: is stored over the last character in numbers: R2 is decremented by one and while the number is not zero or below the loop cycles again. When R2 reaches zero, the read/write is completed and the _write routine prints the new string out.

Although we haven't used immediate constants in these examples, they are certainly available to you and may also be specified as negative values. Here are a couple of examples:

```
STR R0, [R1, #0xF0]
LDR R0, [R1,#-4]
```

In the latter example, R0 would be loaded with data taken from an address which is one word lower than the address contained in R1.

Address Write Back

In calculating the location in memory of the word or byte, the ARM adds the contents of the items held inside the square brackets, the first being a register with an address, and the second being a register or immediate constant. Once the result of the addition of these values has been used it is discarded.

It is sometimes useful to retain the calculated address, and this can be done in pre-indexed addressing, using a method called 'write-back'. This is done by including a '!' at the end of the instruction, after the closing square bracket:

```
LDR R0, [R1, R2]!
LDRB R0, [R2, #10]!
```

In the first example, if we refer to our earlier programs, let's assume that R1 holds the address 0x9300 and R2 contains the index initially set at 26. Now, on the first iteration R1 and R2 point to the address given by 0x9300+26 which is 0x931A. This address is used to source the information and then 0x931A is written back into R1.

To step-through an array of data held in memory we might use the instruction:

```
LDR R0, [R1, #4]!
```

The value 4 will be added to R1 and thus create a single word step. The value in R1 is updated to reflect R1+4. By including this in a loop we can quickly step-through memory with little hindrance.

Post-Indexed Addressing

Post-indexed addressing uses the write-back feature by default. However, the offset field isn't optional and must be supplied. The offset is also handled differently. Post-indexed addressing takes this format:

Raspberry Pi OS Assembly Language

```
LDR (<suffix>) <Destination>, [<Operand1>],<Operand2>
```

The first thing to note is that the compulsory Operand2 is based outside the square brackets to signify the difference in addressing mode. Here are a few examples of how the instruction is formatted:

```
LDR R0, [R1], R2
STR R3, [R4], #4
LDRB R6,[R1], R5, LSL#1
```

When post-indexed addressing is used, the contents of the base register alone are taken as the source or destination address (word or byte depending on the format of instruction). Only after the memory has been extracted or deposited are the contents of the offset field (Operand2) added to the base register and the value written there. Thus, the offset is added post and not pre memory access. Figure 15e illustrates this diagrammatically for the command:

```
LDR R0, [R1], #8
```

The left-hand side of the diagram shows the situation before the command executes. The contents of R0 are undefined at this stage. R1 contains the address 0x9300. The contents of 0x9300 contain 0xFF01, and this is taken and placed in R0. The intermediate value 8 is then added to the contents of R1 (0x9300+08) and the result written back into R1, which now contains 0x9308 as now reflected on the right-hand side of the diagram.

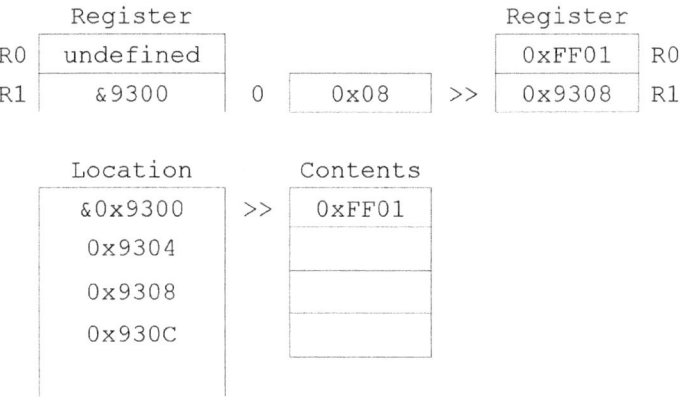

Figure15e. Post-indexed addressing process.

If the LDR line was executed again then the contents of 0x9308 would be extracted and deposited in R0, and after 8 is added to it R1 would contain 0x9310.

Program 15c will create a machine code routine that uses post-indexed addressing to join two strings to create one single string.

Note that in the data definitions for the string we use a slight twist on the '.ascii' directive. Here we use '.asciz' — which will place a zero byte (0x0) at the

151

end of the string, and we use this to see if we have reached the end of the strings during the load and compare portions of the program.

Program 15c. Using post-indexed addressing.

```
/* Post-indexed addr to concatenate strings */

        .global _start
_start:
        LDR R2, =string1      @ load locations
        LDR R3, =string2      @ of both strings
_loop:
        LDRB R0, [R3], #1     @ Get string2 byte & +1
        CMP R0, #0            @ is it end of string?
        BNE _loop             @ no, then get next byte
        SUB R3, R3, #1        @ Yes, decrement back 1

_copyloop:
        LDRB R0, [R2], #1     @ get byte from string 1
        STRB R0, [R3], #1     @ add to end of string 2
        CMP R0, #0            @ is it 0?
        BNE _copyloop         @ if not get next char
_write:
        MOV R0, #1            @ is 0 so print new
        LDR R1, =string2
        MOV R2, #24
        MOV R7, #4
        SWI 0

_exit:
        MOV R7, #1
        SWI 0

.data
string1:
        .asciz "ABCDEFGHIJKL"
string2:
        .asciz "012345678910"
padding:
        .ascii "              "
```

Byte Conditions

Conditional suffixes may be used with the load and store instructions in a similar fashion to others. However, when you are using the byte modifier with conditionals, you should express the conditional instruction first, thus:

    LDREQB R0, [R1]

Note the condition test EQ comes before B, the byte modifier. If they are not in this order, an error message will result when you try to assemble the program.

PC Relative Addressing

Besides pre-and-post index addressing, the GCC Assembler implements an additional pseudo-addressing mode itself — PC relative addressing. We have already used this in previous examples, but it is worth highlighting its usefulness under a separate sub-heading here.

The general format of instructions that use PC relative addressing is as follows:

    LDR <dest>, <address>

As before, the destination is always a register, into which — or from which — the data is transferred. The address is either an absolute number or an assembler label. In the latter case, the label marks the address from where the data will be placed or gathered. Let's look at a couple of examples:

    LDR R0, 0x9300
    STR R0, data

In the first case, the word located at 0x9300 would be loaded into R0. In the second, the location which the label 'data' was assembled at would be used as the destination of the word to be held in R0.

When the assembler encounters an instruction in such a format it looks at the address or location of the address and calculates the distance from where it is to the specified location. This distance is called the offset, and when added to the Program Counter would provide the absolute address of the data location. Knowing this, the assembler can compile an instruction that uses pre-indexed addressing. The base register in this instruction will be the Program Counter, R15. If we ignore effects of pipelining, the PC will contain the instructions address when executed. The offset field contains the absolute offset number as previously calculated by the assembler, with a correction for pipelining. (This is a similar method to the one described for branches in Chapter 10).

It is important to remember that there is a set range restriction in the offset that can be used in pre-indexed addressing. This is -4096 to 4096, and the offset in PC relative addressing must be within this range.

16: Block Transfer

Efficiency is one of the key design concepts behind the ARM chip. With the large number of registers and the consistent need to manipulate and move data, it would be very inefficient to have to sequence a whole series of instructions to transfer the contents block transfer of a set of registers from one place to another. The LDM and STM instructions simplify multiple load and store between registers and memory.

The format of the instruction is:

    LDM <Options>(<Suffix>) <Operand1>(!), {<Registers>}
    STM <Options>(<Suffix>) <Operand1>(!), {<Registers>}

Registers is a list of the registers, inside curly brackets and separated by commas, to be included in the transfer. They can be listed in any order, and a range of registers can be specified with the use of a hyphen, R5-R9.

Operand1 is a register which contains the address marking the start of memory to be used for the operation. This address is not changed:

    STM R0, {R1, R5-R8}

Here, the contents of the registers R1, R5, R6, R7 and R8 (five words or 20 bytes in total) are read and stored sequentially, starting at the address held in R0. If R0 held 0x9300 then R1 would be stored here; R5 at 0x9304, R6 at 0x9308. This is illustrated in Figure 16a.

Reg			Memory	Contents
R0	0x9300	>>	0x9300	0xFF00FF00
R1	0xFF00FF00		0x9304	0x2A0D4AA
R2	0xFF		0x9308	0x953A
R3	0xA8FB		0x930C	0xF36BCA
R4	0xAF2		0x9310	0x101
R5	0x2A0D4AA
R6	0x953A
R7	0xF36BCA
R8	0x101

Figure 16a. Storing register contents in memory.

This example in assumes that we want data to be stored in successively increasing memory address locations, but this need not be the case. The ARM provides options that allow memory to be accessed in an ascending or descending order, and in which way the increment step is handled. In fact, there are four options as listed in Figure 16b.

Suffix	Meaning
IA	Increment After
IB	Increment Before
DA	Decrement After
DB	Decrement Before

Figure 16b. Suffixes for memory direction setting.

The I or D in the suffix defines whether the location point is being moved forwards (increasing) or backwards (decrementing) through memory. The base address is being increased four-bytes at a time or decremented four-bytes at a time.

After each instruction, the ARM will have performed one of the following:

Increment: Address = Address + 4 * n

Decrement: Address = Address - 4 * n

where 'n' is the number of registers in the register list.

The A or B options determine where the base address has the defined adjustment before or after the memory has been accessed. There is a subtle difference, and if you are not careful it can lead to your information being a word askew to what you might have expected. This is illustrated in Figure 16c and Figure 16d.

```
STMIA Base,{R0-R6}              STMIB Base,{R0-R6}

                                 R6      Base+28
R6      Base+24                  R5      Base+24
R5      Base+20                  R4      Base+20
R4      Base+16                  R3      Base+16
R3      Base+12                  R2      Base+12
R2      Base+8                   R1      Base+8
R1      Base+4                   R0      Base+4
R0      <<Base                           <<Base
```

Figure 16c. The effect of IA and IB suffixes on STM.

In Figure 16c the left-hand model shows the storage pointer in Incrementing After mode. After the first register has been stored (R0), the storage pointer has four added to it and is incremented to Base+4 where the contents of R1 are placed. On the right-hand side of the model Incrementing Before is in operation. When the command is executed 4 is added to Base and the contents of R0 is stored at that address.

In Figure 16d the actions are the same except that in each case 4 is subtracted from Base either After or Before as illustrated.

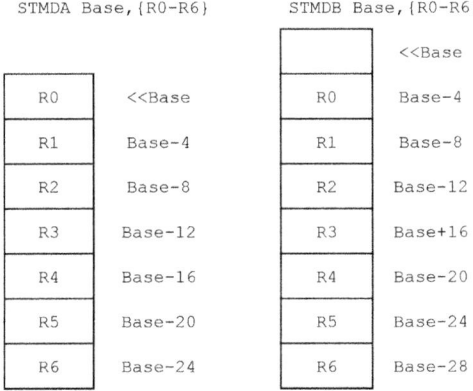

Figure 16d. The effect of DA and DB suffixes on STM.

Write Back

Unless the instruction asks for write-back to occur, then the address held in the specifying register remains unaltered. Its contents remain the same as they were when the command was first fetched. If we want a write-back to take place, the '!' operator must be included:

```
LDMIA R0!,{R2-R4}
STMDA R0!,{R5-R8, R10}
```

The value written into the address register (R0) is the address calculated after the last register in the list has been processed.

The STM and LDM instructions have a variety of applications. One of the most obvious is that used in combination they can be used to preserve and restore the contents of all the registers. If R0 holds the address of a free memory block, then save all the registers with:

```
STMIA R0, {R1-R14}
```

And restore them later with:

```
LDM R0, {R1-R14}
```

if R0 again has the address of the memory block.

A word of caution about including R15 in a list like this. If you block restore with LDM and include R15 you will most likely set your program into a continuous loop.

This write-back feature in this block data transfer instruction is provided to simplify the creation of stacks, the subject of the next chapter.

Block Copy Routine

Program 16a shows just how simple it is to copy a block of data from one place in memory to another. In fact, just four lines of assembler is all it takes, and this routine is robust enough to copy a block of memory that can be any length provided it is divisible by eight.

It uses registers R3 and R4 to first load and then store the data, so any information in them will be destroyed unless preserved first. R0, R1 and R2 hold addresses that point to the start and end of the data and the start address of its ultimate destination, respectively.

To see this work, you can use GDB. Make sure you assemble with the -g option. Enter GDB and load the file:

```
gdb prog16a
```

Set a breakpoint at the _exit routine (this is right after the block copy loop):

```
break _exit
```

Now run the program:

```
run
```

The program will run to the breakpoint, at which point type:

```
x/2x &dest
```

The '&' is used here to mean the 'location of' dest. If you do not use the ampersand, then the data labels will not be recognised. When the two-words of memory are displayed you will see that all the bits are now set (all fs) proving the block copy worked, as they were zeroes originally.

The routine can be extended to handle bigger blocks of memory. For example, by changing the two load and store instructions to read:

```
LDMIA R0!, {R3-R12}
STMIA R2!, {R3-R12}
```

you can work in blocks of 40 bytes (10 registers by 4 bytes each). Your data areas will need to be adjusted accordingly, or rather than using labels you may need to invoke absolute memory addresses.

Program 16a. Moving Blocks of Memory

```
/* Memory block copy routine */

        .global _start
_start:
        LDR R0, =begin      @ load locations
        LDR R1, =end        @ of both strings
        LDR R2, =dest       @ addr of destination

_blockcopy:
        LDMIA R0!, {R3-R4}
        STMIA R2!, {R3-R4}
        CMP R0, R1
        BNE _blockcopy

_exit:
        MOV R7, #1
        SWI 0

.section .data
begin:
        .word 0xFFFFFFFF
        .word 0xFFFFFFFF

end:
        .word 0
        .word 0
dest:
        .word 0
        .word 0
```

17: Stacks

Stacks have been a fundamental feature of computer systems since just after the day dot. In many respects they are exactly what you might think them to be, stacks of data, but they are stacks of data that you as the programmer own and control. Their management is a fundamental component of designing programs. Do it well and the program flows well. Do it badly and you'll be reaching for the power switch.

The general analogy is a stack of plates. In theory, you can continue putting a plate on top of a plate. Unless you are attempting a trick, if you want to take a plate off the stack it will be the last one you placed on it, the top plate. In this respect the last one on is the first one off. We refer to this as a LIFO structure, last in, first out. Try to take a plate out from the middle (or the bottom!) and, unless you do so very carefully, the lot comes crashing down. It's a good analogy.

Push and Pull

In the early days of home computers on systems such as the 6502 microprocessor, stacks were built in a simple fashion. You pushed data onto the stack and pulled (popped) data off the stack. For the most part you didn't even know where the stack was — that was managed by the CPU. However, as a programmer you did need to keep track of what order things went on to the stack. Generally, the concept is still true today in that a sequence of data pulled from the stack is always pulled from it in the reverse order it was pushed.

The instructions STM and LDM and their derivatives are what we use for pushing (STM) and pulling (LDM) data onto and off ARM stacks. These stacks are areas of memory that we as the programmer define. There is no limit to the number of stacks that can be used. The only restriction is the amount of memory available to implement them.

R13, also known as the Stack Pointer or SP, is designated to be used to hold an address relating to the location of the stack, but you can use any of the available registers for the purpose. If you are running several stacks you will need to allocate more registers or manage where you store the addresses in memory. Figure 17a illustrates a simple stack.

Raspberry Pi OS Assembly Language

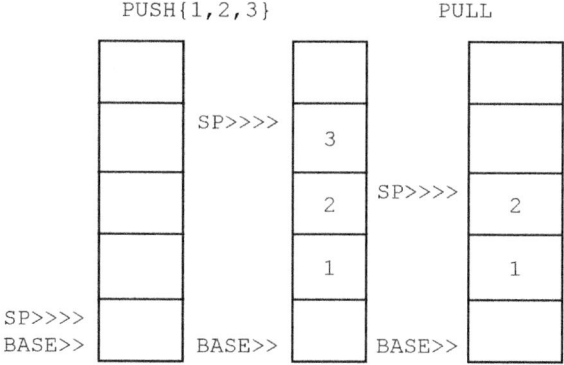

Figure 17a. A simple stack where each stack item is four-bytes wide.

To implement a simple stack can use the following instructions. The important thing to note is that the options for the STM instructions are always reversed for the LDM instruction.

```
STMIA SP!,{R0-R12, LR} @ push registers onto stack
LDMDB SP!,{R0-R12, PC} @ pull registers from stack
```

The IA and DB suffix options (introduced in the last chapter) are used in tandem to move up through memory to push them on, and then down through memory to pull them off. The LR and PC registers are used to save the Program Counter's address—therefore this two-line combination is an effective way to save register contents before calling a subroutine and restoring everything on return.

The use of the write-back function is vital. Without write-back the Stack Pointer will not be updated, and the stack will effectively be corrupted as we will not know our relative positive within it.

You may implement a stack with two pointers. The first is the base point, and this locates to the memory location where the stack begins. The second is the stack pointer which is used to point to the top of the stack. The base pointer remains a static address; the stack pointer might be a moving address or an offset from the base pointer. Hopefully, you can now understand how different addressing modes could be used to organise different types of stacks. Whichever way you fall, you will always need to keep a record of where the stack starts and the point where it must end. Without defining these two end limits, you could get into all sorts of trouble. Also, does the Stack Pointer provide the address of the next free space in the stack or the last space used? To make this situation easier to manage and to manage the balancing of pushes and pulls the pseudo instructions PUSH, and POP can also be used to place and retrieve information to and from the Stack:

```
PUSH {R0, R3, R5}      @ Push R0, R3, R5 onto Stack
POP {R0, R5-R8}        @ Pull R0, R5, R6, R7, R8 off stack
```

Stack Growth

In ARM architecture stacks are grouped by the way they grow through memory. Stacks can ascend through memory as items are pushed onto them, and they can descend through memory as data is pushed onto them. It's like being in space — there is no up or down, and the term is relative. Stand on the 10th floor of an empty 20 storey building. The 10th floor is the only entry and each floor, above and below, has four apartments. Eight families arrive; you can accommodate them on two floors up or two floors down. How do you want to do it?

In computer memory terms a stack that grows up — or ascends through memory — is one where the address grows larger. So as an item is pushed into it, the Stack Pointer increases its address by four-bytes. A stack that grows in memory by going down the memory address decreases; this is called a descending stack. In all, there are four types of stacks as listed in Figure 17b:

Postfix	Meaning
FA	Full Ascending Stack
FD	Full Descending Stack
EA	Empty Ascending Stack
ED	Empty Descending Stack

Figure 17b. The four types of ARM stack.

When the stack pointer points to the last occupied address on the stack it is known as a full stack. When the stack pointer indicates the next available free space on the stack, it is called an empty stack. Note that in this empty stack scenario the stack can have data on it; it is used to signify the condition of the next free word on the stack.

The option of full, empty, ascending or descending will often force itself on you and may just be decided by the way you are looping through your data. It may be easier to implement a descending stack as your code lends itself to a decremented count and it's easier to test for the Zero flag.

There are instructions in the instruction set that cater for these types of stacks and these are shown in Figure 17c.

Instruction Pair	Meaning
STMFD / LDMFD	Full Descending Stack
STMFA / LDMFA	Full Ascending Stack
STMED / LDMED	Empty Descending Stack
STMEA / LDMEA	Empty Ascending Stack

Figure 17c. Instruction set to access stacks.

Here are some examples:
```
STMED R13!, {R1-R5, R6}
LDMFD R13!, {R1-R4, R6}
```

There is nothing to stop you using different types of stacks within the same program. Just don't mix them up! Equally, you will understand now why write-back is compulsory in the construction of these instructions.

Examples of these stacks are illustrated in Figure 17d and Figure 17e. By default the ARM implements a full descending stack.

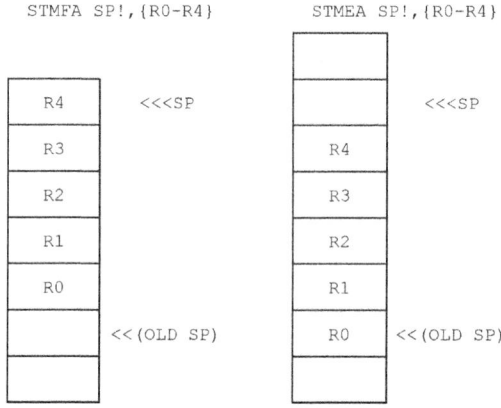

Figure 17d. Full and empty ascending stacks.

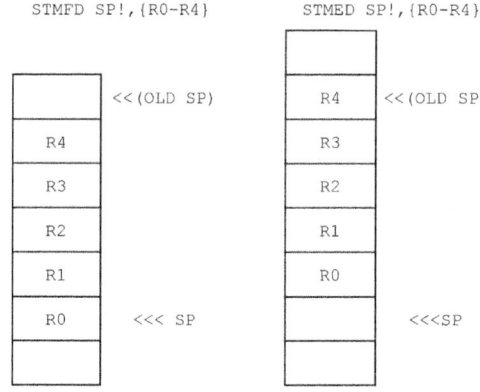

Figure 17e. Full and empty descending stacks.

The best way to understand stacks and their manipulation is to experiment with them. Try seeding an area of memory with known values, and then see if you can move this section of memory to another location via a stack, with the information and its order remaining intact.

Stack Application

Stacks have a multitude of applications, and we have already mentioned a few of them:

- Saving register contents
- Saving and processing data

A third use is to save link addresses when subroutines are called. By pushing the link addresses from the Link Register onto the stack, it is possible to create nested (one inside another) routines without fear of losing control in the program. As you link to a routine you push the link register onto the stack. You can then return from each subroutine by pulling the link addresses off the stack and popping them back into the Program Counter.

The stack also makes it relatively simple to swap register contents around without ever having to go through another register. You simply push the required registers in the stack and then pull them in the order you need them. Imagine this situation where register contents need to be swapped:

```
Source          Destination
R0                  R3
R1                  R4
R2                  R6
R3                  R5
R4                  R0
R5                  R1
R6                  R2
```

At first sight, this looks complex. However, the following four lines will manage it:

```
STMFD SP!, {R0-R6}
LDMFD SP!, {R3, R4, R6}
LDMFD SP!, {R5}
LDMFD SP!, {R0, R1, R2}
```

The first line pushes R0 to R6 onto the stack. The top three items on the stack are (in descending order) R0, R1 and R2. From the chart above these must go into R3, R4, and R6 respectively, and this is what line two does.

The Stack Pointer is now positioned at R3, which is transferred into R5. This leaves just R4, R5 and R6 on the stack which, in the final line, is pulled into R0, R1 and R2, respectively. What looks to be a complex task at the onset is in fact a simple one.

Framed Work

There is only one 'official' stack implement on which the instruction described in this chapter will work. If you implement you own stack, you will need to manage the memory block containing it yourself. This is helped by the use of labels within your assembly listing.

One other method that used the 'real' stack is to create a Stack Frame. This is an area on the stack which we can 'reserve' for our own use. In this scenario we restet the stack pointer to create a gap within the stack for our own use.

For example, of we wanted to store the contents of three registers we would require 12 bytes (3 registers x 4 bytes =12). The segment below shows hoe we can achieve this:

```
SUB SP, #12      @ Take 12 bytes off the stack pointer
STR R1, [SP]
STR R2, [SP, #4]
STR R3, [SP, #8]
```

The three registers R1, R2, and R3 are stored within the gap we have created as illustrated in Figure 17f. You will need to remember to close this gap in the stack when you have finished the operation you needed the space for:

```
ADD SP, #12
```

It is quite common to use this method to preserve register contents before calling a function (see Chapter 21).

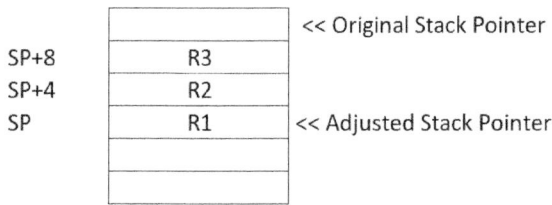

Figure 17f. Forming a stack frame 'gap'.

Frame Pointer

When a lot of use of the stack is being made it can be difficult to remember where things are, and what offset is what. Rather than use the SP and offsets we can invoke a Frame Pointer—this is a pointer to the stack frame. It is common convention to use R11 as the FP, but this is not a hard and fast rule. Just remember to push the registers contents onto the stack, so it can be restored later. After creating the stack frame, we can set the FP to next free spot on the stack (remembering it grows in descending addresses).

```
SUB FP, SP, #4
SUB SP, #12
```

Now we can use the FP to access our variables:

```
STR R1, [SP]
STR R2, [FP, #-4]
STR R3, [FP, #-8]
```

18: Directives and Macros

GCC provides many additional tools to help in the writing of machine code programs. This includes instructions that allow you to store data within your programs and the ability to pass information to them when they are called from the prompt. All assembler directives begin with a period or full-stop and there are a lot of them with GCC. We have already seen several of these in action in earlier programs. In this chapter we'll look at some of them in more detail.

Data Storage Directives

To store character string information within our programs, there are two options:

```
.ascii "This is the string to print."
.asciz "This string has a zero added to the end"
```

A string is written between double quotes. The 'z' in the second option stands for zero and a zero byte (0x00) is appended at the end of the string. This is a useful way to end mark a string in memory as it allows for a simple Zero flag test when you are looking for the end of it. Both directives allow for control or escape code characters to be embedded within them by use of a backslash character, '\'. Figure 18a gives some of the more popular and useful ones:

Option	Effect
\b	backspace
\f	formfeed
\n	new line
\r	return
\t	tab
\\	include '\' in string
\"	include quote in string

Figure 18a. Popular backslash controls for use in strings.

The following:

```
.ascii "1\t2\t3\r\n4\t5\t6\r\n7\t8\t9\r\n"
```

would print out a simple but neatly formatted table using any of the write routines shown in this book. (Remember to change the string length count accordingly.)

As your programs become more sophisticated and have real application you will need to store information in them. This might be in the form of constants, addresses or messages to be printed. For the latter, we have used the string operator. By placing the data within the body of the machine code, we can be safe in the knowledge that it is 'protected'.

In the block move example from Chapter 15 we saw a clear indication how this could be done by using the '.word' directive to write four-byte words of information to memory. As well as '.word' there are other directives that can create space in a similar way. Program 18a shows two of these, '.byte' and '.equ'.

Program 18a. Use of .byte and .equ directives

```
/* Use of byte and equ to sum a set of numbers */
    .global _start
_start:

    LDR R1, =values
    LDR R2, =endvalues
    MOV R0, #0

_loop:
    LDRB R3, [R1], #increment
    ADD R0, R0, R3
    CMP R1, R2
    BNE _loop

_exit:
    MOV R7, #1
    SWI 0

.data
.equ increment, 1

values:
    .byte 1,2,3,4,5,6,7,8,9
endvalues:
```

The '.byte' directive allows for a sequence of values separated by commas to be stored sequentially in memory. As the directive suggests these values must be in the range 0-255.

The '.equ' directive allows an immediate value to be assigned to a name. The name can then be used in your source files. This is handy in that if you need to change the value at any point you just have to change the '.equ' definition and not any and every reference to it in the source.

If you look at the '.data' section of Program 18a you can see that the constant 'increment' has been assigned the value 1. You can see how this is used as the post-indexing counter at the start of the _loop routine.

The label 'values:' is used to mark the start of the '.byte' definition. A second label called 'endvalues:' is used to mark the end of the '.byte' sequence. This is a handy technique to use when dealing with tables or arrays of data as a simple CMP test sees if the end of the sequence has been reached. The program illustrates this.

If you assemble, link, and run Program 18a and then enter:

```
echo $?
```

the value 45 should be returned, which is the sum of the bytes.

Figure 18b below summarises a few important data directives.

Directive	Function
.equ	Assign immediate value to named label. Example: .equ one, 1
.byte	Store byte sized values, separated by commas into memory. Example: .byte 1,2,3,55,255
.word	Store four-byte values, separated by commas into memory. Example: .word 0xFFFFFFFF, 0xFF

Figure 18b. Important data directives..

Aligning Data

If you intend to store data within your executable segments, within the '.text' sections of your program, then this can create problems. All assembled opcodes must start on a word boundary. If you insert text or data that does not completely fill the space to a four-byte boundary then the assembler will freak and issue you with an:

```
Unaligned opcodes detected in executable segment
```

error.

Consider Program 18a. If you add these extra lines at the end of the _start: section:

```
    BAL _loop
_string:
    .ascii "12345"
```

and try to assemble the code you will get the above error. This can be corrected by adding the following after the '.ascii' definition:

```
    .align 2
```

This pads out the space with 0s to the next word boundary. You can check this out using GDB.

There is generally no reason to use the '.align' directive outside of the executable sections of your code. Any definitions made in data sections are normally stored at the end of the file by the assembler to avoid such problems.

Macros

A macro is a fragment of code – which can be of any length – and is defined by a name. The macro definition can be called from within the program by using the macros name. During assembly, the assembler block that constitutes the macro definition is inserted whenever the macro name is encountered in the listing.

Many programmers set about writing their library of macros that they can use in a variety of circumstances. They simply load the macros they need and then call the macro from their program when need. This differs from the pseudo-code given in Figure 2b at the start of the book which uses subroutine calls to jump to different parts of the program. Macros create linear code – one long program! Both permit a group of instructions defined as a single entity.

Macros are not a substitute for subroutines since the macro is replaced with the code and therefore makes the program execution linear in nature. Long macros that are used many times in a program will result in an enormous expansion of the final code size. In this case, a subroutine would be a better choice, since the code in the body of the subroutine is not inserted into source code when called.

Macros are useful when you have some difficult or complex calculations to do and where it may be easy to make a typo mistake. You can use the constant data inside the macro and pass the variable information to the macro each time you can do it. Macros are also useful to avoid the overhead of a subroutine call and return when the subroutine itself is but a few instructions.

Program 18b defines a simple macro, call 'addtwo' that takes two parameters, 'val1' and 'val2', which are passed into R1 and R2 respectively, and are summed together with their addition returned in R0.

Raspberry Pi OS Assembly Language

Program 18b. Implementing a simple macro.

```
/* Implement a simple macro   #1    */
        .global   _start
_start:

.macro addtwo val1, val2
        MOV R1, #\val1
        MOV R2, #\val2
        ADD R0, R1, R2
.endm

        addtwo 3, 4

        MOV R7, #1              @ exit through syscall
        SWI 0
```

The '.macro' directive is used to define the macro which we give a name, 'addtwo' and I have chosen to call the two parameters 'val1' and 'val2'. As you can see the macro definition is terminated by the directive '.endm'.

Note that inside the macro definition the two named parameters are preceded with a backslash '\' character. This is to signify to the compiler that they are parameters and not absolute values. The most common mistake when writing macros is to omit the backslash before parameters.

Calling, or 'invoking' the macro is simple, just insert the name in the assembler and include the parameters. If you run Program 18b and then type:

```
echo $?
```

You'll get the result 7.

It is worth looking at the code produced by Program18b. If you have assembled and linked using the -g option you can look at the code in GDB with:

```
x/20i _start
```

Which will return something similar to what is sho,wn below in Figure 18c.

Note that the disassembly shows that the immediate values have been passed into the assembled code in the first two lines at <_start> and <_start+4>. This is not a subroutine call. The required code is assembled inline at the point required.

```
0x10054   <_start>:       mov    r1, #3
0x10058   <_start+4>:     mov    r2, #4
0x1005c   <_start+8>:     add    r0, r1, r2
0x10560   <_start+12>:    mov    r7, #1
0x10064   <_start+16>:    svc    0x00000000
0x10068   Cannot access memory at address 0x10068
```

Figure 18c. Disassembled output from Program 18b.

Program 18c shows a modified version of this which uses the MLA instruction to add the products of each multiplication together. This time we define the 'multtwo' macro three times to pass three successive sets of values to the macro to calculate:

(2*2)+(3*4)+(5*6)

The caveat here though is that, at this point, there is no error checking.

Program 18c. Multi-calling a macro.

```
/* Implement a simple macro #2   */
        .global    _start
_start:

.macro multtwo val1, val2
        MOV R1, #\val1
        MOV R2, #\val2
        MLA R0, R1, R2, R0
.endm

        MOV R0, #0
        multtwo 2, 2
        multtwo 3, 4
        multtwo 5, 6

        MOV R7, #1          @ exit through syscall
        SWI 0
```

Assemble, link, and execute the program. All being well then when the prompt returns you can obtain the result using:

    echo ?$

Which should return 46.

A disassembly of this same code will provide something like that shown in Figure 18d is you are using GDB and:

```
x/20i _start
```

Note again how the macro has been assembled in absolute terms into the body of the text, and this is a good illustration to allow us to highlight a few of the implications of this, in no particular order:

- The final code size of the assembled file will be larger than might be otherwise expected. (In theory this could create a speed issue but in a RISC environment this is not normally a problem.)
- Debugging can be harder as it is easy to lose yourself in long code repeats.
- You require greater diligence to ensure that your registers contents are saved in the appropriate places if required.

```
0x10054    <_start>:          mov     r0, #0
0x10058    <_start+4>:        mov     r1, #2
0x1005c    <_start+8>:        mov     r2, #2
0x10560    <_start+12>:       mla     r0, r1, r2, r0
0x10064    <_start+16>:       mov     r1, #3
0x10068    <_start+20>:       mov     r2, #4
0x1006c    <_start+24>:       mla     r0, r1, r2, r0
0x10070    <_start+28>:       mov     r1, #5
0x10074    <_start+32>:       mov     r1, #6
0x10078    <_start+36>:       mla     r0, r1, r2, r0
0x1007c    <_start+40>:       mov     r7, #1
0x10080    <_start+44>:       svc     0x00000000
0x10084:   Cannot access memory at address 0x10084
```

Figure 18d. Disassembled output from Program 18c.

Including Macros

Programs 18b and 18c show the usefulness of macros, however that assume that the macro source at this point has the macro definition with the body source. A major benefit of macros is that that you can create a macro library that allows you to simply include the macro or macro library you require as an when assuming that have been written accordingly of course! With this in mind let's re-address this issue by creating a simple math macro file that will supply the two functions offered by Program 18b and Program18c. This Program 18d below which is in fact just a source file that includes the macro definitions of both. Program 18e is the testing program for this.

Program 18d. AddMult macro file

```
/* Macros: Addtwo and MultTwo    *
.macro addtwo val1, val2
        @ On Exit R1,R2 contain val1, val2
        @ R0 contains result
        MOV R1, #\val1
        MOV R2, #\val2
        ADD R0, R1, R2
.endm
.macro multtwo val1, val2
        @ On Exit R1,R2 contain val1, val2
        @ R0 contains accumulated result
        MOV R1, #\val1
        MOV R2, #\val2
        MLA R0, R1, R2, R0
.endm
```

Program 18d can be saved as a normal text source file with the '.s' option. There is no need to assemble and link it as that will be undertaken when it gets included in the main program when called. Just ensure that the filename used in the include (line two of Program 18e) is the one used to save the macro definition file above. (They should also be in the same directory at this point.)

Program 18e. Macro Include Test

```
/* Test External Macros  */
.include "Prog18d.s"
.global _start

_start:
        MOV R0, #0

_add:
        addtwo 3, 4

_mult:
        multtwo 2, 2
_exit:
   MOV R7, #1              @ exit through syscall
   SWI 0
```

Raspberry Pi OS Assembly Language

You can save, assemble and link Prog18e.s in the normal fashion. If you execute and echo the result then the answer, 11, should be forthcoming.

If you disassemble the executable via GDB the output will be along these lines:

```
0x10054    <_start>:       mov     r0, #0
0x10058    <_add>:         mov     r1, #3
0x1005c    <_add+4>:       mov     r2, #4
0x10560    <_add+8>:       add     r0, r1, r2
0x10064    <_mult>:        mov     r1, #2
0x10068    <_mult+4>:      mov     r2, #2
0x1006c    <_mult+8>:      mov     r0, r1, r2, r0
0x10070    <_exit>:        mov     R7, #1
0x10074    <_exit+8>:      svc     0x00000000
0x10078:   Cannot access memory at address 0x10078
```

Figure 18e. Disassembled output from Program 18e.

Additional labels were included in the source file when it was assembled. Using GDB in this way, especially in multi-macro assembly, makes referencing and identifying sections of code easier to distinguish.

The ARM instructions to load 0 into R0 was provided at the start of the code - even though it wasn't needed as the result of 'addtwo' would overwrite the contents of R0 regardless. The result from the 'addtwo' routine was carried in the 'multtwo' routine and accumulated accordingly.

Again, here static values are provided to illustrate how a macro is treated at assemble and link time. However, we can utilise memory to pass values into such macro routines should we not know what their values are at the time of writing the macro, and this can be facilitated using the Stack using the methods illustrated in the previous chapter. Be careful though when using these stack frames within macros as the accumulative effect of adjusting the stack can have catastrophic effects on your data and program management if you are not careful.

Note: When you have code that may contain multiple labels and you are not sure when the start an end may be exactly then a good trick is to make disassembling your code easier is to use something like:

```
disassemble _start, _exit+8
```

This normally works for me as I try to be consistent in the way I enter and exit my assembler code.

Many of the larger programs within this book can be constructed and implemented as macros. There are one or two I have provided.

Mostly though, I have given the assembler as a single linear source file to make it easier to read and understand. However, once you have grasped the concepts you are good to go.

19: File Handling

Files play a big part in the operation of your Raspberry Pi. Almost all the activities you undertake involve the use of a file. Mostly, the Raspberry Pi OS, takes care of the file management. The system provides the infrastructure to allow programs to interface with it and to perform most file operations. This ranges from creating files, to opening and closing files and many other file operations we take for granted.

In Chapter 8 we saw how we can take a line of text and overwrite it or convert it from uppercase to lowercase. That ASCII text was located as a string as part of the program itself. In that instance we knew where the string was located as there was a named label identifying it. What if the information we need was in a file stored on an SD Card or on a USB?

Files are a fundamental element to all computer operations, especially so Raspberry Pi OS (Raspbian). In this chapter we'll look at how to create, open, close, read from and write to files. Figure 19a lists the system calls we will utilise to do this.

```
        Description              Call          No.
Read    Read from a file         sys_read      3
Write   Write to a file          sys_write     4
Open    Open or create a file    sys_open      5
Close   Close a file             sys_close     6
Create  Create a new file        sys_creat     8
Sync    Sync-flush file          sys_fsync     118
```

Figure 19a. File Associated System Calls used in Program 19a.

We've used some of these before, and most require additional information passed to them before being called. Remember that the Syscall number (listed in Figure 19a) must be loaded into R7, and any additional details provided via R0-R6. Not all registers are needed for every call, but assume they are unless you know otherwise. R0 is often used to return information by the Syscall, such as an error number or result.

The listing for Program 19a shows how you can use these calls. In this example, taking the contents of a file, reading the first 26 characters from it into a memory buffer, before writing them out to a new file. This example assumes that the files are in the current directory, or the same directory as the program itself. Nothing special in the 26 characters, other than our input file will comprise an uppercase, alphabet (A-Z), which we'll convert to lowercase, before writing it to the new file. The program will also illustrate some file error checking along the way.

Program 19a. File Creation and Access.

```
/* File Creation and Access Using Syscall            */
/* Create and Open File, Read from File, Write to File */

    .global _start

_start:
@ Open file to read in from.
@ Assumes file exits in current directory
@ Or generates an error message (error1)

    LDR   R0, =inputFile    @ Addr of filename
    MOV   R1, #o_rdonly     @ flag read only file
    MOV   R2, #s_rdwr
    MOV   R7, #sys_open     @ Call open file
    SWI   0

    MOVS  R8, R0            @ Save/Test file flag in R8
    BPL   moveon            @ If positive, moveon
    MOV   R0, #1            @ Set screen as output
    LDR   R1, =error1       @ addr of error1 message
    MOV   R2, #18           @ string length
    MOV   R7, #4            @ Write code
    SWI   0
    B     finish            @ terminate program
moveon:
    @ Create/and-or Open File to write too
    LDR   R0, =outputFile
    MOV   R1, #(o_create+o_wronly)
    MOV   R2, #s_rdwr       @ access rights
    MOV   R7, #sys_open     @ load syscall 5
    SWI   0                 @ Make the call
    MOVS  R9, R0            @ Save file flag
    BPL   readlinein        @ If positive file there
    MOV   R0, #1            @ Non-existent so error2
```

```
        LDR R1, =error2
        MOV R2, #18
        MOV R7, #4
        SWI 0
        B finish                @ terminate program

readlinein:                     @ read line from InFile.txt
        MOV R0, R8              @ File descriptor R8>R0
        LDR R1, =inbuffer       @ location of inbuffer
        MOV R2, #alphabet       @ length of alphabetbuffer
        MOV R7, #sys_read
        SWI 0                   @ InFile >> InBuffer
        MOV R10, R0             @ Save bytes written in R10
        MOV R1, #0
        LDR R0,=inbuffer
        STRB R1, [R0, R10]      @ Write null terminator to buffer

convertUpperCase:
        PUSH {R8}
        PUSH {R9}
        MOV R8, #0              @ counter

loop:
        LDR R0, =inbuffer       @ Move file from in to out
        LDRB R1, [R0, R8]       @ doing ORR conversion
        ORR R1, R1, #0x20
        LDR r0, =outbuffer
        STRB R1, [R0, R8]
        ADD R8, #1              @ increment loop counter
        CMP R8, #26             @ is it alphabet length?
        BNE loop                @ no so loop again
        POP {R9}                @ restore file files
        POP {R8}

writebuffer:
        MOV R0, R9
        LDR R1,=outbuffer       @ addr of outbuffer
        MOV R2, #alphabet       @ length of alphabet
        MOV R7, #sys_write      @ write converted buffer
        SWI 0
        MOV R1, #0
```

```
@ flush and close 'infile'
    MOV R0, R8
    MOV R7, #sys_fsync
    SWI 0
    MOV R0, R8
    MOV R7, #sys_close
    SWI 0

    @ flush and close 'outfile'
    MOV R0, R9
    MOV R7, #sys_fsync
    SWI 0
    MOV R0, R9
    MOV R7, #sys_close
    SWI 0

finish:
    MOV     R0, #0      @ Use 0 return code
    MOV     R7, #1
    SWI     0

.equ    sys_open,   5
.equ    sys_read,   3
.equ    sys_write,  4
.equ    sys_close,  6
.equ    sys_fsync,  118
.equ    o_rdonly,   0
.equ    s_rdwr,     0666
.equ    o_wronly,   1
.equ    o_create,   0100
.equ    alphabet,   26      @ file length in bytes

.data
inputFile: .asciz "infile.txt"
outputFile: .asciz "outfile.txt"
error1: .asciz "Input file error \n"
error2: .asciz "Output file error\n"
inbuffer: .fill (alphabet+1), 1, 65
outbuffer: .fill (alphabet+1), 1, 66
```

If you look at the end of the listing for Program 19a you will notice, there are several 'equ' definitions setting up constants (a few lines after the label finish:). The '.data' section contains areas where string information is stored. These areas are vital to the program as they contain system calls values, flag values and file names. These label names and definitions are commonplace within the industry, and thus enhance program readability. Many programmers create specific macro file definitions that you can then '.include' to help ensure consistency if you so desire.

There is a minimum of three parameters required by the system for opening a file, and these are provided in the first three registers thus:

R0	Pointer to the filename to open, stored as a null terminated ASCII string.
R1	Flag to specify a mode of action for file open, read, write, read/write.
R2	Access mode permission values.

The first five code lines of the program open the file we want to read from. The system number for this is 5. if the file does not exist, an error is generated. Therefore, the filename is essential, and we load the address of this into R0. R1 requires for a code specifying the file operation; we use in this case 0 as it is being open as a read-only file. R2 defines the permission values and 0666 (octal 666) is required here.

On return, R0 will contain details of any errors. If a positive number, then the file was located and opened. If it returns a negative value, the file could not be found or opened. An error occurred, and it's not possible to proceed, therefore the next section of lines prints out the 'error1' message string.

Assuming all is good the value passed into R8 for preservation (contains the descriptor for the file), a small jump is made, and program operation continues at 'moveon'.

Having successfully opened the 'inputFile' we do the same for the 'outputFile'. Although, in this instance, if the file does not exist the syscall will create it for us. Information is passed again through the sys_open call. If all is good, the branch to 'readlinein' takes place, otherwise an 'error2' message is printed to the screen, and the program ends.

At 'readlinein' we first move the file descriptor previously saved in R8 back into R0. R1 is pointed to an address of where we can store the contents of the file we are reading-in, and then takes a number that defines the number of bytes we need to read in, before calling sys-read. The bytes are read and stored in the RPi memory at the defined location. On return from the call the number of bytes written is returned in R0. This is moved to R10, so we have a pointer as to where we have ended. A zero is then written at the end of the buffer.

The 'convertupcase' and 'loop' sections that follow are all about doing something with the information read in from our open file. This can be whatever you want at this stage. For example, here, we are going to read each byte from the 'inbuffer', ORR it with 0x20 to convert to lowercase and the store it back to the 'outbuffer' location. As we need a register or two to work with the contents of R8 and R9 are pushed on the stack for the interim. On completion R8 and R9 are restored, and the 'outbuffer' contents are written to the open output file (using the restored R9 as the file descriptor handle).

Finally, the two files are flushed and closed using sys_fsync and sys_close, again using the relevant file descriptors in R8 and R9.

A few points. Before running the program create the input file 'infile.txt' using a suitable text editor and place:

    ABCDEFGHIJKLMNOPQRSTUVWXYZ

on the first line. Save the file to the same directory as Program 19a. Make sure the filename is the same as used in the .data section of the listing.

In the listing the 'inbuffer' and 'outbuffer' labels are used as buffers for the reading, converting and writing the information. In both cases, I fill the buffers with a string of As (65) and Bs (66) to distinguish them from one another. If the program performs correctly, these will end up with the uppercase and lowercase alphabets in them, respectively. This is handy if you wish to debug the program at any point you can also dump these sections of memory to see what is there, thus helping you to identify where you are up to or otherwise at any point.

Assemble and link Program 19a. Ensure that 'infile.txt' is in the same directory and then execute the program. All being well you should see 'outfile.txt' appear in the directory. Open 'outfile.txt' and examine the result.

If there are any logical errors within your source, they should show up in the contents of 'outfile.txt'. One advantage of using the character strings, including the As and Bs used in the memory buffers, is that if anything other than what you expected turns up in 'outfile.txt' you can pinpoint where the error is.

Once you have the program and any versions you derive from it running correctly, you can always change the As and Bs to 0s should you wish.

File Permissions

When opening and reading files earlier we needed to specify several values which we described as flags and modes. We placed these in R1 and R2 as part of the syscall process. We defined these as numeric values.

Figure19b is the output from a directory containing the files needed and/or created by executing Program 19a. You can get such a listing by entering the following in a terminal window:

```
ls -l
```

Anything in the current directory will be shown in the listing, including directories and files.

```
-rwxr-xr-x    1    pi    pi    2384    Sep 25    09:54    prog19a
-rw-r--r--    1    pi    pi    2496    Sep 25    09:54    prog19a.o
-rw-r--r--    1    pi    pi    2813    Sep 25    09:54    prog19a.s
-rw-r--r--    1    pi    pi    28      Sep 25    09:54    infile.txt
-rw-r--r--    1    pi    pi    26      Sep 25    09:54    outfile.txt
```

Figure 19b. File attributes.

The first column is the one with the file attributes. A string of ten characters makes up this column: an example would be:

`-rwxr-xr-x`

In the first column. In the case of a file then after the first character (-) the following nine characters come as sets of three which define if the file can be read (r), written (w), or executed(x), or not (-). The three groups of three relate to permission of the 'owner', the 'group' and 'other users' have.

So, in the case of the first file in the listing, it can be read, it can be written, and it can be executed. When a 'd' exists as the first letter of the string, then this indicates a directory and not a file.

The attributes for infile.txt are:

`-rw-r--r-- 1 pi pi   28 Sep 25 09:39 infile.txt`

In the example above, we can see the first letter is not d but a hyphen (-). So, we know (infile.txt) is a file, not a directory. Next the owner's permissions are 'rw-' so the owner can read and write but not execute. This may seem odd that the owner does not have all three permissions, but the x permission is not needed as it is a text file, to be read by a text editor, and not executable. The group's permissions are set to r--, so the group can read the file but not write/edit it in any way — it is essentially like setting something to read-only. We can see that the same permissions apply to everyone else as well.

Compare this to 'prog19a' where the attributes are:

`-rwxr-xr-x 1 pi pi 2384 Sep 25 09:54 prog19a`

Here the first letter is a hyphen (-). So, we know it is a file, not a directory. Next the owner's permissions are 'rwx' so the owner has the ability to read, write and execute. The 'Group' and 'Other' permissions are set to r-x, so they can read and execute the file but not write nor edit it in any way.

How does this relate to the numeric values we used in the program? The mode was a three-digit number, in fact it was an octal number.

Raspberry Pi OS Assembly Language

To come up with this three-digit number you need to consider what permissions you want owner, group, and all others to have. Each operation is represented by a number:

```
r=4

w=2

x=1
```

Consider the 'prog19a' attributes. Breaking it down into the three groups of three we have:

```
Owner:    rwx    = 4+2+1 = 7
Group:    r-x    = 4+0+1 = 5
Other:    r-x    = 4+0+1 = 5
```

The value then is 0755. (Remember the 0 at the front signifies an octal value - base 8).

The two text files are:

```
Owner: rw-=4+2+0=6
Group: r--=4+0+0=4
Other: r--=4+0+0=4
```

Which becomes = 0644.

20: Using libc

The assembler and linker we have been using to write and create machine programs so far is just a small part of the GCC Compiler. As I said at the onset the GNU GCC compiler is a C Compiler. It will take programs written in the C programming language and convert them into machine code. Broadly speaking, it takes the C source file and translates it into an assembly language source file, which in turn gets translated into an executable machine code program which is linked together. We have been dealing with the last couple of processes here. But that is only just the tip of the iceberg.

This is not a book about C programming, but that is not to say we cannot use many of the features that C and the GCC Compiler provides. This includes **libc**, which is the standard function library of C. As we saw in an earlier chapter, we can use the operating system Syscall to perform common operations such as input/output, memory management, and string manipulation.

Using C Functions in Assembler

Likewise, the C language has no in-built facilities for performing these functions but provides the interface to allow access to them, without necessarily needing to know a lot about the underlying Syscall itself. In addition, many of the things you may be looking to program for yourself may already be found in libc or available in other C *libraries*, and they can be included and linked into your own assembly source. So, there are libraries to be found that are pre-packed and ready to be included by the compile process. Figure 20a illustrates diagrammatically how libc sits within the overall interface.

Syscalls	User Space	
Kernel	libc	Procedures

Figure 20a. libc and user space.

The kernel in our case is the Raspberry Pi OS. The area above it is the user space. This is where our files sit. Recall the addresses that were being displayed when we used GDB to disassemble our programs. The libc code sits directly on top of the kernel and any of our application code sits on top of this. Although it makes no real difference operationally, diagrammatically we can see how easy it is for the libc functions to tap into the kernel. For the most parts when an application is written, because it is often written in C, it uses the libc interface to access the Syscalls. Rarely in this situation would a programmer go directly to the Syscall.

The main reason for using the Syscalls directly and not using libc would be one of space and speed. Some might also consider it a purer method of programming and not the rather disjointed code that integrating libc creates. The libc library is of a certain size and much of its basic configuration might be redundant. This is not normally an issue, but for a tight, small routine where speed and memory overhead might be critical then it may be a critical consideration. Technically your own program becomes a procedure which uses the resource libc provides.

From a user point of view a copy of 'The GNU C Library Reference Manual' is essential. Not to learn C (but that isn't a bad thing to do — you will become increasingly aware of how fundamental it is to system and application programming) but for the detail of the various functions you can access. This contains information required and returned. In this chapter we'll be looking at some worked examples on these and using the above document as our source. The GNU C Library Reference Manual can be found on the GNU website for download. Another source of instant help is the online manual. At the command line prompt type:

```
man printf
```

and you will get a lot of text output relating to the use and directives available within this C function. Here 'man' stands for 'manual' and it will provide information relating to the function name after it.

Source File Structure

The format of the source file used with the full GCC compiler is a little different from what we have been using to date. It is no more difficult to create and is in fact a lot simpler to compile as we do not need to do the assembly and link stages separately — they can be done with a single command. Have a look at Program 20a. This is a revised version of the write string code that formed Program 7a.

Program 20a. GCC source file structure.

```
/* Printing a string with libc - requirements change */
/* string must end with zero  using printf function  */

        .global main
        .func main
main:
        STMFD SP!, {LR}     @ save LR
        LDR R0, =string     @ R0 points to string
        BL printf           @ Call libc
        LDMFD SP!, {PC}     @ restore PC

_exit:
        MOV PC, LR          @ simple exit
.data
string:
        .asciz "Hello World String\n"
```

The first thing to notice is that the 'global _start' definition has been replaced with 'global main' thus:

```
        .global main
        .func main
 main:
```

The structure used is important as this is used by the compiler to tell libc where the main program is located. Because all C and lib C routines are written as named functions then we must declare this main part of our code as a function and then use a label to impart exactly where the function starts. These three lines do that. (As you can see, they effectively undertake the same task that '_start' label does when using the assembler-linker only, notwithstanding the addition of the function definition.)

The two instructions at the start and end of the main function save and then restore the link register on the stack. These commands and their use were discussed in Chapter 17. Strictly speaking they are not necessary here, but it is often an accepted convention just to preserve the link register when a function is entered. So, we'll stick with it for now.

The libc function **printf** is used to print the asciz string defined at the end of the listing. printf is not a C command but is a function defined in the library that we can use. It is a very versatile function and all that is required before we call it is for R0 to be given the address of the string. In all cases printf requires that the string be terminated with a zero and therefore the asciz directive is — and should always—be used.

Finally, we have abandoned our normal exit function for the much simpler MOV instruction. The SWI version would have worked equally as well, but the full GCC compiler will accept this exit method which is more common in the wider programming world. You can continue to use the SWI method if you like the option of using the echo command to display return contents.

If you have tried to assemble and link this command in the way we have described so far it will have failed because there is no '_start' entry point. Compiling with GCC can be done in a single-step thus:

```
gcc <options> <destination_name> <input_name.s>
```

So, for Program 20a you might use:

```
gcc -o prog20a prog20a.s
```

and execute the program with:

```
./prog20a
```

Investigating the Executable

At this stage it is worth looking at the code that is compiled using GDB. Recompile including the –g option to create the debugging data:

```
gcc -g -o prog20a prog20a.s
```

and then enter the disassembler:

```
gdb prog20a
```

If you now disassemble some code using:

```
disassemble main
```

or:

```
x/44i main
```

you should see by the labels used that the library component of the file is tagged on after '_exit:'. However, if you look through the listing you should also see branches to addresses before your main entry point. Inspect these areas. You will see that the labels associated in the listing indicate that this is libc initialisation code. Your program has almost been wrapped within libc! As you look at the listing you will probably notice some instructions that we haven't discussed so far (but will with the next program example).

Investigating listings in this way is a great way to learn about machine code programming. Remember, you can step-through this code and print register values out at any time using GDB, so you can get a good insight into what is happening and how.

The printf function is amazingly versatile. Program 20b shows how values can be passed into printf and used in printing results.

Program 20b. Passing parameters to printf.

```
/* Printing a string using libc and passing */
/* parameters to function for use in printf  */

        .global main
        .func main
main:
        PUSH {LR}               @ use pseudo directive
        LDR R0, =string         @ R0 points to string
        MOV R1, #10             @ first value in R1
        MOV R2, #15             @ second value in R2
        MOV R3, #25             @ result in R3
        BL printf               @ Call libc
        POP {PC}                @ restore PC with pseudo

_exit:
        MOV PC, LR              @ simple exit

.data
string:
        .asciz "If you add %d and %d you get %d.\n"
```

The first thing to notice here is that the entry and exit instructions for main: have changed. We are using PUSH and POP. These are compiler directives and not ARM instructions, but they have the same effect as the ones used in Program 20a. They are a lot easier to use as you don't have to think too much about what type of stack you are going to use and what order the stack adjusters are used in. (However, it is worth remembering that should you decide to use another assembler, directives may change and not be compatible with your existing code. That said, you will almost certainly have to adjust your code format with a new assembly program.)

The string definition here includes three parameters within it. These are signified by the preceding '%'. If you compile and run this program you will see that its output is:

    If you add 10 and 15 you get 25.

Looking at the listing for Program20b we can see that these three values were passed in R1, R2 and R3. When using libc functions such as printf there is a standard way to pass and return information into them and we'll look at this in the next chapter which deals with writing functions.

The table in Figure 20b below lists some of the output options available to use within printf. This list is by no means extensive, but it does provide some options for you to experiment with, using and editing the above program.

Code	Function
%d	Print an integer as a signed decimal number.
%o	Print an integer as an unsigned octal number.
%u	Print an integer as an unsigned decimal number.
%x	Print an integer as an unsigned hexadecimal numbers using lower-case letters
%X	Print an integer as an unsigned hexadecimal number using upper-case letters.
%c	Print a single character.
%%	Print a literal '%' character.

Figure 20b Output parameters recognised by printf.

Number Input with Scanf

You could be forgiven for thinking that scanf performs the reverse task of printf, but it does not. scanf takes a string of characters entered at the keyboard and converts it into its numerical value and stores it in memory. For example, if when using scanf you typed:

```
255
```

when requested scanf would store the binary equivalent in memory. In hex this would be:

```
0xFF
```

The reason for discussing this routine at this point, rather than the string-input routine equivalent of printf is that it illustrates another way a libc function expects and uses data. Not all functions expect data in the same way. This is a concept that you will need to bear in mind as you come to learn how to access libc functions and write your own.

However, as with printf, scanf recognises many, many different formats and you could spend a great deal of time learning and experimenting with them both. For this example, we'll stick with the use of integer values. This is the %d format introduced in the previous program example.

The format for use of scanf is as follows (this is stylised — it is not how it would be coded in C):

```
scanf <input_format>, <variable>
```

or:

```
scanf "%d", integernumber
```

The steps for using scanf are these:
- Declare a memory variable holding the address of the formatting string. This will be a string "%d" for this example.
- Declare a memory variable holding the address of where the value is to be placed.
- Make space on the stack for the converted ASCII string to be stored.

Notice how in this case we are pointing to the information indirectly; we are passing the addresses of the relevant information. This is important to know because it means that to use the indirect addresses we have to declare the variables, and here we are talking about the '.word' directive, within the text area. The string definitions themselves should remain outside the text section and be defined in the data segment of the code. The other thing you need to know is that scanf stores its result on the stack, so to prevent it being corrupted we need to adjust the stack point by a word to make a safe place for it. Program 20c should help disperse the mist.

The line numbers are there to help in the description of the program and should be omitted when you are entering the listing.

Program 20c. Reading and converting a number with scanf.

```
1   / *Reading a number using scanf */
2   /* via registers and the stack    */
3
4   .global main
5   .func main
6   main:
7       PUSH {LR}
8       SUB SP, SP, #4      @ Make room on stack
9       LDR R0, addr_format @ get addr of format
10      MOV R1, SP          @ place SP in R1 and
11      BL scanf            @ store entry on stack
12      LDR R2, [SP]
13      LDR R3, addr_number
14      STR R2, [R3]
15      ADD SP, SP, #4
16      POP {PC}            @ restore PC
17
18  _exit:
19      MOV PC, LR          @ simple exit
20
21  /* as scanf needs addresses of strings we */
22  /* assemble them in the text area         */
23
```

```
24    addr_format:   .word scanformat
25    addr_number:   .word number
26
27        .data
28    number:        .word 0
29    scanformat:    .asciz "%d"
```

Let's look at the listing. Lines 6 and 18 should be familiar and should be considered part of standard procedure. Line 8 is where we adjust the stack pointer by four-bytes to make some space for scanf. Before we call scanf we need to place the SP address into R1 (line 10) and the address of the format string in R0 (line 9). The format string should indicate the details of the value that will be entered at the keyboard and read by scanf. This ensures that the value is converted correctly.

After calling scanf (line 11) the converted binary value is now held on the stack, so this is retrieved (line 12) and the address of where it is to be saved is placed in line 13. Then using indirect addressing the value is stored (line 14). To tidy up, we should reset the stack point by adding the four additional bytes we originally subtracted from it (line 15).

Lines 25 to 29 show how we create addresses to point to the actual data to be utilised. The actual data is in the .data subsection (lines 27-29) and the addresses of these two places are held in word length addresses within the text area defined by lines 24 and 25. Thus on assembly the four-bytes of space created by line 24 will hold the address of the string "%d". This is the formatting string we encountered earlier. Line 25 creates a place for the address of where the result returned by scanf will be placed.

When you run this program there will be no prompt. Just enter a number such as 255 and press the return key. The prompt will be returned. If you have compiled the program with debugging information enabled (the –g option) then you can use GDB to single step-through the code and interrogate the registers at each stage. This is a very worthwhile exercise and what seems a convoluted way to do something is in fact remarkably simple once you have your head around it!

Program 20d extends the above routine to provide some interaction using printf to request the value and then print the result.

Note that in this program the information is expected to be entered in decimal format, but the result is displayed in hex — see the very last line of the program.

Getting This Information

If you have no experience with C, you may be wondering how best to get all this information and then understand how to use it. Good question. The bald answer is that there is no central resource and that it comes down to investigation and interrogation. Websites and user forums are a good source of detail for one. The other way to look at what the function itself does by generating the source code for it and then using GDB to interrogate it. As your knowledge of ARM machine code increases then this will become a more common option and we'll have a look at just how to go about it in a later chapter.

Program 20d. Combining scanf and printf.

```
/* Reading a number using scanf    */
/* and printing it with prinf      */

    .global main
    .func main
main:
    PUSH {LR}           @ use pseudo directive
    SUB SP, SP, #4      @ make a word on stack

    LDR R0, addr_messin     @ get addr of messagein
    BL printf               @ and print it

    LDR R0, addr_format     @ get addr of format
    MOV R1, SP              @ place SP in R1
    BL scanf                @ and store entry on stack

    LDR R1, [SP]            @ get addr of scanf input
    LDR R0, addr_messout    @ get addr of messageout
    BL printf               @ print it all

    ADD SP, SP, #4          @ adjust stack
    POP {PC}                @ restore PC


_exit:
    MOV PC, LR          @ simple exit

addr_messin:    .word messagein
addr_format:    .word scanformat
addr_messout:   .word messageout
```

```
.data
messagein:      .asciz "Enter your number: "
scanformat:     .asciz "%d"
messageout:     .asciz "Your number was 0x%X\n"
```

21: Coding Functions

Functions are the basic building blocks you can use to construct your programs. A function has a name and a purpose, and it is written in such a way that it provides a result each time it is called. The function will accept information and produce a result based on the information it is given. It may also pass information back to the calling program. All functions have a predefined structure, and if we want to write a function ourselves then we should also follow that structure.

Ideally, before sitting down to write a program you should give its structure some thought and as we saw in Chapter 2, try and plan your program as a set of routines called from within a main controlling program. Each of these routines may themselves call smaller routines. When breaking these down any section of code that is used more than a few times could be worth writing as a function, especially if you may look at using it in other programs. Effectively creating reusable code.

However, there is an overhead in doing this because a function must conform to certain standards which relate to entry and exit conditions. Clearly the length of the function must be more than a few lines to make it worthwhile coding.

Often when programming we don't always plan as well as we should. One thing I like doing is returning to code after completion and trying to re-structure it. This can be rewarding and a way to do this is to look at what can be broken down into functions.

Function Standards

A couple of the libc functions we looked at in the last chapter, namely printf and scanf, both expected to receive and return information. We also saw that we can pass information into these functions using the registers R0, R1, R2, and R3. This is determined by a standard called the Application Binary Interface (ABI standard) which was carefully devised and defines how functions should run. The point being that if everyone follows the standard and writes their functions in the same way, then everyone will be able to use each other's functions. (C programmers use the AAPCS standard which goes into things in a little more detail). As far as we are concerned, they achieve the same result at code level, but it is worth getting online and investigating both in a little more detail at some point.

Register	Role	Contents Preserved
R0	Argument and Result	No
R1	Argument	No
R2	Argument	No
R3	Argument	No
R4	General	Yes
R5	General	Yes
R6	General	Yes
R7	General	Yes
R8	General	Yes
R9	General	Yes
R10	General	Yes
R11	General	Yes
R12	General	Yes
LR	Return Address	No
SP	Stack Pointer	Yes

Figure 21a. Register designations in a function call.

Figure 21a details the purpose of each register when a function is called. In summary a function should adhere to the following:

- It may freely modify registers R0, R1, R2 and R3 and expect to find the information in them that it requires to carry out its task.
- It can modify registers R4-12, providing it restores their values before returning to the calling routine.
- It can modify the Stack Pointer providing it restores the value held on entry.
- It must preserve the address in the Link Register so that it may return correctly to the calling program.
- It should make no assumption as to the contents of the CPSR. As far as the function is concerned the status of the N, Z, C and V flags are unknown.

So, let's break this down in a bit more detail.

Register Use

It is this standard that says R0, R1, R2 and R3 (in that order) will be used as inputs to a function. But this is only if the function requires four inputs. If it only needs one then this goes in the first register R0, if it needs a second that must be placed in R1 and similarly for R2 and R3. If it only needs one input, then it does not matter what is in the other registers as they will not be used. If the function returns a value it will always go in R0 - the first byte at least, so we can use 'echo $?' to return a value.

The second point made is that the other registers R4-R12 inclusive must be preserved so that when the calling program gets control back from the function the contents of R4 through to R12 inclusive must be the same as when the function was called. This is not to say we can't use them. If your function needs them, then one of the first things it should do (but not necessarily the very first as we shall see) is to push their contents onto the stack and then restore them from the stack before finishing. These two complementary instructions would do the job:

```
STMFD SP!, {R4-R12}    @ save registers R4 thro R12
LDMFD SP!, {R4-R12}    @ restore R4 through R12
```

More Than Three

You may be asking at this point what happens if we need to pass more than four items to the function we are calling? The answer lies in the next 'rule' in that we can modify the Stack Pointer (SP) again provided we ensure that it is set correctly on completion of the routine. However, this is not always strictly true, because if we need to pass more information into the function the control of the SP has to be managed by the calling routine, especially if the amount of data is unknown. If a function must have an additional four items of data every time, then the function can manage the SP, but you need to be wary of this.

You will recall in Program 20b we called printf to display three items of information by passing the data through R1-R3. Program 21a extends this to pass six values to the calling routine. The listing has lines numbered for ease of discussion.

The program is pretty much identical until we get to line 13 where we start taking the word values stored in lines 31-33 inclusive and pushing them onto the stack. By the time we reach line 21 we have the address of the string in R0 whilst R1, R2 and R3 hold the values 1, 2 and 3, respectively. Then the stack holds (at the top) 6, and below that 5 and below that 4. Despite being single digits, these are all words with values and occupy four-bytes each. If you run the program the result you will see on screen is:

```
Values are: 1, 2, 3 and 6
```

Program 21a. Passing function values via the stack.

```
1       /** Printing a string using printf **/
2       /** and passing parameters to it   **/
3       /** via registers and the stack    **/
4
5               .global main
6               .func main
7       main:
8               PUSH {LR}               @ use pseudo directive
9               LDR R0, =string         @ R0 points to string
10              MOV R1, #1              @ first value in R1
11              MOV R2, #2              @ second value in R2
12              MOV R3, #3              @ result in R3
13              LDR R7,=value1          @ get address of param
14              LDR R8, [R7]            @ load value1 into R8
15              PUSH {R8}               @ put on stack
16              LDR R7,=value2          @ repeat for value2
17              LDR R8, [R7]
18              PUSH {R8}
19              LDR R7,=value3          @ repeat for value3
20              LDR R8, [R7]
21              PUSH {R8}
22              BL printf               @ Call libc
23              ADD SP, SP, #12         @ balance stack
24              POP {PC}                @ restore PC
25
26      _exit:
27              MOV PC, LR              @ simple exit
28
29              .data
30      string:         .asciz "Values are: %d, %d, %d and %d\n"
31      value1:         .word 4
32      value2:         .word 5
33      value3:         .word 6
```

This is because we only instructed printf to print an extra value, and it looked for it on top of the stack. Adding in a couple more d% into the printf string will provide the means to print the two additional values. You would also need to swap the push order onto the stack if you wanted to ensure that the numbers were displayed in the correct order.

Line 23 is the interesting one. We adjusted the SP by 12 bytes because of the three PUSH instructions. This line moves the SP back those 12 places and ensures that the system is hunky dory. This could have been achieved with three POP instructions equally as well; however, this is a neat way to restore the status quo if you are dumping a lot of data on the stack.

If a function requires the use of registers, then we should save the register contents (and restore them after the function has completed). The simplest way to do this would be to push the values straight onto the stack, but this could force any required data down the stack and out of sync with the function. In situations such as these the best answer is to save the register contents to an area of memory that you have set aside for work space. Alternatively, you can look to push the data on the stack first, adjusting the SP if required, and prior to pushing the function parameters there.

If you are writing a function that needs additional information passed to it on the stack and the registers saved, then you can use the stack for all of it as you are managing the stack. If your function expected three items on the stack and you needed to save R4 then you can access the stack directly at the three locations using a simple immediate offset, something like this:

```
    LDR R4, SP+4     @ Get first data word on stack
```

The second item would be at SP+8 and the third at SP+12.

Remember that these instructions do not adjust the SP so you must reset it on completion as already described. (NB: If you find this difficult to visualise then you can always physically draw the stack and identify where each item of data is being placed.)

Preserving Links and Flags

One thing you must always remember when writing functions is that on completion the function is going to need to return program control back to whence it came. This means that it is imperative to preserve the integrity of the Link Register. If you intend to call another function or routine at some point, then you may well use a BL or BLX instruction to do so. If you do this then the contents of the LR will be overwritten and lost. Therefore, they must be stashed away safely in your memory workspace somewhere or pushed onto the stack for later restoration.

There is no requirement for preserving the Status Flags. As far as the function is concerned these are generally unknown. That said, your function may have a requirement for the flags as a signal back to the calling line and this is a valid way to signal information back, especially as R0 is the one standard way of returning a value. For example, the N flag might be set on return to signal that an error occurred, and an error code placed in R0.

Robust Print Routines

Sort routines are ideal mechanisms for function uses and also illustrate how you can build libraries of routines that can perform consistently across your own portfolio. Data manipulation and sorting is a particularly good use of computer time. We'll look at a flexible sort routine before the end of this chapter.

Robust print routines are also useful. We have looked at a few in earlier chapters so, this one utilises the printf function and is flexible to your needs. This example will print a vector of word width values. Program 21b is the subroutine itself, and Program 21c will allow you to text it is working. There is nothing special it requires the libc library as it utilises the printf function, so will need to be assembled using GCC. To work the routine needs the address of the vector containing the word elements, the number of elements and a couple of pointers to allow the routine to keep track of its position in the vector.

Program, 21b - Print vector of words

```
/* printw - This routine prints a vector of words */
/* R0 = address of vector                         */
/* R1 = number of vector elements                 */
/* R2 = pointer string to print first element     */
/* R3 = pointer string to print next elements     */

.global _printw
.equ _wsize,4
.align 2
_printw:
    STMFD   SP!, {R4, R5, R6, R7, LR}
    CMP     R1, #0          @ exit if no elements
    BLE     _last
    MOV     R4, R0          @ save parameters to locals
    MOV     R5, R1
    MOV     R6, R2
    MOV     R7, R3
    LDR     R1, [R4], #_wsize  @ load first element
    MOV     R0, R6          @ address of first string
    BL      printf          @ print it
    SUBS    R5, R5, #1      @ decrement counter
    BEQ     _last           @ exit if zero
_printw_loop:
    LDR     R1, [R4], #_wsize   @ load next item
    MOV     R0, R7          @ address next string
```

```
        BL      printf              @ print it
        SUBS    R5, R5, #1          @ decrement counter
        BNE     _printw_loop        @ loop if more
_last:
        LDMFD   SP!, {R4, R5, R6, R7, PC} @ restore, return
```

The test harness below has a list of items after the label 'values' - there are 11 in total. These can be changed and edit as you require.

Program 21c - Test printw

```
/* Test subroutine printw */
.equ _size,4
.equ _items, 11
.global main
.align 2
.section .rodata
first:  .asciz "Vector of words - values : %d"
rest:   .asciz ", %d"
final:  .asciz "\n"
values: .word 10, 15, 20, 25, 30, 35, 40, 45, 50, 55, 60

.align 2
.text

main:
        LDR R0, =values
        MOV R1, =_items
        LDR R2, =first
        LDR R3, =rest
        BL      _printw
        LDR R0, =final
        BL printf

        MOV R7, #1
        SWI 0
```

Assuming both source files in your current directory you can assemble them as follows:

```
gcc -o testprint prog21b.s prog21c.s
```

You can then execute the code with:

```
./testprint
```

As we have used both files in the same command line assembly, we do not need to use the 'include' directive.

We will use Program 21b when for printing out the results of the next routine.

Bubble Sort

The bubble sort, sometimes referred to as sinking sort, is the simplest sorting algorithm that works by repeatedly swapping the adjacent elements if they are in wrong order. The pass continues through the list is repeated until the list is sorted. The algorithm, which is a comparison sort, is named for the way smaller or larger elements "bubble" to the top of the list. The comments should help you understand what is going on.

This simple algorithm performs poorly in real world use and is used primarily as an educational tool. More efficient algorithms such as quicksort, timsort, or merge sort are used by the sorting libraries built into popular programming languages such as Python.

Program 21d. Bubble Sort Routine

```
/* Bubble Sort - bubble sorts vectors of words */
/* R0= start of vector of elements             */
/* R1= Number of elements to sort              */
/* R4 = current pointer                        */
/* R5 = inner counter                          */
/* R6 = keep_going flag                        */
/* R7 = first element                          */
/* R8 = second element                         */
/* R9 = swap register                          */

.global _bubble
.text
_bubble:
        STMFD   SP!, {R4, R5, R6, R7, R8, R9, LR}
        CMP     R1, #1          @ must be > 1
        BLE     _exit           @ exit if nothing to do

        SUB     R5, R1, #1      @ Set inner counter
        MOV     R4, R0          @ Set current pointer
        MOV     R6, #0          @ Register set on swap

_loop:
```

Raspberry Pi OS Assembly Language

```
        LDR     R7, [R4], #size  @ load element
        LDR     R8, [R4]         @ and next element
        CMP     R7, R8           @ compare them
        BLE     no_swap          @ branch if second greater

        MOV     R6, #1           @ set keep_going flag
        SUB     R4, #size        @ reset to first element
        LDR     R9, [R4]         @ Load word at address
        STR     R8, [R4]         @ Save lower value back in memory
        STR     R9, [R4, #size]! @ Complete swap process

no_swap:
        SUBS    R5, #1           @ decrement counter
        BNE     _loop            @ loop again if not finished

end_inner:
        CMP     R6, #0           @ check if done
        BEQ     _exit            @ and leave if not set
        MOV     R6, #0           @ clear flag
        MOV     R4, R0           @ reset pointer
        SUB     R5, R1, #1       @ reset counter
        B       _loop            @ And go again

_exit:
        LDMFD   SP!, {R4, R5, R6, R7, R8, R9, PC}
.data
    .equ size,4
```

The listing provided as Program 21d will test the bubble sort. This test has 16 items in total and includes signed, negative numbers. The routine prints then before the sort and then after the sort. The number of items can be changed and adjusted to suit.

Program 21e, Bubble Sort Test

```
/* Bubble Sort Test          */

.global main
main:
        LDR R0, =values
        MOV R1, #items
        LDR R2, =before
```

203

```
        LDR R3, =comma
        BL     _printw
        LDR R0, =new_line
        BL     printf
        LDR R0, =values
        MOV R1, #items
        BL     _bubble

        LDR R0, =values
        MOV R1, #items
        LDR R2, =after
        LDR R3, =comma
        BL     _printw
        LDR R0, =new_line
        BL     printf

        MOV R7, #1
        SWI #0

.equ items,16

.data
before: .asciz "Order before sorting, values are : %d"
after:  .asciz "Order after sorting,  values are : %d"
comma:  .asciz ", %d"
new_line:.asciz "\n"
values: .word 12, 2, 235, -64, 28, 315, 456, 63, 134, 97, 221,
-453, 190333, 145, 117, 5
```

Ensure that the source for Program 21b is in the same directory as Program 21d and Program 21e and assemble the files with:

```
gcc -o testbubble prog21b.s prog21d.s prog21e.s
```

and execute with:

```
./testbubble
```

22: Disassembling C

As I have already stated this isn't a book about learning to program in C, but the fact is as you delve deeper into ARM assembler on your Raspberry Pi you will probably be drawn towards C. At the very least you will probably want to learn more about the libc functions so that you can take advantage of them in your own programs. You might want to look at the machine code that constitutes the libc functions to see how they work, and learn from them. This is called *reverse engineering* and it plays a major part in all software development, as programmers look at how other programmers have achieved certain results and seek to improve on those themselves.

While the libc functions are well documented from a C programmer's perspective, there is not a lot of detail about using them at the lower machine code level. I guess this is understandable. Given that C is relatively straightforward and there are literally thousands of program examples available to you (in manuals, online and in forums) it is extremely easy to write a C program containing a particular function that you can compile into an assembly language source file and then examine it, investigate it and refine it for your own purposes.

With GCC and GDB you have the tools to do so at your disposal. This chapter provides an introductory primer towards that goal. You may well encounter some frustrating times, but as you become more familiar with the way GCC converts C into machine code then you will become more familiar with the code it is generating.

GCC - The Swiss Army Knife

GCC is a bit like a Swiss Army Knife, it must be able to deal with all situations and it goes about it in a methodical manner. The use of the assembler and linker as standalone tools in the earlier part of this book shows that GCC isn't a single beast; it is more a controller for several GNU programs, running them one-by-one in order to produce a result. But the good thing is that we can stop the process at any point in that chain and this is to our benefit.

GCC can compile a C program to an executable file with just a single command line thus:

```
gcc -o tornado   tornado.c
```

This will take a C program called tornado.c and convert it to an executable file called 'tornado'. It does this using several separate steps:

Pre-processor (CPP)   This takes the C source and gathers information about the #defines and #includes so that it has a list of all the variables and additional bits of information and files it will need.

GCC   Creates the assembly language source listing. It does this by using some basic rules and building the sections of code needed as a series of building blocks which calls functions in libc. It effectively organises your data and information using the functions rules we discussed in the previous chapter and then inserts the function call. It then assembles the code required to handle any information returned before starting the process again. Once this is complete the source file, with a '.s' extension, is complete.

AS   The assembler takes the source file and converts it into an object file (.o) as described much earlier in this book.

LD   The linker takes the object code file and adds to it all the additional files and libraries required. Again, this process was described in an earlier chapter.

In Chapter 14 we saw that by using GDB the final executable code produced by GCC is not a straightforward start-to-finish linear flow but an integrated suite of code that can provide a solution to every legal C program given to it!

What GCC does not give you is tight, highly refined machine code. If space and speed are critical then you need to code at the lowest level. The Raspberry Pi OS (Raspbian) itself is written mostly in C and compiled. But critical areas of it are coded directly in assembler. Compiled code can be optimised at the source stage and GCC provides some automated options for doing this. However, this is outside the scope of this book. But in a way, when looking at the assembler source file created to execute a particular function, what we will be doing is to optimise the source, cutting away everything that is not needed, until we have the bare bones assembler to do what we need.

A Simple C Framework

The framework for a C program is simple enough. Program 22a illustrates the use of the C function 'putchar' to print a single ASCII character to the screen. It has six lines.

Program 22a. A simple C program to print an asterisk.

```c
#include <stdio.h>

int main()
{
    putchar('*');
    return 0;
}
```

The first line tells the compiler that the file stdio.h should be included in the compilation. This is the file that includes the standard input-output interfaces including functions such as printf and the one we are interested in now — putchar. This is the part of the file that would be handled by the pre-processor described earlier, and this is the case for any line that begins with a hash.

The actual program starts with the function named main(). All functions begin with an opening brace '{' and end with a closing brace '}'. Everything between the opening and closing braces is considered a part of the function. main(), like all C functions, must state what kind of value it returns. The return value type for main() is int, which means that this function returns an integer to the operating system when it completes. Here, it returns the integer value 0. A value may be returned to the operating system to indicate success or failure or using a failure code to describe the cause of failure.

Hopefully you will have already cottoned onto how the main() in the C program above ties in with the main function in our assembler source files to date (and to a lesser extent the start function in the assembler listings that we looked at the start of this book).

In amongst all this we have the crux of the program – putchar – being instructed to print an asterisk to the screen.

Program 22a can be entered using a text editor (Vim or Geany), but the file should be created with the .c extension:

```
prog22a.c
```

To compile this C program into an executable and run it we use:

```
gcc -o prog22a prog22a.c
./prog22a
```

You should see an asterisk printed on the screen before the prompt. Look carefully it is easy to miss!

Sourcing the Assembler

Given what we have learnt in the past few chapters you might be able to take a good guess at what you would expect to see in the assembly language source code generated for this C program. The function prints a single character. We would expect therefore that, as specified by the AAPCS standard, the ASCII code for the character to be printed would be loaded into R0. No other information is passed. The routine will complete with a return value of 0, so we should also expect to find this passed back in R0 as per standard. Let's C!

To create an assembler listing from a .c file we use the –S directive (note must be capital 'S'), thus:

```
gcc -S -o prog22a.s prog22a.c
```

GCC will create a file called prog22a.s and this will hold the assembler listing. Open this in a text editor and you should see something similar (it may not be identical) to what is shown in Figure 22a.

You should be able to quickly identify the body of the program in here. In fact, of the 30 plus lines of assembler only a handful of them are of significance relative to what we are after. All the additional information can ultimately be discarded but was an important transformation step for GCC when it did the initial conversion. This conversion is very methodical and is a case of one size fits all using a brute force method of working. GCC must create workspace for each function it is dealing with in the conversion process and has to protect this workspace for its needs. In broad terms it does this by partitioning an area on the stack for the function's use. This is called to the stack frame (introduced in Chapter 17 which is tracked using a Frame Pointer (FP), also introduced in Chapter 17.

This marks the start of the stack frame and each function creates its own stack frame to manage local variables. The stack frame is therefore an important aspect of a C program, but they are less important in creating assembler. However, understanding what it does is important in allowing us to deconstruct C derived assembler, more on which in due course.

Back to the listing. It is good at this point to create a backup of this initial assembly file. You will want to start deleting lines and adjusting code to create a smaller compact source file that you can assemble and test. Thus:

```
cp prog22a.s prog22a.so
```

would create a copy with the .so indicating to you that it is source original.

```
        .arch armv6
                .eabi_attribute 28, 1
                .eabi_attribute 20, 1
                .eabi_attribute 21, 1
                .eabi_attribute 23, 3
                .eabi_attribute 24, 1
                .eabi_attribute 25, 1
                .eabi_attribute 26, 2
                .eabi_attribute 30, 6
                .eabi_attribute 34, 1
                .eabi_attribute 18, 4
                .file    "prog21a.c"
                .text
                .align   2
                .global main
                .arch armv6
                .syntax unified
                .arm
                .fpu vfp
                .type    main, %function
main:
                @ args = 0, pretend = 0, frame = 0
                @ frame_needed = 1, uses_anonymous_args = 0
                push     {fp, lr}
                add      fp, sp, #4
                mov      r0, #42
                bl       putchar
                mov      r3, #0
                mov      r0, r3
                pop      {fp, pc}
                .size    main, .-main
                .ident   GCC: (Raspbian 8.3.0-6+rpi1) 8.3.0
                .section .note.GNU-stack,"",%progbits
```

Figure 22a. The assembler generated by GCC from the C program.

Building Blocks

Our purpose here is to cut this source down so that we can assemble and link it directly and produce the same result as the original C program. GCC has constructed the assembler source using some basic building blocks. The first 15 lines provide various items of information. There is a directive identifying the instruction set for which this code is to be compile (armv6) and the specific floating-point unit to be used (VFP). The eabi attributes (embedded-application binary interface) are specifies standard conventions for file formats, data types, register usage, and options that are present or absent on the CPU. The attribute settings listed above are not important, for our purposes and so can be deleted.

There follows the file name and definition of the '.text' section. Again, for our small assembler construct these can both be deleted.

```
     1              .global main
     2              .type    main,  %function
     3   main:
     4              @ args = 0, pretend = 0, frame = 0
     5              @ frame_needed = 1, uses_anonymous_args = 0
     6              push     {fp, lr}
     7              add      fp, sp, #4
     8              mov      r0, #42
     9              bl       putchar
    10              mov      r3, #0
    11              mov      r0, r3
    12              pop      {fp, pc}
```

Figure 22b. The C assembler source with directives removed.

Having done all that we are left with the listing shown in Figure 22b, with line numbers for ease of reference. The first three lines define the main() function, and we will need to edit these slightly for use in our assembly listing. This is followed by a couple of comments (lines 4 and 5) provided by the compiler in relation to management of the stack frame for this routine. Again, we will not need these, and they can be deleted.

Lines 6 and 12 act in tandem to preserve the addresses held in the Frame Pointer and Link Register The FP is of no importance to us here but we do need to preserve the LR before calling the putchar routine so a suitable PUSH and POP instruction can be substituted here. Line 7 can also be removed as we do not need to process anything relating to the FP.

The crux of our code comes down to lines 8 and 9. The ASCII code for the asterisk (42) is moved into R0 and putchar is called. Lines 10 and 11 are then used to place a zero in R0. You will recall that the original C function is to return zero. For our purposes, we do not strictly need these two lines and they can be removed. What we are left with is the listing presented as Program 22b.

Program 22b. The final putchar listing.

```
        .global main
        .func main
main:
        PUSH {LR}
        MOV R0, #42
        BL   putchar
        POP {PC}
```

This listing will assemble and run correctly. Although the original C program was relatively trivial the methodology used to create and reduce the assembler source that it creates is sound and can be applied in virtually all cases.

A printf Example

We have already examined the use of printf in assembly language programs, but we'll look at it again, this time from the C perspective as it provides a good insight into how C programs are constructed that will be useful when looking at the assembler. Program 22c is the C file for the famous "hello world" program. On the face of it, this is not much different from our previous putchar example. But in fact, it is.

Program 22c. C listing for the 'hello world' program.

```
#include <stdio.h>
int main()
{
  printf("hello world");
  return 0;
}
```

You can convert this to assembler using:

```
gcc -S -o prog22c.s prog22c.c
```

Figure 22c lists the derived assembler minus the initial header and footer directives, again this may differ from your output but will fundamentally be the same.

Given our knowledge of printf and applying what we learnt above, the main: section of the program should be straightforward — nothing new to learn here. It is the other areas that are of interest —notably the areas marked by the labels LC0, L4 and L3. The L4 label is not required nor is the '.align 2' directive — the label will clearly be on a word boundary as it comes directly behind code. L3 marks a reserved word to hold the address of the 'hello world' text marked by LC0. This was a technique that we used when playing with the scanf function in Program 20c but is different to the method we used in our original printf program, Program 20a. It is worth comparing the two side by side.

```
                .section    .rodata
                .align      2
        .LC0:
                .ascii      "hello world\000"
                .text
                .align      2
                .global     main
                .type       main, %function
        main:
                @ args = 0, pretend = 0, frame = 0
                @ frame_needed = 1, uses_anonymous_args = 0
                push        {fp, lr}
                add         fp, sp, #4
                ldr         r0, .L3
                bl          printf
                mov         r3, #0
                mov         r0, r3
                pop         {fp, pc}
        .L4:
                .align      2
        .L3:
                .word       .LC0
```

Figure 22c. The compiled assembler for the C printf program.

As a final exercise you might want to try compiling a scanf example, as this combines a few of these techniques and accesses the stack for information. Program 22d is what you will need. If you compile and run this the keyboard will wait for you to enter a number. There will be no additional responses as it is the bare function we are concerned with.

A reminder here that scanf uses the stack to store and pass its converted numeric value, so you will need to manage the stack and Frame Pointer in the assembler.

Program 22d. A C listing for using the scanf function.

```c
#include <stdio.h>
int main()
{
int myvariable;
    scanf("%d", &myvariable);
    return 0;
}
```

Frame Pointer Variables

Just a word to the good about the Frame Pointer relative to dissecting your listings in this way. If the original C programs contains variables then the Frame Pointer will be used to point to these values, so it becomes important in your deconstruction. Consider these two lines of assembler:

```
LDR R2, {FP, #-8}
MOV R0, R2
```

The first line shows that a variable is located at the position given by FP-8 and this result is accessed and moved into R0. If the original C listing has several variables you will need to identify where each one is located on the stack, by seeking out similar code lines. Of course your assembler will not have a Frame Pointer, or it would be assigned a value it is often set equal to the SP by the code, so you will need to translate these into labelled locations.

(In ARM, R11 is normally used as the Frame Pointer register, although this may vary between Operating Systems.)

Disassembling System Calls

In Chapter 7 we had a look at Syscalls and how to interface with the actual operating system calls directly with them. Of course, we have since learnt of libc and how we can make use of its own functions such as printf. Using libc comes with a memory overhead which you might not be prepared to live with when space is tight, and at these times Syscalls can come into their own. This is fine in principle, but the trouble is that hard detail about Raspberry Pi OS (Raspbian) Syscalls is rather scarce on the ground. For popular Syscalls such as printing a string to the screen you will find many examples if you search the net. The same cannot be said if you wanted to create a directory or produce a directory listing. But the information is there if you use a bit of common sense and are prepared to do a little reverse engineering. Doing this with a few examples will test your knowledge of the ARM and the way it works on the Raspberry Pi, and you will learn heaps from doing it.

Appendix B provides a list of the first 195 Syscalls. These are generally the ones you will use most. The book support website also contains links to an unofficial site where you can find out more information on Syscalls. One other option is to have a go at working it out for yourself!

The examples above are ones we have encountered and already explained, and this is done deliberately to make it easier to explain what GCC is doing in its compile process. You may not be forewarned with such knowledge when looking at new functions. But GCC goes about its business in a predefined way and the processes will not vary. Information is passed in registers and on the stack (and via the Frame Pointer), so it is often just a matter of identifying what is where and then working back from there.

You may also find it easier to open a second text editor window and set about creating a new assembly listing alongside the one created with GCC, rather than editing the original one. This is especially sound advice if the listing contains a lot of data access as the tables tend to flop all over the place.

23: GPIO Functions

Pi Eye: This chapter contains programs that may need to be modified depending on the version of the Raspberry Pi you are using. The text and body of the assembler script will contain change details at the relevant points in the chapter.

The GPIO port has been one of the fundamental features of the Raspberry Pi since launch. It has been accessible on all models and on most has a ready installed connector to allow you to plug in and play.

We'll look at how the GPIO interface is connected to the Raspberry Pi and how you can use machine code to access that connection, thereby enabling you to read and write the individual pins. While this isn't a primer on the GPIO interface, understanding how it sits with the Raspberry Pi is fundamental to understanding how to program it.

Many of the kits you can purchase and use with the GPIO, come with special libraries of code you can download and use. This is typically written in Python or Scratch and is certainly an ideal way to check that any hardware connections are sound should you run into debugging difficulties at any time. The code listed this in chapter originated on a Raspberry Pi and has been tested on multiple versions of Raspberry Pi.

GPIO extension and interface boards have evolved since the original Raspberry Pi was released, however I have seen people be quite inventive in connecting them. For my purposes here I have utilised the CamJam/EduKit. However, any suitable interface should work. Other kits such as the RasP.io Breadboard Pi Bridge exist (see Figure 23a) and are worth checking out, (www.rasp.io/bbpi).

Memory Mapping

The Raspberry Pi uses memory mapped I/O. The addresses used for I/O are widely known and specifically retrievable from the associated Broadcom data sheet. For early Raspberry Pi models, addresses 0x20000000 to 0x20FFFFFF, are for I/O devices. In later versions 0x3F000000 to 0x3EFFFFFF are reserved for I/O devices. Be aware that this is not all reserved for the GPIO memory but for *all* peripheral interfaces in total.

The location of these blocks of memory, and specifically in future releases, may well change and the memory allocated to the GPIO port. Obviously, that would make programs that access the GPIO port directly potentially incompatible. Given also that Raspbian has been renamed and effectively re-launched as Raspberry Pi Operating System, it may be possible, however unlikely, that some of the standard underling Linux routines are further modified.

If reading the Broadcom data sheets you should be aware that the ARM cores and the VideoCore GPU *share* the same memory space *but* at *different addresses* on that device. Be clear to distinguish between BUS address, VC address and ARM address. The same thing appears differently to each system which is often the source of much confusion. The GPIO is offset from a 'peripheral base address' by 0x200000 and needs to be added to it to access it. For our purposes the information required for this exercise is provided here.

The kernel includes a driver to a special character file, '/dev/mem', which is a mirror of main memory. Similar to any file, we can open it, read bytes from or write bytes to it, and close it. The "position" of each byte in '/dev/mem' is the byte address in physical memory. In principle, we could program the GPIO device by opening '/dev/mem', moving a pointer to the desired location of a GPIO port, and writing the appropriate value in that byte location.

Writing directly to areas of this I/O memory can be a risky thing, and as such ROS won't allow us to do that. It has a built-in self-protect mechanism meaning only 'root' users can access it. This ensures we don't do anything that might otherwise cause the operating system to lock or crash.

A secure method of accessing this GPIO memory does exist using a scheme that uses a similar memory mapping technique and a driver at '/dev/gpiomem/' which writes changes directly to the GPIO control area via a designated block of memory which is effectively a mirror of the real memory (this is often referred to a virtual memory). Thus, if we make any changes that have an adverse effect (hanging the system for example), we should be able to cycle the power to reset everything. This driver ensures that nothing can go drastically wrong, but obviously only works with the GPIO area.

Because the Broadcom data sheet provides us with the basic start address of each I/O peripheral area we can let the operating system calculate the virtual memory address for us and everything remains pretty transparent from that point.

In Chapter 19 we examined some of the file system calls need to open and close files using Syscalls. Reading and wring to the GPIO is not unlike running a filing system, but this time around we'll make things a little simpler by using the main Linux system calls.

Raspberry Pi OS Assembly Language

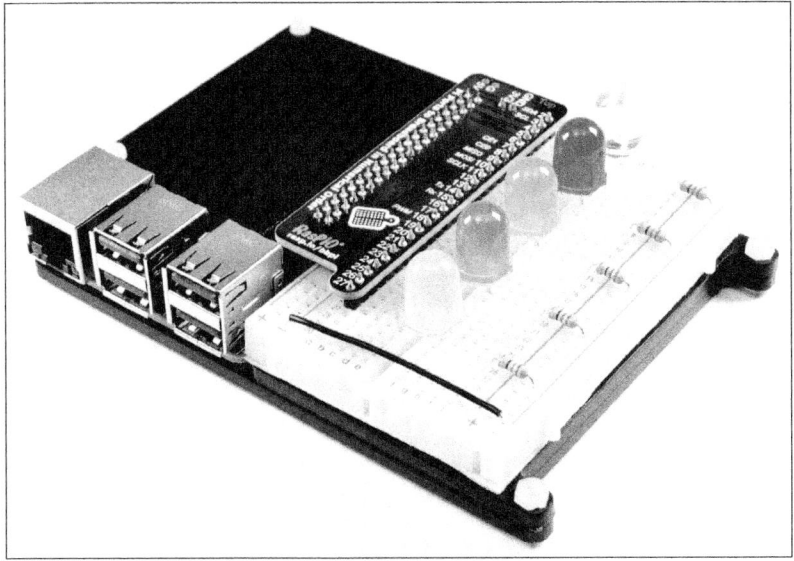

Figure 23a. The Breadboard Pi Bridge from RasP.io.

The GPIO Controller

The GPIO has its own controller and this contains no less than 41 registers. The first five of these registers deal with reading and writing to the 54 GPIO pins. These pins are numbered GPIO 0 through to GPIO 53 although only a handful or so of these are available to us to connect to on the GPIO expansion port itself. And then it depends on the size of the GPIO header, 26-pins on early Raspberry Pi and 40-pin on the more recent ones. (Figure 23f at the end of this chapter defines the GPIO header layout diagrammatically.)

It should be noted also that the GPIO Controller pin numbers do not run concurrently on the main GPIO header connector and may differ again on any expansion board you have attached. Please ensure you familiarise yourself with the system you are using as the pin numbers here relate specifically to the numbers assigned by BCM. Equally, there are several different numbering systems used in the setup, and it can get confusing. I'll try and guide you through these. Note: the header pin number does not correspond to the GPIO pin number.

If you have a Terminal window open on the Desktop you can type 'pinout' at the prompt to get information regarding your GPIO header and various other settings.

The first five of the GPIO Controller registers, their names, and the pins they are associated with are listed in Figure 23b.

217

No	Name		Offset	Pins
0	GPIO Function Select 0	(GPSEL0)	#0	0-9
1	GPIO Function Select 1	(GPSEL1)	#4	10-19
2	GPIO Function Select 2	(GPSEL2)	#8	20-29
3	GPIO Function Select 3	(GPSEL3)	#12	30-39
4	GPIO Function Select 4	(GPSEL4)	#16	40-49
5	GPIO Function Select 5	(GPSEL5)	#20	50-53

Figure 23b. GPIO registers and pin control.

Each of these registers is 32-bits wide and each pin has three bits assigned to it within each register. The 'Offset' column above I related to the number of bytes that must be added to the address of the GPIO. More on which shortly. Note here that 'pin' refers to GPIO pin. Not the connection header pin number. The example we will look at here is GPIO Pin 22 which Program 23a, will utilise.

Looking at Figure 23b, we can see that Pin 22 has an offset of 8 bytes and is therefore located in GPSEL2. Figure 23c below shows that Pin 22 has bits 6,7, and 8 linked with it in the 32-bits of the address where GPSEL2 is located.

Pin 29			Pin 28			Pin 27			Pin 26			Pin 25			Pin 24			Pin 23			Pin 22			Pin 21			Pin 20		
31	30	29	28	27	26	25	24	23	22	21	20	19	18	17	16	15	14	13	12	11	10	9	8	7	6	5	4	3	2	1	0

Figure 23c. Bit association with GPSEL2.

You may have noticed in Figure 23b that not all the bits in Register 5 are used. This is correct. Only the first 12 bits are used, and the others are classed as 'reserved'. Likewise, bits 30 and 31 in each of the other registers are unused.

The base address for the GPIO controller in Raspberry Pi Operating System changes depending on the Raspberry Pi you are using as listed in Figure 23d.

RPi	SOC	Peripheral Base	GPIO Offset
A+	BCM2835	0x20000000	0x200000
B	BCM2835	0x02000000	0x200000
Zero	BCM2835	0x20000000	0x200000
2	BCM2836	0x3F000000	0x200000
3	BCM2837	0x3F000000	0x200000
3+	BCM2837B0	0x3F000000	0x200000
4	BCM2711	0x3F000000	0x200000
400	BCM2711C0	0x3F000000	0x200000

Figure 23d. GPIO Base Addresses

To obtain the address of any GPSEL register we need to add the 'offset' value (Figure 23b) to the sum of the 'peripheral base' and 'GPIO offset' addresses (Figure 23d). GPSEL0 is located at this starting point (as offset is zero). To access the second register, GPFEL1, then we need to add four to the controller's base address. GPSEL2 has an offset of 8, so its address would be either:

    (0x3F000000+0x200000)+8 = 0x3F200008

or:

    (0x20000000+0x200000)+8 = 0x20200008

depending on the model Raspberry Pi you are writing for.

Therefore, to access pin number 22 on the GPIO header, we need to use bits 6-8 at 0x08 relative to virtual address in our program that we get from a call to the mmap function.

GPIO In and Outs

It is important to understand how these bits are assigned as we will need to address them individually at various times to make things happen in their associated registers. And to be sure that we don't corrupt or alter the value of other bits in the register.

Using one of the pins is a two-step process.

1. Select the function of the specific GPIO pin, either as an input or as an output. This only has to be done once, unless the function of the pin changes.
2. Turn the pin on (Set) or off (Clear). There are two separate sets of GPIO registers for doing this, GPSET and GPCLR. You do this as required.

(Note: Do not confuse GPSEL and GPSET, they have totally different functions within the GPIO controller!)

As indicated above the first item on the list is to select the function of the GPIO pin we'll be using. In this example it is 22 (GPIO 22).

To assign a pin as an input we must store a 0 in the three associated bits (000). To make the same pin an output we must write a 1 to those same three bits (111). For example, to make GPIO 22 an output we must place 111 in bits 6, 7 and 8. To achieve this we could write the binary value:

    0b111

to the identified bits in GPSEL2. Of course, we must preserve and not overwrite any other bits that may be set or clear so we would do this using a bitwise operator. (Other bit combinations assign other functions to the pins, so it is important to get this right.

Raspberry Pi Assembly Language

So far, we have looked at configuring the function of a pin as an input or an output. To turn the pin on (set) or off (clear) we must write some values into another register.

There are four registers associated with setting and clearing pins and these are detailed in Figure 23e.

```
No   Name                           Offset   Pins
7    GPIO Pin Set 0    (GPSET0)     #28      0-31
8    GPIO Pin Set 1    (GPSET1)     #32      32-53
10   GPIO Pin Clear 0  (GPCLR0)     #40      0-31
11   GPIO Pin Clear 1  (GPCLR1)     #44      32-63
```

Figure 23e. GPIO registers for setting and clearing.

There is a single bit associated with each pin for the purpose of setting and clearing. To set GPIO 22 we would write a '1' into bit 22 of GPSET0. To clear the same bit, we would need to write a '1' into bit 22 of GPCLR0.

If you were to write a 1 to bit 22 in GPSET0 but GPIO 22 was defined as an input nothing would happen. If you then set GPIO 22 to an output, an attached LED would light. The last value written to either GPSET0 or GPCLR0 in this case is remembered and used when the status of the pin is changed.

As we can see from Figure 23e the offset for GPSET0 is 28 and for GPCLR0 is 40 and this value added to the base address to the GPIO controller to calculate the required address.

Program 23a is the listing needed and this is broken down into several segments marked with comments. Remember the process is as follows:

```
Open file
Memory Map the GPIO
Set GPIO Pin Direction Out
GPIO Pin Turn On
GPIO Pin Turn Off
Unmap Memory and Close file
```

The listing is annotated so it should be easy to follow though, even if some of the offsct and register details are still a bit hazy.

Read the note at the after the end of the listing on how to 'run' the program and the flags that must be used.

Program 23a - File access to GPIO memory.

```
/* Accessing GPIO using virtual memory mapping */
/* Using preferred methodology uses GPIO Pin 22*/

@ Constants for assembler - memory map associated
.equ    gpiobase,0x3F000000     @ RPi 2,3,4,400 peripherals
.equ    offset,   0x200000      @ start of GPIO device
.equ    prot_read, 0x1          @ can be read
.equ    prot_write,0x2          @ can be written
.equ    readwrite,prot_read|prot_write
.equ    mapshare,  0x01         @ share changes
.equ    nopref,    0
.equ    pagesize,  4096         @ memory size

.equ    o_rdwr,   00000002      @ open for read/write
.equ    o_dsync,  00010000      @ values are octal not hex
.equ    o_sync,04000000
.equ    o_allsync,o_sync|o_dsync
.equ    openflags,o_rdwr|o_sync @ open file flags

@ Constants for Function Select
.equ    pinnumber,22            @ pin number-change for others
.equ    output,   1             @ use pin for output
.equ    pinfield, 0b111         @ 3 bits
.equ    input, 0                @ use pint for input

.equ    seconds,2               @ sleep value

@ Constants for assembler pinclear and pinset
.equ    pinbit,       1         @ 1 bit for pin
.equ    registerpins, 32
.equ    GPCLR0,   0x28          @ clear register offset
.equ    GPSET0,   0x1C          @ set register offset

@ addresses of messages and values
devicefile:     .word   device
openMode:       .word   openflags
gpio:           .word   gpiobase+offset
openerror:      .word   openstring1
memerror:       .word   memstring2
```

```
@ Constant program data
        .section .rodata
        .align   2
device:         .asciz  "/dev/gpiomem"
openstring1:    .asciz  "Didnt open /dev/gpiomem\n"
memstring2:     .asciz  "Didnt Map /dev/gpiomem \n"

@ The program starts and runs from here
    .text
    .align  2
    .global main

main:
@ Open /dev/gpiomem for read/write and syncing
    LDR    R0, devicefile     @ address of /dev/gpiomem string
    LDR    R1, openMode       @ flags for accessing device
    BL     open               @ call open
    MOVS   R4, R0             @ error check
    BPL    moveon1            @ If positive, moveon
    LDR    R0, openerror      @ error, tell user
    BL     printf
    B      _exit              @ and end program

moveon1:
@ Map GPIO to main memory location so we can access them
@ Keep a copy of the mapped memory address returned in R0
    MOV    R4, R0             @ use r4 for file descriptor
    MOV    R8, R0             @ Save a copy of file descriptor
    LDR    R9, gpio           @ address of GPIO
    PUSH   {R9}               @ Copy on stack for mmmap
    PUSH   {R8}               @ file descriptor on stack for mmap
    MOV    R0, #nopref        @ let kernel pick memory
    MOV    R1, #pagesize      @ get 1 page of memory
    MOV    R2, #readwrite     @ read/write this memory
    MOV    R3, #mapshare      @ share with other processes
    BL     mmap               @ R0-R3+top of stack has info
    MOV    R9,R0              @ save mapped address
    CMP    R0, #-1            @ check for error
    BNE    moveon2            @ no error, continue
    LDR    R0, memerror       @ error, tell user
    BL     printf
    B      _exit
```

```
moveon2:
@   Select pin number and function.
    MOV     R0, R9              @ programming memory
    MOV     R1, #pinnumber      @ pin number (22)
    MOV     R2, #output         @ pin function (1)
    MOV     R4, R0              @ save pointer to GPIO
    MOV     R5, R1              @ save pin number
    MOV     R6, R2              @ save function code

@ Compute address of GPFSEL register and pin field
    MOV     R3, #10             @ divisor
    UDIV    R0, R5, R3          @ GPFSEL number
    MUL     R1, R0, R3          @ compute remainder
    SUB     R1, R5, R1          @ for GPFSEL pin

@ Set up the GPIO pin function register in programming memory
    LSL     R0, R0, #2          @ 4 bytes in a register
    ADD     R0, R4, R0          @ GPFSELn address
    LDR     R2, [R0]            @ get entire register
    MOV     R3, R1              @ need to multiply pin
    ADD     R1, R1, R3, lsl #1  @ position by 3
    MOV     R3, #pinfield       @ gpio pin field (0b111)
    LSL     R3, R3, R1          @ shift to pin position
    BIC     R2, R2, R3          @ clear pin field
    LSL     R6, R6, R1          @ shift func code to pin position
    ORR     R2, R2, R6          @ enter function code
    STR     R2, [R0]            @ update register

@ setGPIOpin
@ All OK, now turn on the LED
@ Requires mmap address and pin number
    MOV     R0, R9              @ Get memory address
    MOV     R1, #pinnumber      @ Get pin number (22)
    ADD     R4, R0, #GPSET0     @ point to GPSET regs in R4
    MOV     R5, R1              @ save pin number

@ Compute address of GPSET register and pin field
    MOV     R3, #registerpins   @ divisor
    UDIV    R0, R5, R3          @ GPSET number
    MUL     R1, R0, R3          @ compute remainder
    SUB     R1, R5, R1          @ for relative pin position
```

```
        LSL     R0, R0, #2          @ 4 bytes in a register
        ADD     R0, R0, R4          @ address of GPSETn

@ Set up the GPIO pin function register in programming memory
        LDR     R2, [R0]            @ get entire register
        MOV     R3, #pinbit         @ one pin (1)
        LSL     R3, R3, R1          @ shift to pin position
        ORR     R2, R2, R3          @ set bit
        STR     R2, [R0]            @ update register

@ Wait for seconds
        MOV     R0, #seconds        @ wait seconds
        BL      sleep

@ clearGPIOpin
@ Clears a GPIO pin. Requires mmap addr & pin number
        MOV     R0, R9              @ Get GPIO mapped address
        MOV     R1, #pinnumber
        ADD     R4, R0, #GPCLR0     @ pointer to GPSET regs.
        MOV     R5, R1              @ save pin number

@ Compute address of GPSET register and pin field
        MOV     R3, #registerpins @ divisor (32)
        UDIV    R0, R5, R3          @ GPSET number
        MUL     R1, R0, R3          @ compute remainder
        SUB     R1, R5, R1          @ for relative pin position
        LSL     R0, R0, #2          @ 4 bytes in a register
        ADD     R0, R0, R4          @ address of GPSETn

@ Set up the GPIO pin funtion register in programming memory
        LDR     R2, [R0]            @ get entire register
        MOV     R3, #pinbit         @ one pin
        LSL     R3, R3, R1          @ shift to pin position
        ORR     R2, R2, R3          @ clear bit
        STR     R2, [R0]            @ update register

@ unmapGPIOmemory
@ On completion need to remocve memory mapping
@ and close file
        MOV     R0, R5              @ memory to unmap
        MOV     R1, #pagesize       @ amount we mapped
        BL      munmap              @ unmap it
```

```
closeDev:
    MOV     R0, R8          @ file descriptor
    BL      close           @ close file

@ end program here
_exit:
    POP     {R8}            @ restore SP to entry level.
    POP     {R9}
    MOV     R7, #1
    SWI     #0
```

Note that to assemble and generate the executable you will need to use the following, otherwise you will likely generate an error:

```
gcc -march="armv8-a" -g -o gpio22 prog23a.s
```

This will generate an executable called 'gpio22' assuming that you saved the above source file as 'prog23a.s'. The program assumes that an LED or similar is attached to GPIO22 and will turn it on (illuminate), wait for two seconds and then turn it off. Either side of this it will create and open a virtual memory map and then do the reverse on completion. (GPIO22 as it seems to be available on all models of the Raspberry Pi released to date.)

Building the Code

That's quite a lot to take in, so let's work through the program section by section.

The first blocks of code define the constants, and label definitions. These occupy the first page or so of the file. This section ends with three asciz string definitions. From the comments and the previous text the function of each of these should become apparent if not already.

The program itself starts at 'main:'.

Opening the file we want to map, requires two pieces of information. This is the address of device name we want to open and the properties to be assigned for the file when opened. These need to be loaded into R0 and R1 respectively. The address of the:

'/dev/gpiomem'

string is provided by the address pointer specified in 'devicefile'. A quick trip to 'open' in the Linux kernel is all that is needed. On return to our program, R0 will contain the file descriptor or a negative number indicating an error occurred and the file couldn't be opened. In the case of the latter the appropriate error message is displayed, and the program terminates. This should be familiar following on from the knowledge gained in earlier chapters.

All being well the program flow resumes at 'moveon1' where we save a copy of the file descriptor in R4 for program use and a backup for use later (R8). We also need to save a copy of the peripheral address provided to access the GPIO (0x3F200000) and preserve a copy of this in R9. These two items are then pushed on the top of the stack.

The 'mmap' function will undertake the process of mapping the virtual memory for us to use. It takes six arguments as follows:

1. R0=The address where the device should be mapped. Best in this instance to allow the system to choose it, indicated by using a null value or zero.
2. R1=The amount of memory required for the mapping. One 'page' is sufficient, specified as 4096 bytes.
3. R2=A number specifying the protection given to the mapped memory. This must tie in with the protection that was specified in the original open operation. Namely the ability to read and write and allow the mapped memory to be synchronised with information written to it.
4. R3=A value specifying whether the mapped memory can be shared with other devices or not. Normally it is best to allow such sharing as you may want to have other programs accessing the GPIO concurrently.
5. {R9} = The physical memory location of the I/O device.
6. {R8} = Value of the file descriptor to the device being mapped. This came from our call to open.

The last two items in our list have been pushed onto the top of the stack. The mmap function call expects a total of six items of information and therefore looks to the stack to provide them as only four are passed through registers R0-R3.

On return from the mmap call the memory address that the GPIO has been mirrored into is R0. This is saved by the program into R9. If -1 is returned then an error has occurred, and an error message is provided, and the program exited. Otherwise, program flow continues at 'moveon2', and everything is primed and ready for selecting the GPIO pin number and function required of it!

The next block of code (the next six lines straight after 'moveon2') primes the registers ready for the programming of the relative GPFSEL register and pin field. These values are initially R0, R1 and R2 and then copied into R4, R5 and R6 respectively so the originals can be utilised.

The next section is fundamental to computing the address of the GPFSEL register and field. This includes an instruction we haven't looked at before, UDIV, and is one of the reasons why special flags are needed to assemble the listing. UDIV divides an unsigned 32-bit value into another unsigned 32-bit

Raspberry Pi OS Assembly Language

value, producing a 32-bit unsigned result. This provides a quotient, but any remainder is thrown away and the result rounded down to the next whole number. However, we want the remainder to provide us with the GPFSEL pin, so we need to compute this as well. Three lines of code do this.

In our segment of assembler, the quotient is calculated by divining R5 by R3 thus:

```
UDIV R0, R5, R3         @ Unsigned divide R0=R5/R3
    R0=0x16/0x0A
    R0=0x02
```

The use of 10 as the divisor (0x0A)in R3 is the constant in converting the decimal value (base 10). The result, 2, is provided as 0x16/0x0A or 22/10=2.2, thus 0x02 rounded down, this is our GPSEL number. Next, we need to compute the remainder from the quotient to obtain the GPSEL pin number. Multiply the quotient by the divisor (now in R0):

```
MUL R1, R0, R3    @ R1=R0*R3
    R0=0x02*0x0A
    R1=0x14
```

Next, subtract the result in R1 from the value in R5:SUB R1, R5, R1   @ R1=R5-R1

```
    R1=0x16-0x14
    R1=0x02
```

This gives us the GPSEL number and the GFSEL pinfield, so we can set-up the GPIO pin function register. We need to account for there being four bytes (one word) in a register, do this by shifting the value left by two positions:

```
LSL R0, R0, #2
    R0=0X02,<<2
    R0=0X08
```

This provides the offset of 0x08, which is added to the base address returned by mmap. (Note this address was returned for a RPi 3B with 1GB of memory. It is likely different on other configurations of RPi; however you can remain oblivious to this address as it is calculated for you.) Look back at Figure 23a and you will see that the offset for GPFSEL2 is #8. This is calculated below.

```
ADD R0, R4, R0
    R0=0x76FFF8000+0x08
    R0=0x76FFF8008
```

We can then read the contents of this memory address in R0, into R2, 0x40 in this instance.

```
LDR R2, [R0]
    R0=[0x76FFF8008]
    R2=0x40
```

Now the pin number previously stored in R1 is moved into R3:

```
MOV R3, R1          @ need to mov R1 into R3 pin
    R3=0x02
```

And then shifted by three shift its position by three:
```
ADD  R1, R1, R3, LSL #1
    R1=0x02+0x2,<<1
    R1=0x06
```
Consult Figure 23b and see that Pin 22 is 6.
```
MOV R3, #pinfield      @ gpio pin field
    R3=0x07

LSL R3, R3, R1         @ shift to pin position
    R3=0x07<<0x06
    R3=0x1C0
```
The GPIO pinfield value is moved into R3, seven in this case. The pin field value is then shifted left by six to give 0x1C0 in R3.

The BIC instruction performs a bitwise AND between the NOT of a bit pattern and the register value. The net effect is to clear the bits in the register as specified by the bit pattern. Before shifting the function code to the pin position:
```
BIC R2, R2, R3
    R2=0x040 BIC 0x1C0
    R2=0
LSL R6, R6, R1
    R6=0x01 << 0x06
    R6=0x40
ORR R2, R2, R6         @ enter function code
    R2=0x0 ORR 0x40
    R2=0x40
```
Store the contents of R2 at the location specified by the address in R0 = 0x76FFF8008.
```
STR R2, [R0]
    0x76FF8008 = 0x040
```
Now we can turn the pin 'on' using the mmap address and the pin number. These are copied in R0 and R1 having previously been saved.
```
MOV R0, R9
    R0=0x76FF8000
MOV R1, #pinnumber     @ 0x16= GPIO 22
    R1=0x16
```
Add the pin number to the original mmap address. To point to the GPSET registers:
```
ADD  R4, R0, #GPSET0
    R4=0x76FF8000+0x1C
    R4=0x76FF801C
```
Save the pin number for later use:
```
MOV R5, R1             @ save pin number
```

```
           R5=0x16
```
Move the register pins number (32) into R3:
```
    MOV  R3, #registerpins
         R3=0x20
```
Utilise UDIV as previously to calculate the GPSET number and then work out the remained, for relative position:
```
    UDIV  R0, R5, R3        @ GPSET number
          R0=0x16/0x20
          R0=0
    MUL   R1, R0, R3        @ compute remainder
          R1=0x0 x 0x20
          R1=0
    SUB   R1, R5, R1        @ for relative pin position
          R1=0x16- 0x0
          R1=0x16
    LSL   R0, R0, #2        @ 4 bytes in a register
          R0=0 << 2
          R0=0
```
Perform additions to get the address of GPSET in virtual memory:
```
    ADD   R0, R0, R4        @ address of GPSETn
          R0 = 0 + 0x76FF801c
          R0=0x76FF801c
```
Access contents of the entire register at address given in R0:
```
    LDR   R2, [R0]          @ get entire register
          R2=[0x76ff801c]
          R2=0x6770696f
```
Load R3 with pin bit constant (1):
```
    MOV   R3, #pinbit       @ one pin
          R3=1
```
Logically shift left the value by contents held in R1 (relative pin position):
```
    LSL   R3, R3, R1
          R3 = 1 << 0x16
          R3= 0x400000
```
Logically OR this with the contents in R2 to provide new value:
```
    ORR   R2, R2, R3        @ set bit
          R2= 0x6770696f ORR 0x400000
          R2= 0x6770696f
```
And update the register by storing it in virtual memory:
```
    STR   R2, [R0]          @ update register
          R2=0x6770696f
          R0=0x76ff801c
          0x76ff801c=0x6770696f
```

This will now turn the pin (and LED if attached) 'on'.

The same methodology is used to turn the pin off and therefore any attached LED. I'll leave you to work through the code utilising the above technique.

You only require minimal changes to adapt the program to work on other pins. simply change the value assigned to 'pinnumber' in the section marked 'Constants for Function Select' to '17' and re-assemble. The program will work out the rest of the details for you.

The program listing is provided as a single contiguous file. More to make it easier to read. Once you have an understanding of its operation it is a good candidate to section it into a series of macros—see Chapter 18 for a refresher on macros.

Other GPIO Functions

Just as a reminder: There are several other registers that form part of the GPIO Controller that can be used and programmed using these methods. As already mentioned you will need to get a copy of the appropriate BCM peripherals data sheet to get the specific detail that you need relating to the other registers, their functions and what you need to do to use them. It is all there. You can check out the official Raspberry Pi website for more information and links to download these.

One final thing in relation to the data sheet. If you look at the memory maps at the start of the document you will see that the ARM peripherals are mapped as starting at 0x7E000000, whereas in Raspbian or Raspberry Pi OS, on Raspberry Pi Zero and 1, they start at 0x2000000 and 0x3F000000 for Raspberry Pi 2, 3, 4, and 400. All operating systems implement their own memory addressing systems which overlay the ones provided by default by the CPU. This allows the OS in question to implement virtual memory mapping — a technique that allows program and applications to use more memory than is actually available to them by swapping data in and out of memory from the SD Card in use or the hard drive attached. From a practical point of view, when you access the Broadcom data sheet you should remember that all the peripheral addresses specified in the text are bus addresses and must be translated into physical addresses. Thus, the GPIO Controller start address is given as 0x7E200000 but we implement as 0x3F200000 or 0x20200000 in our programs depending on the model.

Finally, a word of warning. The GPIO pins control a whole host of functions on your Raspberry Pi and if you are not careful you can crash the operating system. Always save your work before you try to execute any machine code file for the first time.

GPIO Pins Explained

Figure 23f depicts the 40-pin header that is fitted to the more recent Raspberry Pi modules. The first thing to notice is that there are effectively three columns of information, which are repeated on the left and right side of the 'Header' column) in the centre.

For a Revision 2.0, 26-pin header then Header Pins 1-26 are still relevant and have the same assignments. Revision 1.0 is different. If you have a Raspberry Pi with a 26-pin header, you should check the Raspberry Pi website to determine which Revision you have. Generally, the original Pi 1 Model B was fitted with Revision 1.0.

Bits	Register	Pin	Header		Pin	Register	Bits
+3.3 volts			1	2	+5.0 volts		
6-8	GPSEL0	GPIO 2	3	4	+5.0 volts		
9-11	GPSEL0	GPIO 3	5	6	Ground (0 volts)		
12-14	GPSEL0	GPIO 4	7	8	GPIO 14	GPSEL1	12-14
Ground (0 volts)			9	10	GPIO 15	GPSEL1	15-17
21-23	GPSEL1	GPIO 17	11	12	GPIO 18	GPSEL1	24-26
21-23	GPSEL2	GPIO 27	13	14	Ground (0 volts)		
6-8	GPSEL2	GPIO 22	15	16	GPIO 23	GPSEL2	9-11
+3.3 volts			17	18	GPIO 24	GPSEL2	12-14
0-2	GPSEL1	GPIO 10	19	20	Ground (0 volts)		
27-29	GPSEL0	GPIO 9	21	22	GPIO 25	GPSEL2	15-17
3-5	GPSEL1	GPIO 11	23	24	GPIO 8	GPSEL0	24-26
Ground (0 volts)			25	26	GPIO 7	GPSEL0	21-23
Do Not Connect			27	28	Do Not Connect		
15-17	GPSEL0	GPIO 5	29	30	Ground (0 volts)		
18-20	GPSEL0	GPIO 6	31	32	GPIO 12	GPSEL1	6-8
9-11	GPSEL1	GPIO 13	33	34	Ground (0 volts)		
27-29	GPSEL1	GPIO 19	35	36	GPIO 16	GPSEL1	18-22
18-20	GPSEL2	GPIO 26	37	38	GPIO 20	GPSEL2	0-2
Ground (0 volts)			39	40	GPIO 21	GPSEL2	3-5

Outside edge of board.

Figure 23f. Raspberry Pi GPIO Header Connections

Header Pins: The 'Header' is the physical aspect on your Raspberry Pi, and the numbers 1-40 down the centre represent the 40 pins on the header connector. These numbers are often referred to as the 'Header Pin Numbers' and each one is wired into the Raspberry Pi to provide a specific function.

These functions are defined by the columns that appear to the left and right as already mentioned.

Pin: The Pin column, in most instances provides the number of the GPIO pin itself (FSEL). Thus GPIO 22 is wired into Header Pin 15. In some instances, the Pin is also wired to provide poser or act as a ground. Thus, Header Pin 1 is 3.3 volts, and Header Pin 6 is Ground. The two 'Do Not Connect 'options are in fact GPIO 0 and GPIO 1 but are reserved for other functions.

A GPIO pin designated as an output pin can be set to high (3V3) or low (0V). If designated as an input, the pin can be read as high (3V3) or low (0V). This is made easier with the use of internal pull-up or pull-down resistors. Pins GPIO2 and GPIO3 have fixed pull-up resistors, but for other pins this can be configured in software.

Register: The Function Select Register is listed in this column. Figure 23a has more details on these. GPSEL 0, 1 and 2 are the ones commonly used here.

Bits: These are the three bits in the related GPSEL register that control the GPIO pin. Look at Header Pins 11 and 13. These both have bits 21-23 associated with them however they are in different registers GPSEL1 and GPSEL2.

Other Functions: In addition to being input and output devices, GPIO pins can be used for a variety of alternative more advanced functions. For example, software pulse width modulation (PWM) is available on all pins, whilst hardware PWM is available through GPIO 12, GPIO 13, GPIO 18 and GPIO 19. Serial TX via GPIO14; and RX via GPIO15. Other options exists and these can be found on the Raspberry Pi website.

24: Floating-Point

In our everyday use of computers, we take the use of floating-point numbers point numbers for granted. After all what use would a bank have of a computer that couldn't work out decimal points? When we use spreadsheets, calculators and even some word-processing packages, the ability to perform simple calculations down to several decimal points is accepted without a second thought. But what about assembly language? All the number action we have looked at to date, and there's not been that much in reality, has been dealing with integer numbers, values without any fractional part.

The management and manipulation of floating-point numbers takes a great deal of processing grunt and this is not provided in the first instance by the ARM chip—it is supplied by something called a co-processor. As we will see in Chapter 30, the ARM chip used in the Raspberry Pi forms part of a 'bigger' infrastructure known as a SOC or System-on-Chip. It is more than just the ARM chip itself, and one of these additional items is some additional hardware circuitry that handles floating-point math. This co-processor as it is known is the VFP or Vector Floating-Point co-processor and this supplies additional architecture, including registers and instructions to allow floating-point to be included in assembly language programs. Better still GCC and GDB support these too and do so as the IEEE 754 definition they conform to standardises the format of floating-point numbers to provide a common format across computer platforms.

In these next couple of chapters, we'll look at how the floating-point architecture is implemented and the instructions which we can use to include real numbers in our own programs. This should provide you with more than enough information to use them in a practical way and display your results for the world to see.

VFP Architecture

Modern software, mainly media codecs and graphics accelerators, operate on large amounts of data that is less than word 56sized. 16-bit data is common in audio applications, and 8-bit data is standard in graphics and video, and there is lots of it. When performing these operations on a 32-bit microprocessor, parts of the microprocessor are unused but continue to consume power. To make better use of this excess, wasted processor capacity, Single Instruction Multiple Data (SIMD) technology introduced the use of a single instruction to perform the same operation in parallel on multiple data elements of the same type and size. This way, the hardware that frequently adds two 32-bit values instead performs four parallel additions of 8-bit values in the same amount of time.

The creators of the Raspberry Pi have been keen to utilise the full benefits of the ARM microprocessor, but if you follow the technology world closely you will have noticed that there is a never-ending stream of ARM microprocessors available. This makes compatibility difficult as they all offer something different. For that reason, only three versions of ARM have been used with the various Raspberry Pi at the time of writing. Namely ARMv6, ARMv7 and ARMv8. (There are other reasons but hardware and software compatibility is fundamental to the concept of the Raspberry Pi.)

VFP2 architecture is implemented on the ARM v6 chip fitted to Raspberry Pi 1 models A, B, A+ and B+. On the Raspberry Pi 2 and Raspberry Pi 3 the ARMv7/8 chip supports VFP4 which encompasses VFP2 but includes an expanded instruction set. We'll deal with the basics that are common to both here.

The VFP provides support for single-precision and double-precision numbers. As the name implies the latter can represent numbers in more detail than the former. To this end a single-precision number occupies a word of memory (32-bits or binary32), whilst a double occupies two-words of memory (64-bits or binary64). You will recall that the ARM can use 32-bit numbers for its standard values, and this begs the question: are the single-precision floating-point numbers that are available as big as the integer ones? The answer is yes, they are, and they can be much bigger as it boils down to the way in which they are represented. The following are examples of floating-point or real numbers:

```
0.2345
546.6735268
1.001011010
4E7
```

In the latter case the number is 4*10 to the power of 7 or $4x10^7$. The 7 is the exponent and means 'raised to the power of'. In single and double-precision numbers the values can be encoded into the bits so that they have a sign bit, an exponent portion and a fractional or mantissa portion. In this way large or small numbers can be depicted.

Figure 24a below shows how a single-precision and double-precision number are laid out. In the circumstance of double-precision numbers, the two-words must occupy consecutive memory locations and be word-aligned.

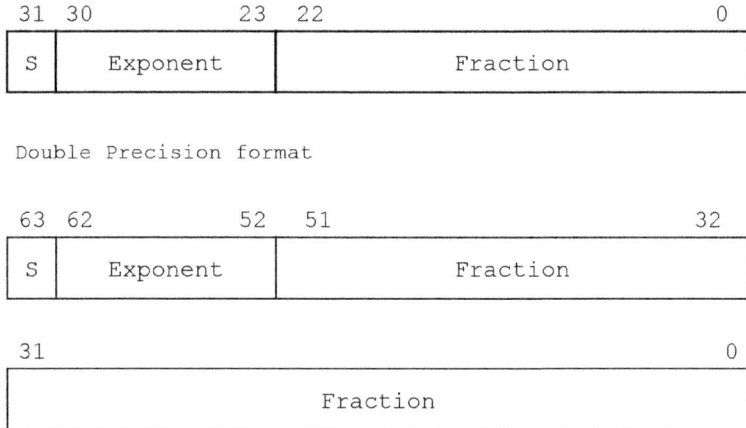

Figure 24a. Construction of single and double-precision numbers.

Sign (S): This can be 0 or 1 to represent positive or negative values, respectively. It is held in the most significant bit of the number.

Exponent: The exponent is the value we need to shift the mantissa along to the left to restore it to its original value. It is held between the sign bit and fraction.

Fractional: Also called the mantissa, this is the number following the point and it can obviously be a binary value to represent the real number. The mantissa will have been normalised, that is shifted along to the right until we are left with a single digit on the left of the dot. In double-precision numbers it occupies the whole of the least significant word and part of the most significant word.

In a single-precision floating-point the mantissa is 23-bits (+1 for the integer one for normalised numbers) and the exponent is 8-bits, meaning the exponent can range from -126 to 127. In a double-precision the mantissa is 53-bits (+1 as for single) and the exponent is 11-bits, so the exponent ranges from -1022 to 1023).

For completeness there is also a third type of number representation. This is called NaN, an acronym for 'Not a Number'. This is used in special circumstances where a value cannot be represented in single or double-precision manner. It is a fascinating topic—not least as there are also two different types of NaN and is worth investigating further if you are interested in this type of thing.

The Register File

The load and store architecture of the ARM chip persists in VFP and to deal with floating-point values it provides a set of registers specifically for the purpose. There are 32 in all with the prefix S and numbered S0-S31. These registers are used to hold single-precision values as they are all one word wide. For the manipulation of double-precision numbers these registers can be paired up to form up to 16 two-word width registers. D is used to denote this, and they are numbered D0 to D15. Figure 24b illustrates this in principle.

S0	S1	<<	>>	D0	
S2	S3			D1	Scalar
S4	S5			D2	Registers
S6	S7			D3	
S8	S9			D4	
S10	S11			D5	
S12	S13			D6	
S14	S15			D7	
S16	S17			D8	
S18	S19			D9	Vectoral
S20	S21			D10	Registers
S22	S23			D11	
S24	S25			D12	
S26	S27			D13	
S28	S29			D14	
S30	S31			D15	

Figure 24b. The VFP Register File. The Sx registers may be used individually or paired to create a double-precision register, Dx.

You should be clear that these registers are one and the same and although the values in registers may be either single or double, they can only contain one value at a time. Thus, S0 and S1 can be used individually for two single-precision values or combined as D0 for a double-precision value. If D0 is loaded with a value, then the contents of S0 and S1 are wiped. It is perfectly possible to have single-precision value in S0 and S1 and a double-precision value in D1 as D1 is composed of S2 and S3.

Please note that there are no warning devices or alarm systems to tell you what is in what register. That is up to you to look after — this is machine code after all. You are the manager. These registers are grouped into *scalar registers* (S0-S7/D0-D3) and *vectorial register* banks (S8-S31/D4-D15) for usage purposes— and the group determines how they are accessed, which we'll look at with some examples later.

As you might expect there are instructions to deal specifically with moving both single and double-precision values to and from memory and registers and a variety of instructions for arithmetic functions. Let's look at a simple example first that will also show how to use printf to display a floating-point number. We'll also use it to highlight a few points.

Managing and Printing

Program 24a illustrates a few basic operations involving floating-point numbers and illustrates a technique to to use printf to display a floating-point value on the screen.

This is important as it will allow you to display the results of any operations you do. The first thing to note is that you cannot load a floating-point value directly into a register; you must do it indirectly via a register. This concept should be familiar and the way the code is structured, as shown below.

Program 24a. Printing a floating-point value with printf.

```
/* Printing a floating-point number */
    .global main
    .func main
main:

    LDR R1, addr_value1     @ Get addr of value1
    VLDR S14, [R1]          @ Move value1 into S14
    VCVT.F64.F32 D5, S14    @ Convert to B64

    LDR R0, =string         @ point R0 to string
    VMOV R2, R3, D5         @ Load value
bp:
    BL printf               @ call function
    MOV R7, #1              @ Exit Syscall
    SWI 0

addr_value1:
    .word value1

    .data
value1:    .float 108.65625
string:    .asciz "Floating point value is: %f\n"
```

The first line of code loads the address of value1 into R1. In the next line this is used as the indirect address of the value to be loaded into S14. The VLDR stands for Vector LoaD Register. The third line then converts the value into a double-precision one. This is because printf can print double-precision values but not single-precision ones, which is the format of the value in S14. The instruction is complex but is surprisingly easy to read and construct when you know how:

```
VCVT        Vector Convert instruction
.F64        Convert to Binary64 - viz double-precision
```

```
.F32        From Binary32 - viz single-precision
D5          Destination double-precision register
S14         The source single-precision registers
```

The order is the important thing to remember here: the target comes before the source.

The next three lines are all about getting printf ready to use. As before R0 must point to the string to print. Normally R1, R2, and R3 are used to pass additional values to printf. However, we can only get one double-precision value in those three registers, so the definition is that R2 and R3 are used (R1 is ignored). VMOV moves D5 into R2 and R3. The %f directive is used in the print string and printf is smart enough to know that this directive indicates a double-precision value and so just looks in R2 and R3 for it. (If you call other libc functions then you may be able to pass two double-precision values through to it as R0-R3 are allocated for the purpose in normal ARM use.)

You can also see in the data section that the '.float' directive is used to store the floating-point value.

Printing more than one double-precision value with printf follows the same route as previously. The additional items are pushed onto the stack. However, PUSH and POP or their equivalents become a little redundant here as we are dealing with two-word values for each double-precision number. Program 22b will build on the previous listing to do this.

The load and conversion process remains the same, but obviously using different registers, and the VPUSH instruction is used to place the value on the stack. Additional values can be added in the same way.

Note that most floating-point numbers that a computer can represent are just approximations. One challenge in programming with floating-point values is ensuring that the approximations lead to reasonable results. If the programmer is not careful, small discrepancies in the approximations can snowball to the point where the results become meaningless.

Assembling and Debugging VFP with GDB

The GCC methodology is ideal for testing and debugging code at this level. One of the advantages using the full gcc compile method is that GCC will invariably handle all the behind-the-scenes leg work for you. So, when it parses the assembler it understands you are using floating-point opcodes and therefore attaches and assembles the additional information required. It will also handle the requirements of utilising functions such as printf. For instance, you can assemble Program24a thus:

```
gcc -g -o prog24a prog24a.s
```

Then utilise the GDB debugging tools to examine and step-through the code. GDB provides debugging tools for operation with the VFP (and Neon which we will cover in in Chapter 26). All the options outlined in Chapter 14 are valid, and GDB will disassemble machine code files correctly. You can also access the VFP registers by adding the extension 'all' to the info command line thus:

```
info r all
```

or:

```
i r a
```

This will list the D and S registers, (plus the Q registers used by Neon which we will discuss in a later chapter). You will notice that this also lists D registers up to D31, whereas we only identified registers to D15 earlier. The D register set is extended to correlate with the Neon Q registers as we shall see.

The 'all' function provides a lot of data. You can limit the amount of data displayed by specifying individual registers. First though insert a breakpoint using the 'bp:' label that was part of the listing assembled by typing:

```
b bp
```

at the GDB prompt. You will get a message confirming this. Remaining within GDB type:

```
run
```

The code will execute up to the breakpoint which is immediately before the call to the printf function. Everything else prior to this break has been executed. We can now look at the contents of the relevant registers by typing:

```
info r s14 d5 r0 r1 r2 r3
```

The output is shown below. For the sake of clarity, I have reformatted slightly this for the D5 register output to make it much easier to read here.

```
s14    108.65625         (raw 0x42d95000)
d5     {u8 = {0x0, 0x0, 0x0, 0x0, 0x0, 0x2a, 0x5b, 0x40},
        u16 = {0x0, 0x0, 0x2a00, 0x405b},
        u32 = {0x0, 0x405b2a00},
        u64 = 0x405b2a0000000000,
        f32 = {0x0, 0x3}, f64 = 0x6c
r0     0x2102c           135212
r1     0x21028           135208
r2     0x0               0
r3     0x405b2a00        1079716352
```

To recap the six registers in the output above are shown immediately prior to the printf call, and therefore have all the information passed into them.

S4 This clearly shows the single-precision value as 108.65625 – also seen its raw binary value of 0x42D95000.

D5	The representation we are normally interested in here is the U32 number. This is shown as: 0x405b2a00 in 32bits and (with 0) in the other 32 bits. You can also see this as 0x405b2a0000000000 in u64 (64-bits).
R0	holds the address of the value the address of the string to be used by printf
R1	Has the address of the single-precision number to be printed.
R2, R3	Hold the value to be printed by printf. This is there same as shown in D5 above.

Therefore, R2 and R3 are holding a double-precision value, stored in two registers. This is because printf only prints double-precision numbers.

The value in D5 is the value 108.656250 represented as a single-precision binary number.

Edit Program24a and change the number to be converted to:

```
108.6000
```

Reassemble the file and execute the program again (no need to go into GDB). The result returned is:

Floating point value is: 108.599998

The value converted back is not 108.60000. This is a rounding error. A small discrepancy, in fact just -0.00000152587890625. However, if compounded, especially by multiplication it might ultimately become quite significant.

The reason for the variation is in the way the way the decimal value is converted into a binary representation. In some cases, these errors can and regularly do occur. It didn't occur in the original example as the initial value converts correctly.

Using GDB is a good way to learn what instructions do, and how the various combinations of actions affect the flags and results.

You can still assemble and link your floating-point code as a two-stage process using 'as' and 'ld' providing you follow the rules laid down in the early chapters of this book. However, you will also need to link the run-time libraries you require for any external functions called, such as printf or scanf etc when you link them. In these instances, we'll stick with the GCC compiler to do the process for us.

The debugger can be used is the -g option is included in the assemble sequence as normal.

Load, Store and Move

As with the standard ARM instruction set the VFP instruction set provides a versatile set of instructions to shift information around. VLDR and VSTR load and store single register quantities using indirect addressing. Here are a few examples:

```
VLDR S1, [R5]       @Load S1 with F32 value at addr in R5
VLDR D2, [R5, #4]   @Load S2 with F64 value addr+4 in R5
VSTR S3, [R6]       @Store F32 value in S3 at addr in R6
```

Pre-indexed addressing is used in the second example to add 4 to the address held in R5 before the operation completes.

We can also use pre-indexed addressing with write-back as well, to update the address in the indexing register. This is useful when dealing with operations working on sets of registers, as shown here:

```
VLDMIAS R5!,{S1-S4} @ Copy S1, S2, S3, S4 & update R5
```

In this example the values in the four registers S1, S2, S3 and S4 are copied sequentially to the word location starting at the address held in R5. When the operation is completed the length of space used for the storage is added to R5. This means that R5 will now point to the next address—the one after S4. If the instruction had read:

```
VLDMIAS R5!, {D1-D4} @ Copy D1, D2, D3, D4 & update R5
```

then the same operation would have taken place, but the instruction would have allowed two-words (8 bytes) per register and added 32 bytes to the value in R5. If you do not wish to update R5 then exclude '!' from the instruction.

The addressing modes in operation here are similar in fashion to those described in Chapter 15 but notice how the registers and information are arranged differently. There is no post-indexed addressing operation.

Program 24b. Manipulating and printing two or more fp values.

```
/* Printing two floating-point numbers */

        .global    main
        .func main
main:
        SUB SP, SP, #16         @ Make space on stack
        LDR R1, addr_value1     @ Get addr of value1
        VLDR S14, [R1]
        VCVT.F64.F32 D0, S14
        LDR R1, addr_value2     @ Get addr of value2
        VLDR S15, [R1]
        VCVT.F64.F32 D1, S15

        LDR R0, =string         @ point R0 to string
        VMOV R2, R3, D0         @ first value
        VSTR D1, [SP]           @ second on stack
```

```
        BL printf
        ADD SP, SP, #16         @ restore stack

        MOV R7, #1              @ Exit Syscall
        SWI 0

addr_value1:    .word value1
addr_value2:    .word value2

        .data
value1:    .float 1.54321
value2:    .float 5.1
string:    .asciz "The FP values are %f and %f\n"
```

VPUSH and VPOP can be used with curly brackets to transfer several items to and from the stack:
```
        VPUSH {S1-S4}   @ put S1, S2, S3, S4 onto stack
        VPOP  {S5-S8}   @ pull them into S5, S6, S7 and S8
```
The VMOV instruction allows values to be freely transferred between different register sets. When there is a transfer between a VFP register and an ARM register then the transfer is done bit-by-bit and no conversion takes place.
```
        VMOV S1, S2             @ Copy S2 into S1
        VMOV S1, S2, R3, R5     @ Copy R3 to S1 and R5 to S2
        VMOV R2, R4, D1         @ Copy loD1 to R2 & hiD1 to R4
```
In the last example a double-precision value (8 bytes) is being transferred into two registers. In such instances it is important to be aware of the order of the hi and lo bytes of the floating-point value as failure to do so can radically alter the value saved. Once again, no conversion is performed, and it is a bit-for-bit transfer. The value is preserved if the transfer is reversed as nothing has changed.

You can use the VMOV instruction to copy information from ARM to VFP registers and thus you can use the command to allow you to store ARM register contents in the Register File if you are looking for extra space:
```
        VMOV S1, R1             @ Store R1 in S1
```

Precision Conversion

Both programs at the start of this chapter included conversion from single to double-precision values. This was done as the printf function directive '%f' requires a double-precision value as its source to work correctly. The VFP architecture allows for conversion to work in several directions. It can also perform double-precision to single-precision transformation, but it can also simplify signed and unsigned integer values conversions. You should bear in mind that conversion can lead to a loss of precision and some rounding of values, particularly where a floating-point number is transformed into an integer.

There are four operators that can be used with VCVT to define the conversion source and targets, two of which must always be used, one as the source and one as the target. These are detailed in Figure 24c.

Suffix	Meaning
.F32	Single Precision, 32-bit one word width values.
.F64	Double Precision, 64-bit two word width values
.S32	Signed integer, 32-bit one word values width values
.U32	Unsigned integer, 32-bit one word values width values

Figure 24c. Suffixes which can be used in number conversion.

The basic syntax of VFP instructions is thus:

```
VCVT <Target><Source>  <Reg-Target>, <Reg-Source>
```

The suffixes '.F32' and '.F64' can be appended to arithmetic or conversion instructions to determine whether the quantities being manipulated are single or double-precision. We have already seen an example of this in the conversion process in both programs above.

The example used in Program 22a was:

```
VCVT.F64.F32 D5, S14
```

This took the single-precision (F32) value in S14 and converted it into a double-provision (F64) value to be stored in D5. A few more examples with short explanations are listed below:

```
VCVT.F32.F64 S10, D2    @ Convert double in D2 to single
                        @ in S10
VCVT.F32.U32 S10, R2    @ Convert Unsigned integer in R2
                        @ to single in S10
VCVT.S32.D64 D4, R2     @ Convert signed integer in R2
                        @ into double in D4
```

Vector Arithmetic

The VFP instruction set provides a comprehensive range of instructions to perform all the arithmetic operations you might expect. The format follows the standard form illustrated so far with F32 and F64 being used to specify single and double-precision values. Operations are performed on one precision format value in each instruction line as single and double-precision values cannot be mixed. An example for each instruction available is given below, remembering that there are '.F32' and '.F64' flavours of each:

```
VADD.F32  S0,  S1,  S2      @ Addition S0=S1+S2
VSUB.F64  D0,  D2,  D4      @ Subtraction D0=D2-D4
VDIV.F64  D4,  D5,  D1      @ Divide D4=D5/D1
VMUL.F32  S2,  S4,  S1      @ Multiply S2=S4*S1
VNMUL.F64 D4,  D3,  D2      @ Multiply and negate
                            @ D4=-(D3*D2)
VMAL.F64  D4,  D3,  D2      @ Multiply and accumulate
                            @ D4=D4+(D3*D2)
VSUB.F64  D0,  D1,  D2      @ Multiply and Subtract
                            @ D0=D0-(D1xD2)
VABS.F32  S0,  S1           @ Absolute S0=ABS(S1)
VNEG.F32  S2,  S3           @ Negate S2=-S3
VSQRT.F64 D0, D1            @ Square Root D0=SQR(D1)
```

25: VFP Control Register

The VFP co-processor provides three system registers. The most important of these from our perspective is the Floating-Point Status and Control Register or FPSCR. You can think of this as the CPSR for the normal ARM instruction set, in that it provides flag status information. Indeed, the N, Z, C and V flags are all present and have the same application. Figure 25a shows how the register is set out for the programmer whilst Figure 25b details the function of the register bits that we'll be discussing here.

FPSCR Format		Rd				Vector			Exception		CEB	
31 28	24	23	22	21	20	18	17	16	12	7	4	0
N Z C V		Rmode		Stride		Len						

Figure 25a. Floating-Point Status and Control Register layout.

The operation and function of several of these flag sets will be covered in these pages. However, the operation of exceptions, although introduced in a forthcoming chapter for the ARM chip itself is not detailed to any degree.

Bits	Flag Set	Detail
31-28	Condition Flags	Negative, Zero, Carry, Overflow
23-22	Rounding Mode	Controls rounding of values
21-20	Stride	Controls step size taken in vector banks
18-16	Len	Controls the vector length
12-8	Exception Status	Enables trapping of exception types
4-0	Cumulative Exception	Trap cumulative exceptions

Figure 25b. Register function summary.

Conditional Execution

We first looked at these condition codes in Chapter 10. The precise meanings of the condition code flags differ depending on whether the flags were set by a floating-point operation or by an ARM data processing instruction. This is because floating-point values are never unsigned, so the unsigned conditions have no meaning. (There is also another reason involving NaN values but as we have not delved into these in this overview, they are not significant at this point.)

Without exception the only VFP instruction that can update the status flags is VCMP and this sets the relative bits in the FPSCR. However, condition flags and instructions are controlled by the APSR (Application Program Status Register—CPSR) and so the FPSCR flags should be copied across into the APSR. There is a specific instruction to do this:

```
VMRS APSR_nzcv, FPSCR
```

The VCMP instruction comes in .F32 and .F64 flavours and can be used thus:

```
VCMP.F32 S0, S1        @ S0-S1 and set condition flags
VCMP.F64 D2, D3        @ D2-D3 and set condition flags
```

The entire contents of the FPSCR can be transferred to an ARM register thus:

```
VMRS R4, FPSCR         @ Copy FSPCR into R4
```

And likewise, the FPSCR can be loaded with the contents of an ARM register allowing the bits to be predetermined and set:

```
VMSR FSPCR, R4         @ Copy R4 into FPSCR
```

Using the bitwise operators (AND, ORR, EOR) this instruction allows you to mask individual bits and provides a mechanism to test specific condition flags. This is used specifically in dealing with the bits associated with 'len' and 'stride' which we'll discuss shortly. Figure 23c overleaf details the meanings of the condition code mnemonics for both ARM and VFP side by side for comparison.

Remember that one of the huge befits of using conditional execution is to reduce the number of branch instructions required and thereby reduce the overall size of your code. Branch instructions also carry a bigger overhead in execution timings — typically three cycles to refill the processor pipeline. For example:

```
VADDEQ.F32 S0, S1, S2   @ Execute only if C=1
VSUBNE.F64 D0, D2, D4   @ Execute only if negative
```

Suffix	After ARM Instruction	After VCMP Instruction
EQ	Equal	Equal
NE	Not Equal	Not Equal or unordered
CS	Carry Set	Equal, Greater Than or unordered
HS	Unsigned Higher or same	Equal, Greater Than or unordered
CC	Carry Clear	Less Than
LO	Unsigned Lower	Less Than
MI	Negative	Less Than
PL	Positive or Zero	Equal, Greater Than or unordered
VS	Overflow	Unordered
VC	No Overflow	Not unordered
HI	Unsigned Higher	Greater Than or unordered
LS	Unsigned Lower or same	Less Than or unordered
GE	Signed Greater Than or Equal	Greater Than or Equal
LT	Signed Less Than	Less Than or unordered
GT	Signed Greater Than	Greater Than
LE	Signed Less Than or Equal	Less Than or Equal or unordered
AL	Always	Always

Figure 25c. Condition code comparison ARM v VFP

Program 25a shows how easy it is to use these commands. This simply loads values into S14 and S15 and then compares them using the VCMP instruction. This sets the flags in the FPSCR. The VMRS instruction is then used to copy the NZCV flags across into the ARM Status Register. Then depending on the status of the C flag, register R0 is loaded with 0 or 255. After running the program, you can use:

```
echo $?
```

to display the result.

You can play with the values of the constants being loaded into the two single-precision registers and use GDB to check the register values to watch the process for yourself. You might like to try extending the program to create a loop that counts down in 0.1 increments, printing them on the screen as you do so and exiting when zero is reached.

Program 25a. Conditional VFP-based execution.

```
/* Conditional execution in VFP code */

        .global    main
        .func main
main:
        LDR R1, addr_value1      @ Get addr value1
        VLDR S14, [R1]
        VCVT.F64.F32 D1, S14

        LDR R1, addr_value2      @ Get addr value2
        VLDR S15, [R1]
        VCVT.F64.F32 D2, S15

        VCMP.F32 S14, S15        @ Compare S14 and S15
        VMRS APSR_nzcv, FPSCR    @ Copy flag set across

        MOVEQ R0, #0             @ If C=1, R0=0
        MOVNE R0, #255           @ If C=0, R0=255

        MOV PC, LR

addr_value1:    .word value1
addr_value2:    .word value2

        .data
value1:    .float 1.54321
value2:    .float 5.1
```

Scalar and Vector Operations

In the previous chapter when looking at the Register File I mentioned that the registers can be divided into scalar and vectorial banks for access purposes. Figure 25d illustrates how this architecture is arranged.

In the earlier examples we have implied that all operations are working on individual registers. However, the VFP can group registers into vectors or sets of registers. For vector operations, the VFP register file can be viewed as a collection of smaller banks. Each of these smaller banks is treated either as a bank of eight single-precision registers or as a bank of four double-precision registers. The number of registers used by a vector is controlled by the LEN bits in the FPSCR. Practically the register banks can be configured as one of the following:

- Four banks of single-precision registers, S0 to S7, S8 to S15, S16 to S23, and S24 to S31
- Four banks of double-precision registers, D0 to D3, D4 to D7, D8 to D11, and D12 to D15
- Any combination of single-precision and double-precision banks.

Bank 0	Bank 1	Bank 2	Bank 3
S0 — S7	S8 — S15	S16 — S23	S24 — S31
D0 D1 D2 D3	D4 D5 D6 D7	D8 — D11	D12 — D15

Figure 25d. The four VFP banks and associated registers.

Normally the value of LEN in VFP is set to 1 so that an instruction will only operate on the registers defined in the instruction. However, by increasing the value of LEN we can make the instruction operate on the rest of the registers in the associated bank of registers. So, a vector can start from any register and wrap-around to the beginning of the bank. In other words, if a vector terminates beyond the end of its bank, it wraps around to the start of the same bank. Figure 25e shows how this works in tabular form.

It is important to note that a vector cannot contain registers from more than one bank, so if the length wraps back to the start the operation stops at that point, once the bank is full.

Referring to Figure 25e, the first entry is LEN 2. This means that the number of registers to be operated on is two. The start register is D11. Looking at Figure 25d we can see that D11 is at the last register in Bank 2. Wrap around means that the next register in the bank is in fact D8 (D12 is in Bank 3).

The first register used by an operand vector is the register that is specified as the operand in the individual VFP instructions. The first register used by the destination vector is the register that is specified as the destination in the individual VFP instructions.

LEN	Start Register	Registers Used
2	D11	D11, D8
3	D7	D7, D4, D5
4	S5	S5, S6, S7, S0
5	S22	S22, S23, S16, S17, S18

Figure 25e. LEN and its effect on bank wrapping.

In the table above the registers accessed have been consecutive ones, in other words they followed the numeric order allowing for wrap-around. However, they can also occupy alternative registers, and this is defined by the setting of the STRIDE bits in the FPSCR. In the examples given in Figure 25e the STRIDE setting would have been 1 as the registers used are consecutive. But a STRIDE setting of 2 would have forced alternative registers to be used. Figure 25f illustrates this in tabular form also.

LEN	STRIDE	Start Register	Registers Used
2	2	D1	D1, D3
3	2	S1	S1, S3, S5
4	2	S6	S6, S0, S2, S4
5	1	S22	S22, S23, S16, S17, S18

Figure 25f. How LEN and STRIDE affects vector wrap-around.

As we have said, a vector cannot use the same register twice, so the combinations of LEN and STRIDE settings are limited.

Consider the following instruction:

```
VADD.F32  S8, S16, S24       @ S8=S16+S24
```

By default, LEN=1, and STRIDE=1 and so the contents of S16 and S24 are added together with the result placed in S8. However, if we set LEN=2 and STRIDE=2 and execute the same instruction, it will be the same as executing the following two instructions with 1+1 settings:

```
VADD.F32  S8, S16, S24       @ S8=S16+S24
VADD.F32  S10, S18, S26      @ S10=S18+S26
```

In turn setting LEN=4 and STRIDE=2 and performing the same instruction would execute as though the following four instructions had taken place:

```
VADD.F32  S8, S16, S24       @ S8=S16+S24
VADD.F32  S10, S18, S26      @ S10=S18+S26
VADD.F32  S12, S20, S28      @ S12=S20+S28
VADD.F32  S14, S22, S30      @ S14=S22+S30
```

As you can see this is a potent programming method and is especially useful when it comes to matrix operations on blocks of numbers.

Which Type of Operator?

Essentially VFP arithmetic can be performed on scalars, vectors or both together. When LEN=1 (default) then all VFP operations are scalar in nature. When LEN is set to anything else then they can be any scalar, vector or mixed. How this works is in your control only by your selection of the register banks used or source and destination registers.

For most purposes Bank 0 (S0-S7/D0-D3) is a scalar bank and the remaining three banks are vector banks. A mixed operation (scalar and vector) occurs when the destination register is in one of the vector banks. Figure 25g provides some examples followed by brief descriptions of the type of action being performed. Although VADD is used through these examples, the action is applicable to all VFP arithmetic instructions.

STRIDE	LEN	Instruction	Result
1	1	VADD.F64 D0, D1, D2	D0=D1+D2. Operation is Scalar as destination (D0) is in Bank 0.
1	1	VADD.F32 S4, S8, S20	S4=S8+S20. Operation is Scalar as destination (S4) is in Bank 0.
2	4	VADD.F32 S10, S16, S24	S10=S16+S24; S12=S18+S26; S14=S20+S28; S8=S22+S30. Operation is vectoral. Notice wrap around on final iteration.
2	2	VADD.F64 D4, D8, D0	D4=D8+D0; D6=D10+D2. Operation is mixed as the second source register is in Bank 0.

Figure 25g. Examples of Scalar, Vector and Mixed operations.

Len and Stride

The bits associated with LEN and STRIDE in the FPSCR can be set up using VMRS and VMSR instructions to transfer the required bit pattern into the FPSCR. This has to be done through an ARM register and is a two-part process, as the FPSCR must be copied across first so that the flag settings may be maintained, and a mask applied just to affect the settings of LEN and STRIDE. Any ARM register can be used, and the two-way process would look like this:

```
    VMRS R4, FPSCR          @ Copy FSPCR into R4
                            @ carry out bit setting here
    VMSR FPSCR, R4          @ Copy R4 into FPSCR
```

The LEN field occupies three bits (b16-b18) whilst the STRIDE field occupies two bits (b20-b21). Figure 25h shows the various bit combinations for LEN and STRIDE and the outcomes for each as well as their reliability with single and double-precision numbers.

Not all combinations return predictable results and should be avoided. Use the table to select what combination works for the type of values you are dealing with. You will see from this that STRIDE bits are only ever 00 or 11 to represent 1 and 2, respectively. LEN operates so a value of 1 is represented by 000 (ie, the actual binary stored is one less than value).

	STR	Bits	LEN	Bits	Single (Sx)	Double (Dx)
1		b00	1	b000	All scalar	All Scalar
2		b11	1	b000	Normal	Normal
3	1	b00	2	b001	Normal	Normal
4	2	b11	2	b001	Normal	Normal
5	1	b00	3	b010	Normal	Unpredictable
6	2	b11	3	b010	Normal	Normal
7	1	b00	4	b011	Normal	Unpredictable
8	2	b11	4	b011	Normal	Unpredictable
9	1	b00	5	b100	Normal	Unpredictable
10	2	b11	5	b100	Unpredictable	Unpredictable
11	1	b00	6	b101	Normal	Unpredictable
12	2	b11	6	b101	Unpredictable	Unpredictable
13	1	b00	7	b110	Normal	Unpredictable
14	2	b11	7	b110	Unpredictable	Unpredictable
15	1	b00	8	b111	Normal	Unpredictable
16	2	b11	8	b111	Unpredictable	Unpredictable

Figure 25h. STRIDE and Vector LEN combinations and their effect on single and double-precision numbers.

Program 25b demonstrates how vector addressing delivers the third option listed in Figure 25g. The bulk of the listing is given over to first seeding values and then printing them out using printf. The theory behind the latter should be familiar to you now, and as we will ultimately be printing four double-precision values, three of these have to be pushed onto the stack so the main: function begins by reserving 24-bytes for just this purpose, 24-bytes being three words.

The actual instruction being executed is:

```
VADD.F32 S10, S16, S24
```

This involves three vector banks in Bank 1, Bank 2, and Bank 3. As we will be using STRIDE=2, LEN=4 as our vector control settings. Bank 1 is used to hold results (S10, S12, S14, S8), Bank 2 will hold the first set of values (S16, S18, S20, S22) and Bank 3 the second set of values (S24, S26, S28, S30).

Five values have been defined for use. To make things easier to check, a single value is assigned into the Bank 2 registers and then four separate values assigned to each of the registers in Bank 3.

The lenstride: entry point marks where the FPSCR is seeded with the settings for STRIDE and LEN. We require settings of 2 and 4, respectively. Looking at Figure 23h we can see in line 8 the binary settings to achieve this for single-precision are 11 and 011 (a 'normal' operation for single-precision).

As STRIDE and LEN are separated by a single bit the bit pattern, we need to seed is 110011. This in turn needs to be shifted so the leftmost bit starts at b21 in the FPSCR, an LSL #16 achieves this.

Looking at the program listing, the 'convert:' routine transforms the Sx registers in Bank 1 into double-precision values in Bank 0. In this program Bank 0 is not touched so these registers are free, but beware, you must ensure that you have at least one double-precision register that you can use if you plan to utilise printf, otherwise you will be doing a lot of register moving and restoring.

Program 25b Using LEN and STRIDE to sum vectors.

```
/*** Using LEN and STRIDE to sum vectors ***/
    .global   main
    .func main

main:
    SUB SP, SP, #24         @ room for printf
    LDR R1, addr_value1     @ Get addr of values
    LDR R2, addr_value2
    LDR R3, addr_value3
    LDR R4, addr_value4
    LDR R5, addr_value5

    VLDR S16, [R1]          @ load values into
    VLDR S18, [R1]          @ registers
    VLDR S20, [R1]
    VLDR S22, [R1]
    VLDR S24, [R2]
    VLDR S26, [R3]
    VLDR S28, [R4]
    VLDR S30, [R5]

lenstride:
/* Set LEN=4 0b101 and STRIDE=2 0b11 */
    VMRS R3, FPSCR          @ get current FPSCR
    MOV R4, #0b110011       @ bit pattern
    MOV R4, R4, LSL #16     @ move across to b21
    ORR R3, R3, R4          @ keep all 1's
    VMSR FPSCR, R3          @ transfer to FPSCR

    VADD.F32 S10, S16, S24  @ Vector addition
    VADD.F32 S12, S18, S26
```

```
        VADD.F32 S14, S20, S28
        VADD.F32 S8, S22, S30

convert:
/* Do conversion for printing, making sure not */
/* to corrupt Sx registers by overwriting      */
        VCVT.F64.F32 D0, S10
        VCVT.F64.F32 D1, S12
        VCVT.F64.F32 D2, S14
        VCVT.F64.F32 D3, S8
        LDR R0, =string         @ set up for printf
        VMOV R2, R3, D0
        VSTR D1, [SP]           @ push data on stack
        VSTR D2, [SP, #8]
        VSTR D3, [SP, #16]
        BL   printf
        ADD SP, SP, #24         @ restore stack

_exit:
        MOV R0, #0
        MOV R7, #1
        SWI 0

addr_value1:    .word value1
addr_value2:    .word value2
addr_value3:    .word value3
addr_value4:    .word value4
addr_value5:    .word value5

        .data
value1:     .float 1.0
value2:     .float 1.25
value3:     .float 1.50
value4:     .float 1.75
value5:     .float 2.0

string:
.asciz " S10 is %f\n S12 is %f\n S14 is %f\n S8 is %f\n"
```

I make no apologies for the simplicity of this program, but it does provide a good way to get to grips with the FPSCR and the STRIDE and LEN bits.

Raspberry Pi OS Assembly Language

26: Neon

At the time of writing, this chapter is not relevant to the original Raspberry Pi 1 series nor the Raspberry Pi Zero board. This is because Neon was introduced with the Raspberry Pi 2 release, or more specifically the version of the ARM chip that was used in its design. Neon is closely tied in with the VFP architecture introduced in the 'Floating-Point' chapter. However, it is *not* the floating-point unit (FPU) of the ARM processor. (Refer back to Figure 1c, in Chapter 1 to see the evolution of the chips used on the Raspberry Pi.)

Neon is an advanced SIMD (Single Instruction, Multiple Data) processing unit that can apply a single action too many pieces of data at one time, without the data ever leaving the registers! So much so it appears you are just loading and then storing data. In this way, you can get more 'speed' (or completed operations) out of Neon than you can a standard SISD (Single Instruction, Single Data) processor running at the same clock rate. Neon's importance comes in the fact that it can sort repetitive complex information quickly using a process called *interleaving*.

Figure 26a depicts the philosophy behind how Neon operations work. While a normal processor would do A0+ B0=C0, A1+B1=C1 (on left), the Neon system does this in one instruction producing the same output (on right).

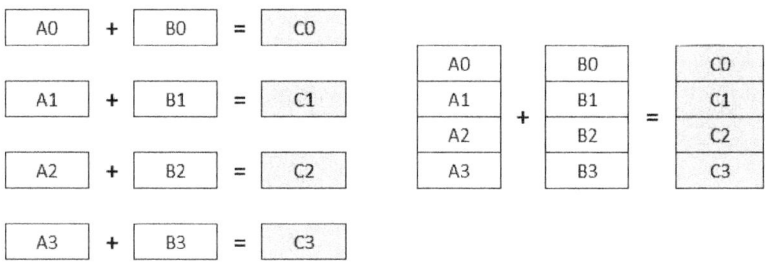

Figure 26a. Neon operations can be carried out in parallel.

255

Neon supports several data types:

- 32-bit single-precision floating-point
- 8, 16, 32 and 64-bit signed and unsigned integers
- 8 and 16-bit polynomials

The convention used to distinguish types is to put the first letter of the type before the size. For example, an unsigned 32-bit integer would be U32, 32-bit floating-point would be F32 and so on.

You should consider a few differences between the Neon and VFP systems:

- Neon does not support double-precision floating-point numbers.
- Neon only works on vectors and does not support advanced operations such as square root and divide.
- VFP offers some specialised instructions not supported by the Neon unit (SQRT for example).

Neon is used to crunch lots of numbers quickly. If you need floating-point precision, then use the VFP. However, bear in mind that the Neon hardware shares the same floating-point registers supplied by the VFP, so if you are using both formats together ensure your register management is up to-scratch.

As illustrated in Figure 26b the Neon system uses a bank of 32 by 64-bit registers which can also be configured as 16 by 128-bit registers:

- 32 x 64-bit ('double-word') registers: D0-D31
- 16 x 128-bit ('quad-word') registers: Q0-Q15

Here the D registers of the VFP are doubled up to make the Q or Quad registers. These registers are aliased so that **the data in a Q register is the same as that in its two corresponding D registers**. For example, Q0 is aliased to d0 and d1, and the same data is accessible through either register type.

To enhance Neon performance and reduce code density the Neon instruction set includes structured load and store instructions that can load or store single or multiple values from or to single or multiple 'lanes' in a vector register. These load and store operations are incredibly versatile and can manipulate data during the load and store operation, pulling data from memory and simultaneously separate values into different register.

D0	D1	<< >>	Q0
D2	D3		Q1
D4	D5		Q2
D6	D7		Q3
D8	S9		Q4
D10	D11		Q5
D12	D13		Q6
D14	D15		Q7
D16	D17		Q8
D18	D19		Q9
D20	D21		Q10
D22	D23		Q11
D24	D25		Q12
D26	D27		Q13
D28	D29		Q14
D30	D31		Q15

Figure 26b. The Neon register configuration. Compare this to Figure 22b to see how the register structure is built.

Neon Assembler

Program 26a is a simple example for you to try, and ensure that Neon is operating on your Raspberry Pi. It will also confirm that you have the assemble and link operations correct. Assuming a source file name of:

    prog26a.s

To assemble and link the code:

    as -mfpu=neon-vfpv4 -g -o prog26a.o prog26a.s
    ld -o prog26a prog26a.o

The option:

    -mfpu=neon-vfpv4

on the assembler command line, specifies that Neon instructions are permitted. If you leave out the option, then you will almost certainly get multiple error message. Include the '-g' option if you wish to look at the operation in GDB.

Program 26a. A Simple Neon Test.

```
/* Simple Neon test */
    .global _start
_start:
```

```
        LDR R0, =number1
        LDR R1, =number2

        VLD1.32 {Q1}, [R0]
        VLD1.32 {Q2}, [R1]
        VADD.I32 Q0, Q1, Q2

        MOV R7, #1
        SWI 0

.data
number1:        .word 1,0,0,0,0,0,0,0,0,0,0,0,0,0,0,0
number2:        .word 2,0,0,0,0,0,0,0,0,0,0,0,0,0,0,0
```

The source only has three lines that you will be seeing for the first time, and you could probably hazard a good guess at least one of these does! The program puts the values 1 and 2 into Q1 and Q2 respectively and then adds them, storing the result in Q0. VLD moves the numbers into registers, and the VADD sums them to provide a result.

GDB can be used to interrogate Neon, provided the -g option is used during assembly. The Neon registers are accessed by number. For example, a break point after the VADD operation in Program 26a would allow you to see the result of the operation with:

```
        info r q0 q1 q2
```

Because the Q registers can be used to contain so many formats, and much of the detail you provide in the Neon commands specify just this, all possible outputs can be seen when you use this method in GDB. The result should be clear though, as shown here (which I have formatted to make it easier to see):

```
q0 {u8 = {0x3, 0x0 <repeats 15 times>},
    u16 = {0x3, 0x0, 0x0, 0x0, 0x0, 0x0, 0x0, 0x0},
    u32 = {0x3, 0x0, 0x0, 0x0},
    u64 = {0x3, 0x0},
    f32 = {0x0, 0x0, 0x0, 0x0},
    f64 = {0x0, 0x0}}
q1
    {u8 = {0x1, 0x0 <repeats 15 times>},
    u16 = {0x1, 0x0, 0x0, 0x0, 0x0, 0x0, 0x0, 0x0},
    u32 = {0x1, 0x0, 0x0, 0x0},
    u64 = {0x1, 0x0},
    f32 = {0x0, 0x0, 0x0, 0x0},
    f64 = {0x0, 0x0}}
```

q2
```
    {u8  = {0x2, 0x0 <repeats 15 times>},
     u16 = {0x2, 0x0, 0x0, 0x0, 0x0, 0x0, 0x0, 0x0},
     u32 = {0x2, 0x0, 0x0, 0x0},
     u64 = {0x2, 0x0},
     f32 = {0x0, 0x0, 0x0, 0x0},
     f64 = {0x0, 0x0}}
```

Neon Instructions and Data Types

Figure 26c lists the data type specifiers available in Neon instructions. Data types are represented using a bit-size and format letter although. As the chart shows not all data types available in all sizes.

In Program 26a the VADD instruction specifies I32. From the table we can see this is a 32-bit integer (or unspecified type) addition. It is important to understand that registers can hold one or more elements of the same data type. Thus, we may not be looking at an overall value in the register but the individual values of the elements in the vector.

Type	8-Bit	16-Bit	32-Bit	64-Bit
Unsigned Integer	U8	U16	U32	U64
Signed Integer	S8	S16	S32	S64
Integer of unspecified type	I8	I16	I32	I64
Floating-Point number	N/A	F16	F32 (or F)	N/A
Polynomial over {0,1}	P8	P16	N/A	N/A

Figure 26c. Neon data type specifiers.

The number of elements to be operated on is indicated by the specified register size:

```
    VADD.I16 Q0, Q1, Q2
```

indicates an operation on 16-bit integer elements stored in 128-bit Q registers. These operations are carried out by dividing the vector into a series of lanes – such that the operation is performed on eight 16-bit lanes in parallel. This is illustrated below in Figure 26d which also shows pictorially how 'lanes' are organised. The instruction performs a parallel addition of eight lanes of 16-bit elements from vectors Q1 and Q2, storing the result in Q0.

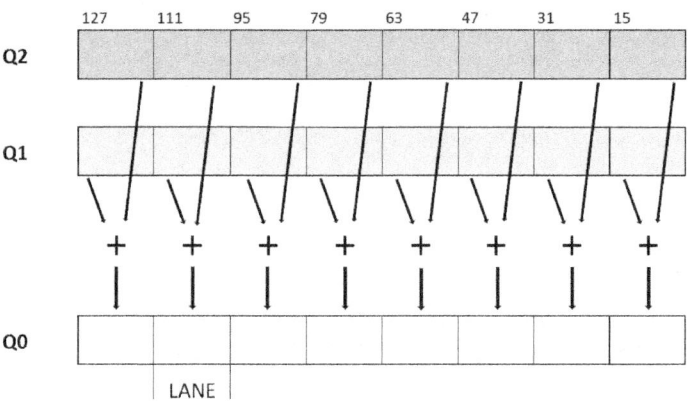

Figure 26d. Manipulating data lanes in Neon.

With larger register sizes register split into equal size any of type elements and the operation is performed on the same element of each register.

Here's an example where the unsigned 16-bit contents of D0 and D1 are summed in four 16-bit parallel lanes. The elements of D0 and D1 being added to create four result elements in D2:

```
VADD.U16 D2, D1, D0
```

Assuming that the contents in D0 and D1 are as shown below, then the result is as per D2.

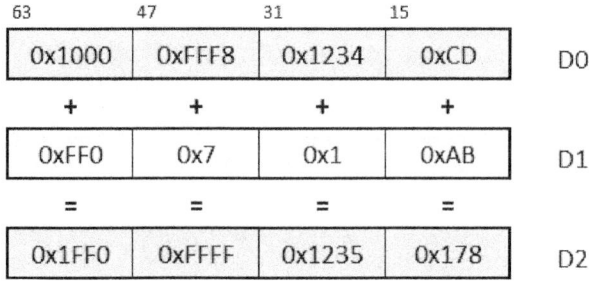

Figure 26e. Adding lane data in Neon

Of course, D0 and D1 combined are also Q0, whilst D2 is the lower 'half' of Q1. There is nothing to stop you using this to your advantage is you wish to manipulate individual lanes of data. There are some examples of this later in this chapter.

Some instructions take different size input and output registers. For example:

```
VMULL.S16 Q0, D2, D3
```

multiplies four 16-bit lanes in parallel, producing four 32-bit products in a 128-bit destination vector! Instructions specify what's in the vectors.

For Neon there are no status flags organised on a per lane basis. If an overall result is required and there is a chance that a carry would be significant then it must be handled using the wider result. As per the example above for instance. Otherwise, the Neon registers use the summary flags in the VFP FPSCR, and there are instructions to act on the results therein.

The datatype always corresponds to the source – you cannot promote past 64-bit or demote to less than 8-bit. Some instructions can promote and demote as part of its operation:

```
VADDL.S32 Q0, D0, D1    @ 2x signed 32-bit promotion to
                        @ 64-bit and then add
VADDW.S32 Q0, Q0, D2    @ Promotes D2 to S64 and does
                        @ 2x64-bit adds with Q0
```

Addressing Modes

Neon has limited ability when used as an addressing mode source. For example, this loads D0 with the contents of the address held in R0:

```
VLD1.64 {D0}, [R0]
```

This addressing mode was used in combination with the Q register to load a vector in Program 26a.

This next example does the same but adds the size of transfer to R0 after the transfer has taken place, which is handy when you are storing data in sequential blocks of memory.

```
VLD1.64 {D0}, [R0]!
```

Finally, this next instruction adds the contents of R1 to R0 after D0 is loaded with the contents of the address held in R0:

```
VLD1.64 {D0}, [R0], R1
```

VLD and VST in their Stride

The Neon load and store instructions are number-crunchingly good. The syntax of the instruction is made up of five parts.

- The instruction itself, either VLD for load or VST for store.
- A number specifying the gap between corresponding elements in each structure (interleave pattern).
- An element type specifying the number of bits in the accessed elements.
- A set of 64-bit Neon registers to be read or written. (Up to four registers can be listed, depending on the interleave pattern.)

- An ARM register containing the location to be accessed in memory. The address can be updated after the access, dependent on the addressing mode used.

Program 26a used the VLD instruction to load Q1 and Q2 with the contents of some numbers stored in memory and pointed to by R0 thus:

```
VLD1.32 {Q1}, [R0]
```

This is the load instruction at its very simplest. The interleave pattern here is 1. In this case the data is accessed as is and it's a straight transfer – one item after the other sequentially and in order. It is common to use 1, 2, 3 or 4 for the interleave pattern for one to four equally sized elements, where the elements are the usual Neon supported widths of 8, 16 or 32-bits:

- VLD1 loads one to four registers of data from memory, with no de-interleaving. Use this when processing an array of non-interleaved data.
- VLD2 loads two or four registers of data, de-interleaving even and odd elements into those registers. Use this to separate stereo audio data into left and right channels.
- VLD3 loads three registers and de-interleaves. Useful for splitting RGB pixels into their own channels.
- VLD4 loads four registers and de-interleaves. Use it to process ARGB image data, for instance.

These instructions have great uses in the audio-visual processing environment. You can use '2' for separating stereo audio data into left and right channels; '3' for splitting RGB pixels into separate streams, and '4' to process ARGB image data. These are just some applications. In all these examples the VST instruction can also do the same before it stores data to memory.

```
VLD 2.8 {D14, D15}, [R0]
```

Breaking down as:

2:	This is the interleave pattern (stride). It may be 1, 2, 3 or 4.
8:	This is the data type: 8, 16 or 32.
D14, D15	This is the list of Neon registers to be used. Up to four registers can be included.
[R0]	The ARM register containing the address of the data.

Figure 24f below illustrates part of the operation of:

```
VLD2.16 {D0, D1},[R0]
```

Would load the D0 and D1 (Q0) registers with four 16-bit elements in the first register (D0), and four 16-bit elements in the second (D1), with adjacent pairs (the Xs and Ys) separated to each register.

Raspberry Pi OS Assembly Language

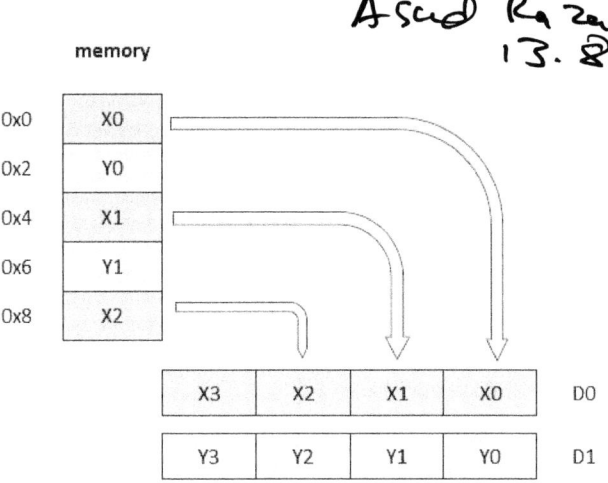

Figure 26f. Selectively loading data from memory into registers with VLD2.16 {D0, D1},[R0].

Changing the size to 32-bits loads the same amount of data, but now only two elements make up each vector, again separated into X and Y elements. The operation of:

```
VLD2.32 {D0, D1},[R0]
```

is illustrated in Figure 24g:

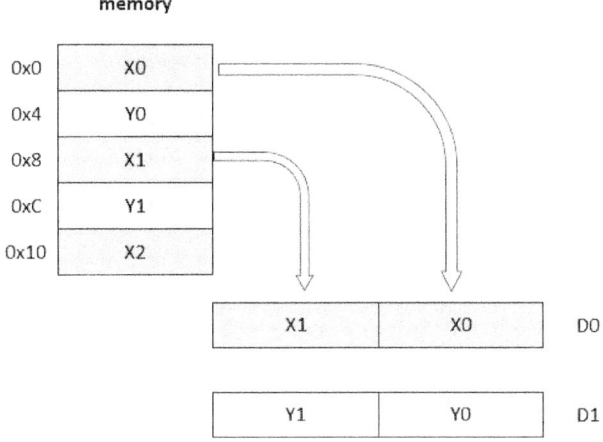

Figure 26g. Selectively loading data from memory into registers with VLD2.32 {D0, D1}, [R0]

263

Element size potentially affects the data entity and, as a rule, if you specify the correct element size to the load and store instructions, bytes will be read from memory in the appropriate order. If not, then you may need to undertake some manual adjustment at some point. Getting your data sitting right in memory in the first instance is always a good bit of housekeeping. For example, when loading 32-bit elements, align the address of the first element to at least 32-bits.

Program 26a can be used as the basis of some investigation. This takes some simple visual data and performs a VLD on it. If you compile this with the -g option, you can jump into GDB and inspect the registers to see what has happened to your data. You can add to the program simply using different values using additional registers so you can get a good visual idea of what is happening.

One of the most common uses for this sort of Neon instruction is to read and sort RGB video data. If you imagine that the information was stored as a sequence of R,G,B, R,G,B, R,G,B as 24-bit data then you could sort the three channels into R, G and B using:

```
VLD3.8 {D0, D1, D2}, [R0]
```

Here the red information will be in D0, the green in D1 and the blue in D2.

Some instructions can reference individual scalar elements, which are referenced using the array notation Vn[x]. (Array ordering is always from the least significant bit.)

Consider this command:

```
VLD4.8 {D0[2], D1[2], D2[D2], D3[2]}, [R0]
```

This would take the element in the third lane from the four vectors and store them at the address in R0, leaving the other lanes intact.

Load of Others

In addition to structural loads and stores Neon also provides two other formats for the instruction:

VLDR and VSTR to load or store a single register as a 64-bit value.

VLDM and VSTM to load multiple registers as 64-bit values.

The latter can be useful for pushing and pulling registers from the stack.

Neon Intrinsic

Because of the complexity of Neon applications (decoding video or sound for your Raspberry Pi for example), the C language, or derivatives of it (C++ for instance) is invariably used to write code for compiling into ARM machine code. However, the most direct way to utilise Neon is writing assembler code, not least because, as we have seen in earlier chapters, the code produced by the compiler out of the C file is not always 'tight' and can be wasteful of resources. Equally, C doesn't always make the best register decisions when compiling.

The term 'Neon Intrinsic' is often used to refer to C compilation of Neon. An intrinsic function is a function available for use in a programming language whose implementation is handled specifically by the compiler. Typically, it substitutes a sequence of automatically generated instructions for the original function call, like an inline function. Unlike an inline function, though, the compiler should have an intimate knowledge of the intrinsic function and can, therefore, better integrate it and optimise it for the situation.

Intrinsic functions are often used to explicitly implement vectorization and parallelisation in languages which do not address such constructs as part of their syntax. The compiler parses the intrinsic functions and converts them into vector math or multiprocessing code appropriate for the target platform.

Neon Intrinsics are a set of definitions that induces use of Neon when compiling the C program. Some programmers love them; some hate them. For performance-critical programs then I am not a fan. It's too easy for the compiler to inject extra register unload/load steps between your intrinsic operations. The effort to get it to stop doing that is more complicated than just writing the stuff in raw Neon assembler. At this level, it's good to know what's happening and control it yourself. Especially if speed is critical.

Neon Arrays

Because Neon can manipulate large amounts of data with one instruction, it is often used to code graphics software. For example, if you rotate a picture on your smartphone or tablet the process is probably done by manipulating blocks of data using Neon instructions.

The following code will rotate the contents of a block of four Q registers through 90 degrees. Figure 26h shows the matrix before and after rotation. The numbers on the left refer to the Q registers, and the grid numbers are placeholders for each lane so you can see the before and after state. The data is loaded into the Q registers and as array ordering is always from the least significant bit, the D registers aliased against them will have the appropriate values in them also.

Q0	0	1	2	3
Q1	4	5	6	7
Q2	8	9	10	11
Q3	12	13	14	15

Before Position

	12	8	4	0
	13	9	5	1
	14	10	6	2
	15	11	7	3

After Position

Figure 26h. Rotating data through 90 degrees.

Program 26b lists the assembly code that will produce this. The data used is simple numbers just so that you can visually inspect the start and end results via a GDB register dump. Let's work through each block and look at the a few of the instructions operation as we encounter them.

Program 26b. Rotate a 2D matrix by 90 degrees (clockwise).

```
/* Rotate 4x4 Matrix Through 90 Degrees */

    .global _start
_start:

    @ Get data pointers
    LDR R0,=matrix0
    LDR R1,=matrix1
    LDR R2,=matrix2
    LDR R3,=matrix3

    @ Load Q0-Q3 with the data
    VLD1.32 {Q0}, [R0]
    VLD1.32 {Q1}, [R1]
    VLD1.32 {Q2}, [R2]
    VLD1.32 {Q3}, [R3]

    @ Transpose Matrix and then interleave inner pairs
bp1:
    VTRN.32 Q0, Q1
    VTRN.32 Q2, Q3
    VSWP D1, D4
    VSWP D3, D6
```

```
    @ Mirror flip matrix
    VREV64.32 Q0, Q0
    VREV64.32 Q1, Q1
    VREV64.32 Q2, Q2
    VREV64.32 Q3, Q3

    @ Swap high and low halves
    VSWP D0, D1
    VSWP D2, D3
    VSWP D4, D5
    VSWP D6, D7

    @Store result
bp2:
    VST1.32 {Q0}, [R0]
    VST1.32 {Q1}, [R1]
    VST1.32 {Q2}, [R2]
    VST1.32 {Q3}, [R3]

    MOV R7, #1
    SWI 0

.data
matrix0:        .word 0,1,2,3
matrix1:        .word 4,5,6,7
matrix2:        .word 8,9,10,11
matrix3:        .word 12,13,14,15
```

There are some instructions we have used for the first time here, and if you are interested in digging deeper, you might want to work through these diagrammatically substituting the numbers for colour in a 4 x 4 grid.

The data for our array is stored at the end of the listing as mart of the '.data' block. The numbers 0 through to 15 are used as per the matrix. After starting R0, R1, R2 and R3 are pointed their respective lines and these are loaded as 32-bit values into Q0, Q1, Q2 and Q3, respectively. If you look at the registers prior to the two transpose commands executing you should see these quite clearly. Especially if you look at the u32 register output. The registers at this point will show:

Q0	0	1	2	3
Q1	4	5	6	7
Q2	8	9	A	B
Q3	C	D	E	F

The first operation is to deal with transposing the matrix itself. VTRN (Vector Transpose) treats the elements of its operand vectors as elements of 2 x 2 matrices and transposes them.

```
@ Transpose Matrix
VTRN.32 Q0, Q1
VTRN.32 Q2, Q3
```

The first line transposes Q0 and Q1, therefore '1' and '4' are transposed, as are '3' and '6'. The second line deals with Q2 and Q3 where '9' and 'B' and 'E' are transposed, respectively.

Q0	0	4	2	6		Q0	0	4	2	6
Q1	1	5	3	7		Q1	1	5	3	7
Q2	8	9	A	B		Q2	8	C	A	E
Q3	C	D	E	F		Q3	9	D	B	F

VSWP (Vector Swap) is then utilised to exchange the contents of two vectors. The vectors can be either double-word or quadword. There is no distinction between data types. In fact, it is used to interleave:

```
VSWP D1, D4
VSWP D3, D6
```

D1 is the 'high' two elements of Q0 and D4 is the 'low' two elements of Q2. You can see on the left-hand matrix below that '8 and C' have swapped places with '2 and 6'. On the right-hand matrix '9 and D' have been swapped with '3 and 7' as the elements of D3 and D6 are swapped.

Q0	0	4	8	C		Q0	0	4	8	C
Q1	1	5	3	7		Q1	1	5	9	D
Q2	2	6	A	E		Q2	2	6	A	E
Q3	9	D	B	F		Q3	3	7	B	F

VREV64 instruction is used to reverse the order of the 32-bit elements within each double-word of the vector. This is done on each of the four Q registers using:

```
@ Mirror flip matrix
VREV64.32 Q0, Q0
VREV64.32 Q1, Q1
VREV64.32 Q2, Q2
VREV64.32 Q3, Q3
```

The matrix now looks thus:

Q0	4	0	C	8
Q1	5	1	D	9
Q2	6	2	E	A
Q3	7	3	F	B

Now all that is required is to realign some of the elements by swapping the low and high halves of each full register thus:

```
@ Swap high and low halves
VSWP D0, D1
VSWP D2, D3
VSWP D4, D5
VSWP D6, D7
```

Q0	C	8	4	0
Q1	D	9	5	1
Q2	E	A	6	2
Q3	F	B	7	3

Which completes the rotation, prior to being stored back in memory.

If you compile Program 26b you can use the two labels 'bp1' and 'bp2' as breakpoint specifiers. Then display the Q0, Q1, Q2 and Q3 registers at both points. I have only shown the U32 data in the output below.:

Raspberry Pi OS Assembly Language

```
        Breakpoint 1, bp1 () at Prog26b.s:21
        21          VTRN.32 Q0, Q1
        (gdb) info r q0 q1 q2 q3
        q0          u32 = {0x0, 0x1, 0x2, 0x3}
        q1          u32 = {0x4, 0x5, 0x6, 0x7}
        q2          u32 = {0x8, 0x9, 0xa, 0xb}
        q3          u32 = {0xc, 0xd, 0xe, 0xf}

        Breakpoint 2, bp2 () at Prog26b.s:42
        42          VST1.32 {Q0}, [R0]
        (gdb) info r q0 q1 q2 q3
        q0          u32 = {0xc, 0x8, 0x4, 0x0}
        q1          u32 = {0xd, 0x9, 0x5, 0x1}
        q2          u32 = {0xe, 0xa, 0x6, 0x2}
        q3          u32 = {0xf, 0xb, 0x7, 0x3}
```

Order Correctly

It is important that your order you data correctly, and consistently when you do any matrix calculations. This is to ensure that you are calculating on the same elements as required in the matrix being processed. At some point you will need to move information from a source to place where the information can be manipulated. Think of a vector as a one-dimensional array. Memory occupies a linear space, so it is also a one-dimensional area. A matrix is a two-dimensional object. A 4x4 matrix provides 16 'cells' arranged in an array consisting of four rows and four columns. How is this moved into a vector that is both sensible and convenient to be processed?

In computing, row-major order and column-major order are the most popular methods for storing multidimensional arrays in linear storage These are illustrated in Figure 26i.

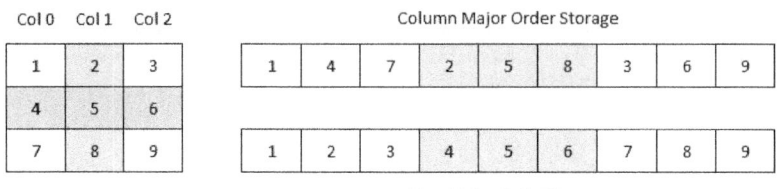

Figure 26i. Illustrating column-major order and row-major order storage options.

In column-major order the data is stored placing the columns one after the other. So, in Figure 24i Column 0 data 1, 4, 7 and placed in the first three spaces in the vector. These are followed immediately by Column 1 (2, 5 and 8) and finished with Column 3 (3, 6 and 9).

In row-major order each row is done sequentially. Therefore, the first row (1, 2, 3) and then the second (4, 5, 6) and finally the third (7, 8, 9). The process is the same for whatever sized matrix in use. If you know the size of the array and the method of storage, then it can safely be deconstructed and reconstructed with no errors. It is also another method which allows you to sort and move data quickly and efficiently. Look at Fig 26i again. If you took the column-major data and then deconstructed it using row-major, you have a method or rotating the matrix.

Generally, you will decide the data storage you want to use. It may also be stipulated by the routine you want to use or the language environment you ultimately working in (C or Python for example). But with knowledge of Neon it is possible to manipulate the data between the two regardless, although it is better to stick to one for simplicity.

Matrix Math

Matrix math is a relatively straight forward operation utilising the with the VFP and/or Neon Co-processor. The next two examples show how to add and multiply them together. There are many other operations that can be performed and, applying some principles here along with a good understanding of matrix manipulation, should allow you to develop what you need.

To add two matrices, you sum the corresponding elements in each column to create a third matrix containing the result. As shown in Figure 26j.

MATRIX 1

	Col 0	Col 1	Col 2	Col 3
Row 0	106.6	105	104	103
Row 1	2.4	4	6	8
Row 2	4.5	6	8	10
Row 3	6.2	8	10	12

+

MATRIX 2

2	3	4	5
3	4	5	6
4	5	6	7
5	6	7	8

RESULT = (M1+M2)

108.6	108	108	108
5.4	8	11	14
8.5	11	14	17
11.2	14	17	20

Figure 26j. Adding two matrices together.

This example forms the basis of Program 26c.

Program 26c. Adding two 4x4 Matrices together.

```
/* Add two 4x4 matrices together   */
/* column-major Order              */

@ Pointers:
@ R10 = pointer to where 4x4 matrix result will be stored
@ R11 = pointer to 4x4 matrix 1, single-precision floats
@ R12 = pointer to 4x4 matrix 2, single-precision floats
@ d16-d19 and d20-d23 (Q8, Q9, Q10, Q11) for Matrix 1
@ d8-d11 and d12-d15 (Q4, Q5, Q6, Q7) for Matrix 2
@ d24-d27 and d28-d31 (Q12-Q15) contains result on exit

      .global main
      .func main
main:

      LDR R10, =result
      LDR R11, =matrix1
      LDR R12, =matrix2

      VLD1.32 {D16-D19},[r11]!       @ Q8-Q9    load M1, 2 lines
      VLD1.32 {D20-D23}, [r11]!      @ Q10-Q11  load M1, 2 lines
      VLD1.32 {D8-D11},[r12]!        @ Q4-Q5    load M2, 2 lines
      VLD1.32 {D12-D15}, [r12]!      @ Q6-Q7    load M2, 2 lines

      VADD.F32 Q12, Q8, Q4           @ Q12=Q8+Q4
      VADD.F32 Q13, Q9, Q5           @ Q13=Q9+Q5
      VADD.F32 Q14, Q10, Q6          @ Q14=Q10+Q6
      VADD.F32 Q15, Q11, Q7          @ Q15=Q11+Q7

      VST1.32 {D24-D27}, [r10]!      @ D24-D27 store 1st eight
      VST1.32 {D28-D31}, [r10]!      @ D28-D31 store 2nd eight

@ Following code will print out results
matrixprint:
      .equ Num, 4            @ number of bytes
      .equ Cells, 16         @ umber of matrix cells
      LDR R10, =result       @ R10 hold address of result matrix
      MOV R7, #Cells         @ R7  holds matrix cell counter
loop:
      LDR R0, [R10]          @ Get data item into R0
      VMOV S2, R0            @ Get into FPU register
```

```
        VCVT.F64.F32 D0, S2  @ Convert to single-precision
        VMOV r2, r3, D0      @ Into R2 and R3 for fprint
        LDR R0, =string      @ Point R0 to string
        BL printf            @ call fprint function
        ADD R10, #Num        @ increment address of next result
        SUBS R7, #1          @ decrement cell counter
        BNE loop             @ do next cell if not complete

        MOV R7, #1           @ otherwise exit
        SWI 0

string:                 .asciz "Result is: %f\n"
.data
matrix1:    .single 106.6,2.4,4.5,6.2
            .single 105,4,6,8
            .single 104,6,8,10
            .single 103,8,10,12

matrix2:    .single 2,3,4,5
            .single 3,4,5,6
            .single 4,5,6,7
            .single 5,6,7,8

result:     .word 0,0,0,0
            .word 0,0,0,0
            .word 0,0,0,0
            .word 0,0,0,0
```

Assemble and link the program with:

```
gcc -mfpu=neon-vfpv4 -g -o prog26c prog26c.s
```

If you execute with:

```
./prog26c
```

The output you see should be:

```
Result is: 108.599998
Result is: 5.400000
Result is: 8.500000
Result is: 11.200000
Result is: 108.000000
Result is: 8.000000
Result is: 11.000000
Result is: 14.000000
```

```
Result is: 108.000000
Result is: 11.000000
Result is: 14.000000
Result is: 17.000000
Result is: 108.000000
Result is: 14.000000
Result is: 17.000000
Result is: 20.000000
```

Again, if you interrogate the program using GDB, you will see the results. Notice in the results printed via the program that the rounding error we discussed previously is also present.

Program 26c contains a routine called 'matrixprint' that can be used to print the 4x4 matrix. This is also used in Program 26d and can be adapted to provide an easy visual output of results or values during points of a programs execution. It's always nice, simply displaying memory and register contents have we have done, show that it's just as easy to check on progress as we have done in the samples beforehand.

Multi Matrix

There are two types of multiplication for matrices: scalar multiplication and matrix multiplication. Scalar multiplication is easy. You just take a regular number (called a "scalar") and multiply it on every entry in the matrix, thus:

0	1	2
3	4	5

X 2 =

0	2	4
6	8	10

Figure 26k. Multiply a matrix by a scalar.

On matrix multiplication (non-scalar) you multiply each of the elements of a row in the left-hand matrix by the corresponding elements of a column in the right-hand matrix, and then sum the resulting 'n' products to obtain one element in the result matrix.

Program 26d given below keeps things simple by using two matrices of equal size and assumes that the matrices are stored in memory in column-major order. The process for multiplication is the same, as illustrated below (Figure 26j), where the math for first column result is shown. The same will be done for the next three columns to calculate the result:

	C0	C1	C2	C3
R0	X0	X4	X8	X12
R1	X1	X5	X9	X13
R2	X2	X6	X10	X14
R3	X3	X7	X11	X15

X

	C0	C1	C2	C3
R0	Y0	Y4	Y8	Y12
R1	Y1	Y5	Y9	Y13
R2	Y2	Y6	Y10	Y14
R3	Y3	Y7	Y11	Y15

=

	C0
R0	=(X0*Y0)+(X4*Y1)+(X8*Y2)+(X12*Y3)
R1	=(X1*Y0)+(X5*Y1)+(X9*Y2)+(X13*Y3)
R2	=(X2*Y0)+(X6*Y1)+(X10*Y2)+(X14*Y3)
R3	=(X3*Y0)+(X7*Y1)+(X11*Y2)+(X15*Y3)

Figure 26l. Calculating the first column of a 4 x 4 matrix multiplication.

In the program, each column from the matrix is loaded into a Neon register; we can use the vector-by-scalar multiplication (VMLA) instruction to calculate the result for each column. We must also add the results together for each element of the column, which we do use the accumulating version of the same instruction.

Remember that the D registers are aliased with the Q registers so that we can access the contents of these register, either way, remembering that Q0 is the combination of D0 and D1 and so forth.

The program beings by loading the first eight elements matrix (Matrix 1) into D16-D19, and the second eight elements in D20-D23 which correspond to Q12 and Q13. It then loads the contents of Matrix 2 into D0-D7 (Q0- Q1).

The crux of the program then operates through these instructions which can calculate a single column using just four Neon instructions:

```
VMUL.f32   Q12, Q8,  D8[0]
VMLA.f32   Q12, Q9,  D8[1]
VMLA.f32   Q12, Q10, D9[0]
VMLA.f32   Q12, Q11, D9[1]
```

Here, the first instruction (VMUL.F32) takes x0, x1, x2 and x3 (in register Q8) and each is multiplied by y0 (element 0 in D0), and the result is stored in Q12. The three subsequent VMLA.F32 instructions operate on the other three columns of the first matrix, multiplying by corresponding elements of the first column of the second matrix. Results are accumulated into Q12 to give the first column of values for the result matrix.

This set of instructions must be executed three more times to calculate the second, third and fourth columns. Here we use values Y4 to Y15 from the second matrix in registers Q1 to Q3.

This makes this calculation part ideal for implementation as a macro, however although this is ideal for ease of coding it can create a timing issue due to an effect known as 'Scheduling'. Often when adjacent multiply instructions that write to the same register are placed next to one another, the Neon processor must wait for each operation to complete before it can move the next one into the pipeline.

By separating the instructions out so that the accumulate operations do not overlap Neon register access they can continue to be feed into the Neon pipeline to ensure speed is maintained to achieve real parallel operations.

Program 26d. Single-Precision Matrix Multiplication

```
/* Neon 4 x 4 Single-Precision Matrix Multiplication */
/* Column-major order   */

@ Pointers:
@ R10 = pointer to where 4x4 matrix result will be stored
@ R11 = pointer to 4x4 M1, single-precision floats
@ R12 = pointer to 4x4 M1, single-precision floats
@ d16-d19 and d20-d23 (Q8, Q9, Q10, Q11) for M1
@ d8-d11 and d12-d15 (Q4, Q5, Q6, Q7) for M2
@ d24-d27 and d28-d31 (Q12-Q15) contains result

    .global main
    .func main
main:

    LDR R10, =result
    LDR R11, =matrix1
    LDR R12, =matrix2

    VLD1.32 {D16-D19},[R11]!   @ Q8-Q9    load M1, 2 lines
    VLD1.32 {D20-D23}, [R11]!  @ Q10-Q11  load M1, 2 lines
    VLD1.32 {D8-D11},[R12]!    @ Q4-Q5    load M2, 2 lines
    VLD1.32 {D12-D15}, [R12]!  @ Q6-Q7    load M2, 2 lines

    VMUL.f32 Q12, Q8, D8[0]    @ RC0 = (M1 C0) * (M2 C0 E0)
    VMUL.f32 Q13, Q8, D10[0]   @ RC1 = (M1 C0) * (M2 C1 E0)
    VMUL.f32 Q14, Q8, D12[0]   @ RC2 = (M1 C0) * (M2 C2 E0)
    VMUL.f32 Q15, Q8, D14[0]   @ RC3 = (M1 C0) * (M2 C3 E0)
```

```
        VMLA.f32 Q12, Q9,  D8[1]      @ RC0 += (M1 C1) * (M2 C0 E1)
        VMLA.f32 Q13, Q9,  D10[1]     @ RC1 += (M1 C1) * (M2 C1 E1)
        VMLA.f32 Q14, Q9,  D12[1]     @ RC2 += (M1 C1) * (M2 C2 E1)
        VMLA.f32 Q15, Q9,  D14[1]     @ RC3 += (M1 C1) * (M2 C3 E1)

        VMLA.f32 Q12, Q10, D9[0]      @ RC0 += (M1 C2) * (M2 C0 E2)
        VMLA.f32 Q13, Q10, D11[0]     @ RC1 += (M1 C2) * (M2 C1 E2)
        VMLA.f32 Q14, Q10, D13[0]     @ RC2 += (M1 C2) * (M2 C2 E2)
        VMLA.f32 Q15, Q10, D15[0]     @ RC3 += (M1 C2) * (M2 C3 E2)

        VMLA.f32 Q12, Q11, D9[1]      @ RC0 += (M1 C3) * (M2 C0 E3)
        VMLA.f32 Q13, Q11, D11[1]     @ RC1 += (M1 C3) * (M2 C1 E3)
        VMLA.f32 Q14, Q11, D13[1]     @ RC2 += (M1 C3) * (M2 C2 E3)
        VMLA.f32 Q15, Q11, D15[1]     @ RC3 += (M1 C3) * (M2 C3 E3)

        VST1.32 {D24-D27}, [R10]!     @ d24-d27 store 1st eight
        VST1.32 {D28-D31}, [R10]!     @ d28-d31 store 2nd eight

@ Following code will print out results if required

matrixprint:
    .equ Num, 4                   @ Number of bytes
    .equ Cells, 16                @ Number of matrix cells

    LDR R10, =result              @ R10 address of result matrix
    MOV R7, #Cells                @ R7  matrix cell counter

loop:
    LDR R0, [R10]                 @ Get data item into R0
    VMOV S2, R0                   @ Get into FPU register
    VCVT.F64.F32 D0, S2           @ Convert to single-precision
    VMOV R2, R3, D0               @ Into R2 and R3 for fprint
    LDR R0, =string               @ Point R0 to string
    BL printf                     @ Call fprint function
    ADD R10, #Num                 @ Inc address of next result
    SUBS R7, #1                   @ Decrement cell counter
    BNE loop                      @ Next cell if not complete
                                  @ Otherwise finish
    MOV R7, #1                    @ exit
    SWI 0
```

```
string:         .asciz "Result is: %f\n"

.data
Matrix1:        .single 106.6,2.4,4.5,6.2
                .single 105,4,6,8
                .single 104,6,8,10
                .single 103,8,10,12

Matrix2:        .single 2,3,4,5
                .single 3,4,5,6
                .single 4,5,6,7
                .single 5,6,7,8

result:         .word 0,0,0,0
                .word 0,0,0,0
                .word 0,0,0,0
                .word 0,0,0,0
```

As with previous program the 'matrixprint' routine is used to display the matrix results. Thus:

```
gcc -mfpu=neon-vfpv4 -g -o prog26d prog26d.s
./prog26d
Result is: 1459.199951
Result is: 80.800003
Result is: 109.000000
Result is: 136.399994
Result is: 1877.800049
Result is: 101.199997
Result is: 137.500000
Result is: 172.600006
Result is: 2296.399902
Result is: 121.599998
Result is: 166.000000
Result is: 208.800003
Result is: 2715.000000
Result is: 142.000000
Result is: 194.500000
Result is: 245.000000
```

Figure 26m below shows Matrix1 and Matrix2 as used in Program26d. The third Result matrix (M1*M2) is also shown. Referring to Figure 26l we can see that the top left cell is calculated as:

```
=(X3*Y0)+(X7*Y1)+(X11*Y2)+(X15*Y3)
=(106.6*2)+(105*3)+(104*4)+(103*5)
=1459.2
```

MATRIX 1

	Col 0	Col 1	Col 2	Col 3
Row 0	106.6	105	104	103
Row 1	2.4	4	6	8
Row 2	4.5	6	8	10
Row 3	6.2	8	10	12

X

MATRIX 2

2	3	4	5
3	4	5	6
4	5	6	7
5	6	7	8

RESULT (M1xM2)

1459.2	1877.8	2296	2715
80.8	101.2	121.6	142
109	137.5	166	194.5
136.4	172.6	208.8	245

Figure 26m. Matrix Multiplication

Macro Matrix Example

If you remove the 'matrixprint' routine from the code listed in Program26d then there is a lot of repetition within the body of the matrix calculations. This makes it a prime candidate for the use of a macro. The example above was important to illustrate how to use Neon to undertake the multiplication process. Now that is done, let's look at the macro version of the same assembly code, which is listed below as Program26e, in this instance minus most of the comments for clarity. The macro itself uses just six lines of code including the enclosing directives.

Program 26e. Single-Precision Matrix Multi - Using Macro Version

```
/* Floating-Point 4x4 Matrix Multiplication */
/* Using a macro to reduce coding           */
.global main
.func main
main:
    LDR  R10, =result
    LDR  R11, =matrix1
    LDR  R12, =matrix2

.macro matrixf32 resultQ, col0_d, col1_d
VMUL.f32   \resultQ, Q8,  \col0_d[0]    @ ele0 by Matrix C0
VMLA.f32   \resultQ, Q9,  \col0_d[1]    @ ele1 by Matrix C1
VMLA.f32   \resultQ, Q10, \col1_d[0]    @ ele2 by Matrix C2
VMLA.f32   \resultQ, Q11, \col1_d[1]    @ ele3 by Matrix C3
.endm
```

```
VLD1.32 {D16-D19}, [R11]!   @ first eight elements of M1
VLD1.32 {D20-D23}, [R11]!   @ second eight elements of M1
VLD1.32 {D0-D3}, [R12]!     @ first eight elements of M2
VLD1.32 {D4-D7}, [R12]!     @ second eight elements of M2

@ Call macro
matrixf32 Q12, D0, D1       @ matrix 1 * matrix 2 col 0
matrixf32 Q13, D2, D3       @ matrix 1 * matrix 2 col 1
matrixf32 Q14, D4, D5       @ matrix 1 * matrix 2 col 2
matrixf32 Q15, D6, D7       @ matrix 1 * matrix 2 col 3

VST1.32  {D24-D27}, [R10]!  @ save first 8 elements of result.
VST1.32  {D28-D31}, [R10]!  @ save second 8 elements of result.

@ Insert printmatrix code below if you wish to print results
@ Or download full program from www.brucesmith.info

    MOV R7, #
    SWI 0

string:         .asciz "Result is: %f\n"

.data
matrix1:        .single 106.6,2.4,4.5,6.2
                .single 105,4,6,8
                .single 104,6,8,10
                .single 103,8,10,12

matrix2:        .single 2,3,4,5
                .single 3,4,5,6
                .single 4,5,6,7
                .single 5,6,7,8

result:         .word 0,0,0,0
                .word 0,0,0,0
                .word 0,0,0,0
                .word 0,0,0,0
```

27: Thumb Code

Thumb is the name given to a subset of the ARM instruction set. More significantly it is a 16-bit (two-byte) implementation, so instructions can in theory be coded in half the space of an equivalent ARM program but in reality, achieving the same result in a third less space. This higher code density makes Thumb code popular where memory constraints are tight. You will probably not see a lot of Thumb programs around on the forums. This is mainly because most Thumb code seems to be written and compiled from C. But that isn't to say we can't hand assemble it.

In terms of hardware there is no real difference between the way in which ARM and Thumb instruction sets function — they are one and the same. Although Thumb is a 16-bit implementation register sizes do not change. R0 is still a word wide, as are the other registers. What is different is how they are fetched and interpreted before execution. Thumb instructions are expanded into their 32-bit equivalents internally by the hardware, so it doesn't slow down their execution in any way— ARM speed is maintained. This makes it perfectly acceptable to mix normal sections of ARM and Thumb code and jump from one to the other; in fact, jumping from ARM to Thumb is the preferred way to enter Thumb code.

If you flick back to Chapter 5 and look at Figure 5c the diagram shows the Status Register configuration. Bit 5 is the 'T' bit, and this is normally clear to indicated ARM State. When the T bit is set (T=1) then the chip is in Thumb State. We'll look how to move between states and write a simple program that can be the shell for any Thumb code you may wish to write. But first....

Differences

The Thumb instruction set will be very familiar to you, but there are differences that need to be borne in mind. If you understand these, you should have no difficulties implementing and writing a Thumb program from your existing ARM knowledge (which should be quite extensive at this point). And of course, GCC supports Thumb as does GDB, so the tools to do so are readily available.

The major architectural difference is that your code does not have direct access to all the ARM registers; only R0 to R7 inclusive are available. Registers R8 to R12 inclusive can only be used in conjunction with MOV, ADD, SUB and CMP. There is limited access to R13 (SP), R14 (LR) and R15 (PC) and only indirect access to the CPSR. There is no access to SPSR and the VFP instructions cannot be accessed from Thumb State.

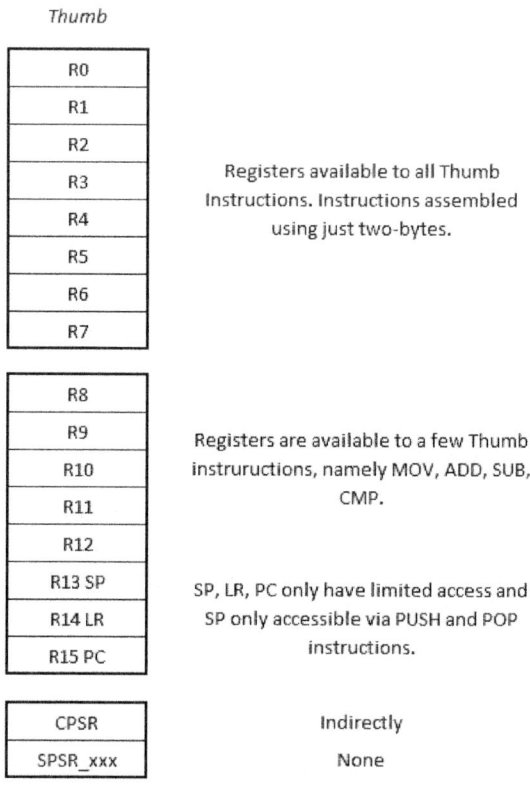

Figure 27a. Thumb registers accessibility.

The registers and code that are not available can be accessed from the program, but only after ARM State is switched back in. In other words, you must first come out of Thumb State to execute what you want to do and then switch back into Thumb State to continue. Figure 27a summarises these register restrictions. However, the advantage of all this is that when you move between ARM and Thumb State the contents of registers are preserved!

The other significant difference is that mnemonic representations of Thumb instructions are shorter, often with one less operand. Compare these ARM and Thumb versions of ADD:

```
    ADDS R2, R2, #16        @ ARM State immediate addition
    ADD R0, #3              @ Thumb equivalent, dest implied
```

The conditional code modifiers for instructions are not available, with only branch relative instructions conditionally executable. Therefore, you *cannot* execute instructions like:

```
ADD CC R0, #3
```

in Thumb State.

The shift and rotate operators, ASR, LSL, LSR and ROR are implemented as standalone instructions and are no longer available as a modifying operand. The following code segment illustrates the format for use:

```
LSL R2, R3    @ Shift R2 left number positions in R3
```

In the example above, if R2=4 and R3=1 then R2 would become 8.

Thumb branch instructions are limited in scope. The B variant, as used in Program 27a, is the only one that is conditional, but the range here is limited to a label that must be within a signed single byte value, effectively -256 to 254. A non-conditional branch instruction can be extended to a range within an 11-bit signed immediate value, -2048 to +2046 bytes.

The BL instruction is not conditional but because it can be used in an indirect manner the address range can be up to 4Mb in either direction. An example of this is provided at the end of the next section.

There are also significant changes to multiple load-store and stack access instructions, and these are covered below separately.

Assembling Thumb

To switch between ARM and Thumb states, you should use the GCC directives:

```
.arm
```

or:

```
.thumb
```

These directives replace the oft seen older versions '.code32' and '.code16', which will work on the current version of GCC on the Raspberry Pi, but these should be considered as old hat now. If necessary, these directives will also automatically insert up to three bytes of padding to align to the next word boundary for ARM, or up to one byte of padding to align to the next half-word boundary for Thumb. Thus, use of '.align' is unnecessary.

Both '.arm' and .'thumb' must be used to direct the assembler what to compile. They do not assemble any instructions themselves; they just direct the assembler as to what follows. Rather than having to play with bit-5 directly in the CPSR the state change will be handled directly for you if you follow the correct protocol for doing so which involves using the BX instruction.

Program 27a. How to invoke Thumb State and run Thumb code.

```
@ Use of Thumb code on Raspberry Pi
@ This divide routine is R0/R1
@ with R2=MOD and R3=DIV

        .global main
        .func main
        .arm
main:
        ADR R0, thumbcode+1
        MOV LR, PC
        BX R0

exit:
        MOV R0, #0
        MOV R7, #1
        SWI 0

        @ All Thumb code to be placed here
        .thumb

thumbcode:
        MOV R3, #0

loop:
        ADD R3, #1
        SUB R0, R1
        BGE loop
        SUB R3, #1
        ADD R2, R0, R1
        BX LR                   @ Return to ARM
```

Essentially, if you load the link address of the start of the Thumb code into R0 and set the least significant bit of R0 (that is b0=1) then Thumb State will be invoked automatically when the Thumb code is reached with BX. This implies that you must always start from ARM State, but that must be the case anyway as that is the state the chip fires up in. Program 27a above shows how this works in practice. (Note the use of '@' for comments. GCC Thumb code does not like the inclusion of '/* */' style comments and these can sometimes cause an error.)

The thumb instructions are located from the 'thumbcode:' label. This address is loaded into R0 at the start of main: and 1 is added to the address to set the least significant bit of R0. The BX (Branch with eXchnage) is executed and the address in R0 is swapped into the PC. Because ARM and Thumb instructions are word or half-word-aligned respectively, bits 0 and 1 of the address are ignored because these bits refer to the half-word and byte part of the address.

The instructions at thumbcode perform a division routine (although we have not loaded any data into them to work with!) before the BX LR returns code back to the calling ARM code. ARM State is switched back in due to the requirement to execute an ARM instruction. Note that you must switch back to ARM State to call a SWI call or a function such as printf.

You must use a BX LR instruction at the end of the ARM subroutine to return to the caller. You cannot use the MOV PC, LR instruction to return in this situation as it will not update the T bit for you thereby delivering the State change.

It is worth having a look at how GDB sees the assembled program as it confirms some of the differences outlined earlier. Figure 27b shows output from GDB using:

```
x /13i main
```

As usual the addresses listed in the first column may be different on your Raspberry Pi. (You can use the gcc route to compile in the normal fashion, nothing special needed.)

```
(gdb) x /13i main
        0x103d0    <main>:        add    r0, pc, #17
        0x103d4    <main+4>:      mov    lr, pc
        0x103d8    <main+8>:      bx     r0
        0x103dc    <exit>:        mov    r0, #0
        0x103e0    <exit+4>:      mov    r7, #1
        0x103e4    <exit+8>:      svc    0x00000000
        0x103e8    <thumbcode>:   movs   r3, #0
        0x103ea    <loop>:        adds   r3, #1
        0x103ec    <loop+2>:      subs   r0, r0, r1
        0x103ee    <loop+4>:      bge.n  0x103ea <loop>
        0x103f0    <loop+6>:      subs   r3, #1
        0x103f2    <loop+8>:      adds   r2, r0, r1
        0x103f4    <loop+10>:     bx     lr
```

Figure 27b. Disassembling Program 27a.

Notice how the 'S' suffix in Thumb is applied to the data instructions in the 'thumbcode:' portion of the listing. When dealing with registers R0-R7 all data processing instructions update the Status Flags and so the S suffix is enforced automatically by the assembler.

Also note that the BGE instruction has a '.N' appended to it. In Thumb the '.N' specifier forces the assembler to generate a 16-bit encoding. In this case, if the instruction cannot be encoded in 16 bits, the assembler generates an error.

The process of mingling segments of ARM and Thumb code together is called *interworking* and you are free to write code that moves between the two instructions sets if you so desire. The same ADR-BX process can be used throughout. If for example an ARM routine was located at the label 'armroutine' then it could be called with:

```
ADR R0, armroutine
BX  R0              @ Branch exchange to armroutine
```

Before making any calls that utilise the Link Register you should preserve its contents on the stack so that you can return to the original point of entry, and then recall the program originally entered at main, so that the program can complete its flow correctly.

Although BX is used in the examples above, the BLX instruction can also be used to jump into Thumb code. This instruction automatically saves the PC into the LR, so the MOV LR, PC instruction included in the listing is not needed. The +1 is still required for the entry address to switch state. The BX instruction should still be used to return from any called routine.

```
main:
ADR R0, thumbcode+1
BLX R0
```

Program 27b shows how these come together in practice using the printf function to print the result of a division performed in an extended program. Note that the additional ARM code follows the Thumb code. This is necessary otherwise the compiler will create an error when trying to create the relative branch address to the ARM code. Note also that the '.arm' and '.thumb' directives should be before the label marking the section of appropriate code.

Program 27b. Using external functions by interworking code.

```
@ Interworking ARM and Thumb code to call printf
    .global main
    .func main
    .arm
main:
    ADR R5, thumbstart+1
    BX R5

    .thumb
```

```
thumbstart:
        MOV R0, #9              @ Do 9/3
        MOV R1, #3
        MOV R3, #0
loop:
        ADD R3, #1
        SUB R0, R1
        BGE loop
        SUB R3, #1              @ R2=MOD
        ADD R2, R0, R1          @ R3=DIV
        ADR R5, divprint
        BX  R5

thumbreturn:
        @ Continue adding code as required
        @ Call ARM functions as and when needed
        ADR R5, exit
        BX  R5                  @ Return to exit

        .arm
divprint:
        LDR R0, =string
        MOV R1, R3              @ DIV in R3,MOD in R2 already
        BL printf
        ADR R5, thumbreturn+1
        BX  R5

exit:
        MOV R7, #1
        SWI 0

.data
string:     .asciz "Result of 9/3 is: %d MOD %d\n"
```

Accessing High Registers

Only a handful of instructions can access the full set of ARM registers. As already stated most Thumb instructions are limited to R0-R7 and automatically update the CPSR in doing so. Figure 27c lists the instructions and format use for accessing the higher registers R8-R14 and the PC. Apart from CMP these instructions do not update the CPSR.

MOV	<dest>,	<operand1>
ADD	<dest>,	<operand1>
CMP	<operand1>,	<operand2>
ADD	<dest>,	<operand1> | <#immediate>
ADD	<dest>,	<operand1>, <operand2> | <#immediate>
SUB	<dest>,	<operand1> | <#immediate>
SUB	<dest>,	<operand1>, <operand2> | <#immediate>

Figure 27c. Thumb instructions that can access all ARM registers.

Stack Operators

The Thumb stack instructions are the most significant departure from the ARM instruction set, in fact opting to use the more traditional PUSH and POP terms. We have seen these before as they are provided as pseudo-instructions by the GCC Compiler. In Thumb their action is similar so you should have little difficulties in getting to grips with them. However, there is a significant difference in that no stack pointer (SP) is available to the instruction. This is because R13 is fixed as the Stack Pointer in Thumb operations and is automatically updated by the instructions.

```
PUSH {R1-R4}    @ Push R1, R2, R3 & R4 onto stack
POP  (R2-R3}    @ Pop top 2 items into R2 and R3
```

PUSH can include the LR in its list and POP can include the PC, otherwise registers are limited to R0-R7 inclusive. In the first instance the SP address is adjusted by four-words: in the second by two-words. In ARM terms PUSH performs:

```
STMDB SP!, <REGLIST>
```

and POP performs:

```
LDMIA SP!, <REGLIST>
```

Single and Multi-Register

The LDR and STR instructions are supported by Thumb but not all addressing modes are. In fact, only three are available for use with these and associated commands. Figure 27d lists these, which are based on the pre-indexed addressing concept, and supply offset by register or by an immediate operand.

Multi-register access is limited to the use of increment after addressing modes using LDMIA and STMIA instructions. Note also that the '!' update operator is not an option as it is in ARM State, it is mandatory:

```
STMIA R1!, {R2, R3, R4}
```

Addressing Mode	Example
Load/Store Register	LDR R0, R1
Base + Offset	LDR R0, [R1, #5] LDR R0, [R1, R2]
Relative	LDR R0, [PC, #8]

Figure 27d Addressing mode samples in Thumb State.

Functions in Thumb

The example given in Program 27b illustrates how an ARM, or more exactly libc, function can be called from Thumb code. As mentioned previously, you switch back to ARM State. There is nothing stopping you creating your own functions in Thumb code—a function consisting entirely of Thumb code that runs exclusively in Thumb State. But when calling the function, it must have the least significant bit of the pointer to it set. As the linker in the compiler cannot do this, you yourself must do it within your calling code, especially if you use an absolute address.

Thus, when you call any standalone Thumb code from another section of Thumb code, the entry condition is identical as if you were entering Thumb code from ARM State. You add one to the link address.

Interestingly, you can have two functions with the same name—one for ARM and one for Thumb. The linker allows this provided they operate within different instruction sets. However, this shouldn't be considered good practice and should generally be avoided.

ARMv7 Thumb Instructions

As part of the release of ARMv7 architecture (Raspberry Pi 2B and later), seven new instructions were added to the Thumb instruction set, the most significant of which is Compare and Branch on Zero, or Non-Zero. This instruction compares the value in the register with zero and conditionally branches forward a constant value. It does not affect the condition flags.

```
CBNZ R0, newdest @ R0<>0 then branch to 'newdest'
CBZ R0, next     @ R0=0 then branch to 'next'
```

Both instructions can take a 'N' or '.W' modified as follows:

```
CBZ.N R0, next
```

'.N' is 'narrow' and informs the assembler to generate a 16-bit encoding. '.W' is 'wide' and signifies a 32-bit encoding. A 'N' (16-bit) is selected by default, whereas assembling in the A32 state will result in a 32-bit or wide encoding.

```
NOP
```

Is 'No Operation' and does nothing other than providing padding which may be needed to ensure the following instruction sits on a 64-bit boundary. It also delays the program by a cycle.

Other new instructions include YIELD, SEV, WFE and WFI which are concerned with events and interrupts as they happen.

An 'IT'(if-then) instruction was added which permits up to four successive instructions to execute based on a tested condition, or on its inverse. IT is ignored when compiling into ARM code, but when compiling into Thumb, it generates an actual instruction. For example:

```
CMP R0, R1     @ if (R0 == R1)
ITE EQ         @ R0 = R2;
MOVEQ R0, R2   @ Thumb: condition via ITE 'T' (then)
               @ else R0 = R3;
MOVNE R0, R3   @ Thumb: condition via ITE 'E' (else)
```

28: Unified Language

It was a long way back, but in Chapter 1, under the sub-heading 'Raspberry Pi OS', we examined the differentiation between 32-bits and 64-bits and the use of terms A32 and A64 to distinguish between 32 and 64-bit ARM.

A Thumb-2 instruction set was introduced with ARMv6T2 (and included in subsequent releases) and added more instructions to the base set but also allows most of the new Thumb instructions to be conditionally executed. If you like, Thumb-2 offers a 'best of both worlds' compromise in that it has access to both 16-bit and 32-bit instructions allowing programmers who are tight for space to extract the maximum bang-per-byte by combing the two. Thumb-2 was therefore a significant step towards the development of a Unified Assembler Language (UAL).

UAL is a standard syntax model for ARM implemented from ARMv7 onward for A32 and T32 instructions. It supersedes earlier versions of both the A32 and T32 assembler languages. Code that is written using UAL can be assembled for A32 or T32 for any ARM processor. However, not every assembler provides full coverage. GCC generally does and can assemble code written in pre-and-post UAL format.

From ARMv4T to ARMv7-A there are two instruction sets: ARM and Thumb. They are both '32-bit' in the sense that they operate on up to 32-bit-wide data in 32-bit-wide registers with 32-bit addresses. In fact, where they overlap, they represent the exact same instructions—it is only the instruction encoding which differs, and the CPU effectively just has two different decode front-ends to its pipeline which it can switch between.

Based on the combined A32 and T32 instruction sets, UAL forms a consistent programming model. This way you should produce the most economical and productive code possible. UAL implements some changes to both ARM and Thumb code to help in this standardisation, as well as the addition of new instructions. Use of this new syntax *will* affect backwards compatibility of code, unless your assembler is smart enough to figure out how to deal with it, whilst assembling it.

The GCC compiler (and I would assume other compatible compilers) will be able to assemble code written in pre-UAL and UAL syntax. If it is your intention to use UAL, ensure that your source code contains the directive:

```
.syntax unified
```

With any other definitions at the start of your code. You may also need to specify the architecture you are utilising – discussed later.

T32 extends the Thumb instruction set with bit-field manipulation, table branches and conditional execution operations. At the same time, the ARM instruction set is extended in areas to maintain equivalent functionality in both instruction sets.

This combination produced a Unified Assembler Language (UAL), which supports assembly of either Thumb or ARM instructions from the same source code; versions of Thumb first seen on ARMV7 processors are essentially as capable as ARM code (including the ability to write interrupt handlers).

With this knowledge, we should re-address the concept of Thumb-2 for clarity. From ARMv6 there are two instruction sets: ARM (A32) and Thumb-2 (T32). They are both '32-bit' in the sense that they operate on up to-32-bit-wide data in 32-bit-wide registers with 32-bit addresses. Where they overlap they represent the same instructions, it is only the instruction encoding which differs, and the CPU effectively just has two different front ends to its pipeline which it can switch between to decode the instruction.

T32 encompassed not just additional instructions (mostly with 4-byte encoding, although there are a few two-byte encoding) to bring it almost to parity with ARM, but also allows conditional execution of most Thumb instructions. A mixed 16/32-bit instruction stream provides the economy of space of Thumb combined with most of the speed of pure ARM code. A stated aim for T32 was to achieve code density similar to Thumb with performance like the ARM instruction set on 32-bit memory.

If performance is critical, then it is important to have at least half the instructions encoded as 16-bit to get maximum speed.

The general rules for generating the 16-bit form of the instructions are:

- Use registers in the range R0-R7
- Set the condition flags unless the instruction is conditional wherever possible
- Use immediate constants in the range 0-7 or 0-255

Thumb Changes

Changes have been made to the original Thumb syntax to bring T32 in line with A32. In original Thumb code where the first operand and destination operand were the same, you need only specify it once. Now they must both be specified so:

```
ADD R0, R1        @ Old Thumb format
ADD R0, R0, R1    @ UAL format
```

In a similar fashion, where the instruction sets the condition flags you must enforce this with the standard 'S' suffix:

```
ADD R0, R1, R2    @ Old Thumb format
ADDS R0, R1, R2   @ UAL format
```

Now, the MOV instruction is used as an addition operation with zero as an immediate value:

```
MOV R0, R1        @ Old Thumb format
ADD R0, R1, #0    @ UAL format
```

And to confuse matters, the CPY instruction becomes a MOV instruction:

```
CPY R0, R1        @ Old Thumb format
MOV R0, R1        @ UAL format
```

Increment after becomes the default addressing mode for the LDM instruction:

```
LDMIA R0!, {R0, R1}   @ Old Thumb format
LDM R0!, {R1, R2}     @ UAL format
```

And write-back is not specified in LDM now if the base register is in the register list:

```
LDMIA R0!, {R0, R1}   @ Old Thumb format
LDM R0, {R0, R1}      @ UAL format
```

New A32 Instructions

Figure 28a lists the new instructions added to the A32 instruction set as part of UAL. For T32 the BL and BLX instructions are confirmed 32-bit operations. Below are a few examples, and all can be used with an optional condition if required. Use of narrow and wide directives are also permitted.

BFC clears any number of adjacent bits at any position in a register and does so without affecting any of the other bits:

```
BFC R0, #5, #3
```

Clears bits 5, 6, and 7 of the value held in R0.

Mnemonic	Action
BFC	Bit Field Clear
BFI	Bit Field Insert
MLS	Multiply and Subtract
MOV	New wide variant that loads a 16-bit immediate value into bits 0:15 of a register
MOVT	Move Top. Loads a 16-bit immediate value into bits 16:31 of a register
RBIT	Reverse Bits in a word
SBFX	Signed Bitfield Extract
UBFX	Unsigned Bitfield Extract

Figure 28a. New A32 instructions.

BFI copies any number of low order bits from a register into the same bits of the specified destination register:

```
BFI R0, R1, #5, #3
```

Copy bits 5, 6 and 7 from R1 into bits 5, 6, and 7 of R0.

MLS multiplies two register values and then subtracts the least significant 32-bits of the result from a third register and writes the result to a destination register:

```
MLS R0, R1, R2, R3
```

Multiply the contents of R1 and R2, subtract the least significant 32-bits from R3 and place into R0.

Compare by Zero

One of the most common cases is a comparison by zero. Figure 28b illustrates the differences between ARM, T32 and T16 for this operation:

State	Mnemonics	Length
ARM	CMP R0, #0 ; BEQ <label>	8 bytes
T32	CMP R0, #0 ; BEQ <label>	4 bytes
T16	CBZ R0, <label>	2 bytes

Figure 28b. Compare by Zero – code options.

As we can see, in T16, CBZ has replaced CMP+BEQ from the ARM and Thumb states and condensed it into one instruction which is two bytes long.

Assembling UAL

The ARM processor can only work in either ARM State or Thumb State. It's the case even in pre-UAL supporting processors. You cannot intermix A32 and T32 code. To use A32 and T32 code in the same program, you must do so in blocks and switch between states at the appropriate point. Called 'interworking' the technique was introduced in Chapter 27 – nothing has changed. However, you should use the directive:

```
.syntax unified
```

At the top of your source along with your other directives to invoke UAL. When you compile the source, you should also specify the architecture you are compiling for, for example:

```
march=armv8-a
```

Code written using UAL can be assembled for A32 or T32 for any ARM processor using this technique.

As we have seen some T32 instructions can have either a 16-bit encoding or a 32-bit encoding. If you do not specify the instruction size, by default:

- For forward reference LDR, ADR, and B instructions, the compiler should generate a 16-bit instruction, even if that results in failure for a target that could be reached using a 32-bit instruction.

- For external reference LDR and B instructions, the compiler should generate a 32-bit instruction.

- In all other cases, the compiler should generate the smallest size encoding that can be output.

If you want to override these defaults, then you should use the '.W' or '.N' to specify instruction width (wide or narrow) to ensure a particular instruction size. The '.W' post-fix is ignored when assembling A32 code, so you can safely use this specifier in programs that might assemble as A32 or T32 code.

Because instruction may be a mix of 16-bit and 32-bit wide, it is important to monitor address alignment. From ARMv7 architecture on, the A bit in the System Control Register (SCTLR) controls whether alignment checking is enabled or disabled. The exception is in ARMv7-M, the UNALIGN_TRP bit, bit 3, in the Configuration and Control Register (CCR) controls this. (See Chapter 29 regarding these registers.)

If set alignment checking is enabled, all unaligned word and halfword transfers cause an alignment exception. If disabled, unaligned accesses are permitted for the LDR, LDRH, STR, STRH, LDRSH, LDRT, STRT, LDRSHT, LDRHT, STRHT, and TBH instructions. Other data-accessing instructions always cause an alignment exception for unaligned data. For STRD and LDRD, the specified address must be word-aligned.

Program 28a. Unified Assembly Language

```
@   Use of UAL code on Raspberry Pi
@   Add two values using short subroutine call
@   gcc option can be used also

        .syntax unified
        .global _start
_start:
        MOV     r0, #10         @ set up parameter
        MOV     r1, #5          @ set up parameter
        MOV     r2, #5
        MOV     r3, #20
        BL      doadd           @ Call subroutine

        MOV     R4, #0xFF00
        MOVT    R4, #0xFFFF
        MLA     R0, R1, R2, R3
stop:
        MOV R7, #1
        SWI 0
doadd:
        ADD     r0, r0, r1      @ Subroutine code, UAL format
        BX      lr              @ Return from subroutine
```

Assemble and run the above with:

```
as -g -o prog28a.o prog28a.s
ld -o prog28a prog28a.o
./prog28a
echo $?
45
```

The result 45 will be printed with the echo$? command.

UAL is a common syntax for A32 and T32 instructions. However, it supersedes earlier versions of both the A32 and T32 assembler languages. Code that is written using UAL can be assembled for A32 or T32 for any ARM processor. Investigate some of the source files on the ARM website and you will notice that the '.syntax unified' directive is largely common to them all.

29: Exception Handing

This chapter provides an overview of exception handling, the various modes of ARM operation, vectors, and interrupts. This is a fundamental design aspect of the ARM chip and provides a clever and versatile way to customise the way your chosen operating system works. It should be considered an advanced topic and as such its detail is beyond the scope of this book. However, it is fascinating as is the whole concept of interrupts which are fundamental to everyday Raspberry Pi operation. As such an overview here is provided which will certainly help you should you delve into areas such as bare metal programming or look at writing your own OS to run on your Raspberry Pi. And these are all tasks you should consider a next step on the learning curve.

As an Operating System Raspberry Pi OS is defensive in the way it is configured, and its core, the kernel memory management prevents you from accessing something that is not mapped into the process memory map., it will not let you just read and write to arbitrary memory locations. It is for this reason that the GPIO pins and other hardware components of the Raspberry Pi cannot be accessed from a standard machine code program running under ROS. This is different from an OS such as RISC OS where the whole system is deployed in a way to make it easy to configure and reconfigure for the programmer's needs. Indeed, a whole wave of SYS calls are provided in RISC OS just for this purpose. I say this just to indicate that it is an OS worth trying if you wish to play with interrupts and events in a controlled manner. (RISC OS is free as a downloadable OS from the Raspberry Pi website, and you can find out about RISC OS Assembly Language programming by going to www.brucesmith.info.)

Direct memory access can only be performed by operating as a root user or by writing a standalone OS that replaces Raspberry Pi OS — bare metal programming in effect.

Modes of Operation

In Chapter 5, we examined the Current Program Status Register and saw how the individual bits within it were used as flags to denote certain conditions. The figure presented then is shown again as Figure 29a.

31	30	29	28	27...8	7	6	5	4	3	2	1	0
N	Z	C	V		I	F	T	MODE

Figure 29a. The Status Register configuration.

The N, Z, C and V flags should be familiar. The ones we are concerned with now are held in the low byte of the register in bits 0 to 7.

The Mode bits are located from 0 to 4 (five in total), and their setting determines which of the six operating modes the ARM operates in. Figure 29b summarises these modes. Any of them can be entered by changing the CPSR. Except for User Mode and Supervisor Mode all modes can be entered when an exception occurs.

Mode	Description
FIQ	Entered when a high priority (fast) interrupt is raised
IRQ	Entered when a low priority (normal) interrupt is raised
Supervisior and Reset	Entered on reset and when a Software Interrupt (SWI) instruction is executed
Abort	Used to handle memory access violations
Undef	Used to handle undefined instructions
User	Unprivileged mode under which mosts task run

Figure 29b. The ARM's six modes of operation.

User Mode is the one used by default by programs and applications. This is the environment we work in, and in truth, we as programmers never have to leave it, unless we are looking to be more adventurous and take over total control of the ARM chip itself. This is not for the novice and care needs to be taken when that line is breached.

Referring again to Figure 29a, bits 7 and 6 are used for enabling and disabling IRQ and FIQ interrupts, respectively. If a bit is set the associated interrupt is disabled. If the bit is clear, then the interrupt is enabled. Bit 5 is the Thumb mode bit and is discussed in Chapter 27. For all interrupts, this bit is clear, and the processor is operating in ARM State.

Vectors

Vectors play an important role in the operation of the ARM chip. A vector is a known location in memory that is exactly one word, or 32-bits wide. (Not to be confused with vectors in VFP.)

There are two types of vectors: hardware and software vectors. Hardware vectors are hardwired to the ARM chip itself and they never change, and as Figure 29c shows, they are located at the very beginning of the memory map.

However, in the ROS, the vector table can be located at a higher address in memory, here starting at 0xFFFF0000.

Hardware vectors control the ultimate flow of information and are a set of memory addresses that are 'known' to the ARM chip. The term 'known' here means that they are physically 'hardwired' and are thus termed hardware vectors. Hardware vectors typically control the flow of abnormal events which the chip itself cannot deal with. They are often referred to as exception vectors and they reside smack bang at the start of the memory map from 0x00000000 to 0x0000001C. Figure 29c lists the hardware vectors.

Address	Hi Address	Vector
0x00000000	0xFFFF0000	ARM reset
0x00000004	0xFFFF0004	Undefined Instruction
0x00000008	0xFFFF0008	Software Interrupt (SWI)
0x0000000C	0xFFFF000C	Abort (pre-fetch)
0x00000010	0xFFFF0010	Abort (data)
0x00000014	0xFFFF0014	Address exception
0x00000018	0xFFFF0018	IRQ
0x0000001C	0xFFFF001C	FIRQ (or FIQ)

Figure 29c. The ARM Hardware vectors.

One common reason for manipulating the hardware vectors is to change the machine's response to memory access faults. If some non-existent memory is accessed then one of the memory faults vectors, 0x0000000C to 0x00000014, is called. The normal effect of this is for the Operating System to report a fatal error and stop executing the current task. Sometimes, for example when writing a memory editor, this is not a very desirable occurrence. It would be better simply to warn the user that a particular location is invalid and allow editing to continue for the rest of memory.

Vectors are useful to the programmer as they allow programs to access standard routines without directly calling the physical address where the machine code for the routine is stored.

In the early days of computers Operating Systems were small and everything was 'hard-coded', meaning address where used in absolute terms. The problem with using absolute addresses and by this, I mean a real physical address rather than a branch offset for example, is that you are always tied to that address. If the OS is updated then, a pound to a pinch of salt, that address will change. Now any external or third-party code that uses that absolute address might be snookered. If the code is updated and its execution point is changed, all that needs to happen is for the address in the vector to be changed.

The second advantage to using vectors is that we, as the programmer, can also change the address in the vector—we can intercept it. By doing this we can modify and change the way the Raspberry Pi operates. This is not easy under ROS but if you plan to write bare metal code then you will be required to take control of the vector table yourself and manage its requirements.

When an exception interrupt occurs, the processor stops what it is doing and jumps to the appropriate location in the vector table. Each location contains an instruction pointing to the start of a specific handling routine. These instructions normally take one of three forms as shown in Figure 29d.

Instruction	Description
B <address>	Jump to the address given as a relative offset to the PC.
LDR PC, [PC, #offset]	Load address from memory to the PC. This address is a 32-bit value stored close to the vector table. This is slightly slower than the previous method due to the extra memory access. The bonus is that you can branch to any legal address in the memory map.
LDR PC, [PC, #-0xFF0]	Load address of a specific interrupt routine service routine from 0xFFFFF030 to the PC.
MOV PC, #value	Copies an immediate value into the PC. This will normally be a single byte value that is rotated right by an even number of bits. Thus provides access to the full memory map but with gaps.

Figure 29d. Instructions that may be used in a vector.

For example, when an IRQ interrupt occurs it ultimately goes via the IRQ vector. This location is 32-bits wide and is just big enough to contain an instruction that facilitates an instruction to branch elsewhere.

Register Arrangements

Each of the modes has an associated set of registers available to it. The registers available to the programmer vary according to the current CPU operating mode.

Raspberry Pi OS Assembly Language

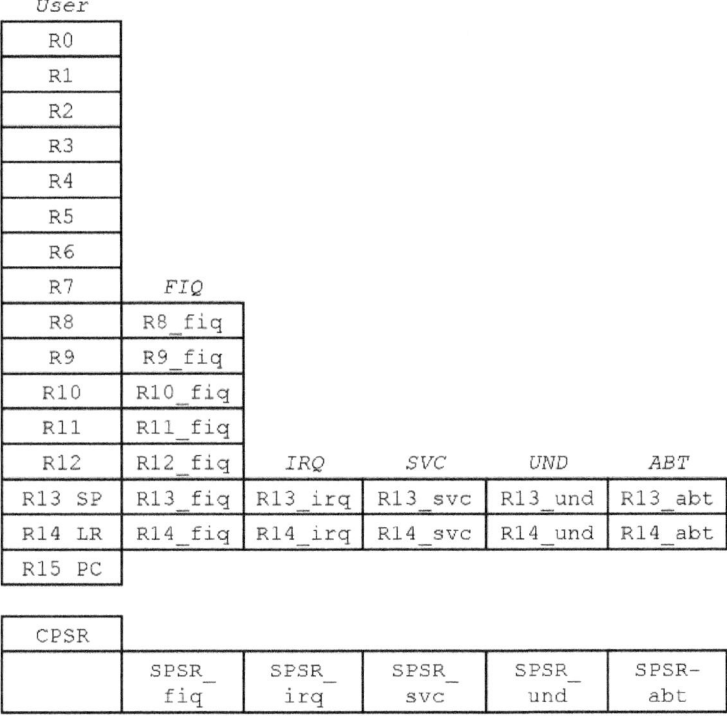

Figure 29e. The ARM programmer's model.

When executing in User Mode the full set of registers, R0 to R15, are available for use. However, when the CPU switches into another operation mode, this all changes. Figure 29e shows the register arrangement depending on the mode of operation. All modes have dedicated stack pointers and link registers associated with them. Whilst all modes except for User Mode have a new register, the Saved Program Status Register, available to them, only FIQ mode has several dedicated registers from R8-R12. Otherwise registers remain unchanged.

The SPSR is used to hold a copy of the User Mode Status Register when one of the other modes is entered. The User Mode does not have, and it does not need an SPSR. An important point to note here is that the CPSR is only copied into the SPSR when an exception or interrupt is raised; it is not changed if you physically write to the CPSR to change mode.

The idea behind this banked register system is that each processor mode has some private registers which it can make use of without affecting the values of the normal registers, thus ensuring that the programmer does not have to worry about saving the contents of their own User Mode registers when an alternative mode is entered.

Figure 29f shows how the low byte of the CSPR looks when one of the modes is invoked. Except for User Mode, all modes are privileged. When power is first applied to the ARM chip it starts off in Supervisor Mode.

	I	F	T	MODE			
	7	6	5	4	3	2	1	0
Abort	1	1	0	1	0	1	1	1
FIQ	1	1	0	1	0	0	0	1
IRQ	1	uc	0	1	0	0	1	0
Supervisor	1	uc	0	1	0	0	1	1
System	1	1	0	1	1	1	1	1
Undefined	1	uc	0	1	1	0	1	1
User	0	0	0	1	0	0	0	0

Figure 29f. Bit settings for Mode changes in CPSR.

Interrupts can be enabled and disabled very easily in ARM — using masking. Bits 7 and 6 enable or disable IRQ and FIQ interrupts, respectively. If either bit is set, then the associated interrupt is disabled and will not be processed. When an exception or interrupt occurs, the interrupt mask bit will normally be set by the chip. For a number of modes, the FIQ bit remains unchanged (uc).

Exception Handling

An exception handling is a condition that requires the halting, temporary or otherwise, of whatever code is executing. A segment of code called an exception handler is called at this point. It identifies the condition and passes control to the appropriate route to handle the exception. When an exception causes a mode change the following sequence of events needs to happen:

- The address of next instruction is copied into the appropriate LR
- The CPSR is copied into the SPSR of the new mode
- The appropriate mode is set by modifying bits in the CPSR
- The next instruction is fetched from the vector table.
- When the exception has been dealt with, control can be returned to the code that was executing when the exception occurred.

Control can be returned as follows:

- The LR (minus an offset) is moved into the PC
- The SPSR is copied back into CPSR and by default this automatically changes the mode back to the previous one

- If set, the interrupt disable flags are cleared. Clear the interrupt disable flags to re-enable interrupts.

Figure 29g. Swapping registers on at a privileged exception.

The illustration above in Figure 29g illustrates what happens at a register level when a SWI call is made. The concept is the same for any of the privileged mode exceptions. The SP and LR of the accessing Mode are switched in over the User Mode ones to allow the exception to be serviced, whilst preserving the status of the interrupted program. The return address is copied from the User Mode PC and stored in the LR of the privileged mode being invoked. R14_svc in the example above.

By preserving the status of the three User Mode registers shown, the status quo of program execution can be maintained when the SVC Mode call has been serviced simply by swapping them back. As stated earlier the CPSR is only saved into the requesting mode's SPSR when an exception occurs. It does not happen when the mode is changed by flipping the Mode bits.

MRS and MSR

There are two instructions which can be used directly to control the contents of the CPSR and SPSR and they can be used on the whole contents or at bit level.

The MRS instruction transfers the contents of either the CPSR or SPSR into a register. The MSR instruction works the opposite way and transfer the contents of a register into either the CSPR or SPSR. The instruction syntax is as follows:

```
MRS (<suffix>) <Operand1>, <CSPR|SPSR>
MSR (<suffix>) <CSPR|SPSR|Flags>, <Operand1>
MSR (<suffix>) <CSPR|SPSR|Flags>, #immediate
```

Some examples will make their operation clearer. The following three lines of code could be used to enable IRQ Mode:

```
MRS R1, CPSR
BIC R1, R1, #0x80
MSR CPSR_C, R1
```

First the CPSR is copied into R1 where it is then masked with 10000000 to clear the bit at b7 – the position of the I flag. (see Figure 26a). R1 is then written back to CPSR. Note the use of the '_C' as an addition to the CPSR operand. For programming, the CPSR and SPSR are divided into four different sectors. These are illustrated below in Figure 29h.

Flags (F) [24:31]	Status (S) [16:25]	Extension (X) [8:15]	Control (C) [0:7]
N Z C V Q			I F T Mode

Figure 29h. The CPSR/SPSR segments to control updating.

By using the correct adjunct(s) on the appropriate instruction we can ensure that only the correct bits of the associated register are updated. The F, S, X and C suffixes may be used in like fashion.

To disable the IRQ, the following segment of code would suffice:

```
MRS R1, CPSR
ORR R1, R1, #x080
MSR CPSR_C, R1
```

The same commands can be used to effect a mode change thus:

```
MRS R0,CPSR            @   copy the CPSR
BIC R0,R0,#0x1F        @   clear mode bits
ORR R0,R0,#new_mode    @   select new mode
MSR CPSR,R0            @   write CPSR back
```

In User Mode you can read all the bits of the CPSR, but you can only update the condition of the field flag, ie, CPSR_F.

Interrupts When?

Interrupt Request Mode (IRQ) and Fast Interrupt Mode (FIQ) are called when an external device pages the ARM chip and demands its attention. For example, the keyboard generates an interrupt whenever a key is pressed. This is a signal to the CPU that the keyboard matrix should be read, and the ASCII value of the key entered into the keyboard buffer. If the ASCII value is 0x0D (RETURN), the keyboard buffer must be interpreted.

The analogy here can be you, sitting at your own keyboard learning Raspberry Pi Assembly Language. At some point your phone starts to ring. You have been interrupted. So, you stop what you are doing (you may make a quick note to remind you or you may save your work) and answer the phone (you deal with or process the interruption). When you have completed the phone call, you hang up and return to what you were doing before the interruption.

The process with the ARM chip is much the same. It receives an interrupt signal at which point it saves what it is doing in line with what we have already discussed and then hands control to the calling interrupt routine by invoking the appropriate mode of operation. When the interrupt has finished its work (in the keyboard example this would be reading the key press and placing the ASCII code in the keyboard buffer) it hands control back to the ARM which restores all its previously saved information and returns to User Mode, picking up where it left off.

So here the interrupt is a function of the ARM chip itself, but how it is dealt with and what happens thereafter is a feature of the software handling it — Raspberry Pi OS in this case.

Without an effective interrupt system, the Raspberry Pi at software level would have to spend a lot of its time checking all attached components just to see if anything has happened, taking up time and resources. Think of all the connections to your Raspberry Pi — keyboard, mouse, USB ports, disk drives... They all require servicing, and often.

Fast Interrupts (FIQs) are deemed to have the highest priority and are the ones that must be serviced first. For example, connected disk drives, otherwise data might be lost. The only time a FIQ is not serviced first is when another FIQ is in the process of being serviced. The Interrupt Request (IRQ) line is deemed to be of lower priority where a slight delay will not create any problems.

The need for speed in processing an FIQ interrupt is signified by its position in the hardware vector table. It is the last in the list. This is because it actually begins executing right at that point—the other vectors all perform other branch instructions further into the system software. The FIQ code resides in the space after the vector at 0x1C. It is then the job of the appropriate interrupt coding to identify which device caused the interrupt and process it accordingly and as quickly as possible.

Your Interrupt Decisions

When dealing with interrupts you need to make the decision about other interrupts. What happens if a new interrupt occurs whilst you are handling an existing interrupt? The easiest method is to invoke what is called a non-nested interrupt handling scheme. In this all interrupts are disabled until control is handled back to the interrupted task. The downside of this is that only one interrupt can be serviced at a time, and if a succession of interrupts are occurring you may lose some of the requests. This could have consequences.

A nested interrupt scheme allows more than one interrupt to be handled at a time and in this case, you would look to re-enable interrupts before fully servicing the current interrupt. This is more complex, but it solves the problems that can occur with interrupt latency, which is the interval of time from an external interrupt signal being raised to the first fetch of an instruction of the raised interrupt signal.

For an FIQ, the IRQs are disabled as the FIQ is deemed critical in relation.

In all cases the implementation of a stack for interrupt handling (interrupt stack) is considered essential for context switching between the modes and preserving information. If several interrupts occur at the same time the details need to be stored somewhere for processing as the sequence is dealt with.

Returning from Interrupts

When the interrupt service routine has been performed, the Operating System must return to the original program which was interrupted by the FIQ or IRQ. This is done by using the following instruction:

```
SUBS R15, R14, #4
```

This restores the Program Counter so that the interrupted program can be resumed from exactly the point at which it was suspended. The 'subtract 4' calculation is required to correct for the effects of pipelining. Providing that the interrupt handling routine has not corrupted any shared registers or workspace, the program will continue executing as if the interrupt had never happened.

Writing Interrupt Routines

Usually, you will not need to create interrupt routines service routines of your own because the OS provides a well-defined system for doing so. If you intend to write direct interrupt handling routines, you should observe the following rule to avoid potential disasters:

- Do not re-enable interrupts in the handling routine. If this is done, a second IRQ/FIQ could interrupt the processor before it has finished handling the first. Sometimes this may be permissible, but you could be walking on thin ice if you do it. Be very aware!

- The interrupt routine must be written as economically as possible. Processing the interrupt at maximum speed should be a major goal. If it keeps interrupts disabled for too long, then the normal Raspberry Pi background activities will grind to a halt. The keyboard will lock, various software clocks will lose time etc.

- All shared processor registers should be preserved. They should contain the same values on exit from the interrupt routine as they did on entry to the interrupt. This is vital if the interrupted task is to be resumed correctly.

- The interrupt handling routine should avoid calling OS routines. It is possible that one of these routines would be only half executed when it is interrupted by IRQ/FIQ. If re-entered in the interrupt routine, work space could be disturbed, potentially causing the routine to corrupt when resumed.

30: System on a Chip

The square chip in the centre of the Raspberry Pi board is the one that this book has been all about. Everything we have been doing in the preceding pages has been taking place inside that square. Figure 30a shows it in all its glory. In fact, that bit of silicon is much more than just an ARM chip. It is a System-On-Chip device.

Broadly speaking, a SoC is a microchip that has all the components required to drive a computer. The composition of the SoC has changed for each version of Raspberry Pi that has been released., However the basic components are an ARM compatible CPU and an on-chip graphics processing unit GPU (a VideoCore IV). The CPU speeds range from 700 MHz (Raspberry Pi 1) to 1.2 GHz for the Raspberry Pi 3. Similarly, the on-board memory range from 256 MB to 1 GB RAM.

Figure 30a. A Raspberry Pi with the SoC at its heart.

Built specifically for the Raspberry Pi 4, the BCM2711B0 –the silverish item in Figure 30a – is a 64-bit quad core Cortex-A72 (ARMv8-A) System-On-Chip running at 1.5GHzs .It includes the Broadcom VideoCore VI – the first upgrade to the graphics processor, for the Raspberry Pi, as well as the various co-processors discussed in this book.

The large black chip is the memory that comes in 1GB, 2GB, 4GB or 8GB flavours.

The SoC technology is increasingly popular, and the packaging of numerous components onto a single integrated circuit (IC) means that the devices they are embedded into become ever smaller. If you have a close look at the Raspberry Pi board then you will see that much of the space is taken up by components that allow us to connect to it! The actual computer part probably occupies only about 10% of the printed circuit board! Indeed, more and more has been placed onto the Raspberry Pi board with each version release.

Make no mistake, the SoC technology used on the Raspberry Pi is on the cutting edge, and you can expect to see it become prevalent in major advances in technology as the physical size of the SoC device continues to implode. Because of its great digital capabilities, you might expect to see similar silicon devices restoring sight to the blind and providing sound for the deaf in the not-too-distant future.

Another major advantage of the SoC design is the fact that it doesn't require a lot of power and it becomes very efficient because of the small distances that signals travel. Remember how much heat standard PCs throw out and where much of the space is given over to cooling?

There is a downside to SoC technology from the consumer point of view and a reason why those devices do not easily dominate the consumer and general market, and that is their lack of ability to be upgraded. Essentially you can't do this because everything is metaphorically glued into one place, so you can't readily add new memory or upgrade the core processor. When you are finished with the device, you effectively throw it away. So, your Raspberry Pi will no doubt become out-dated but then you would have to simply replace it with the newer model. Does this make the Raspberry Pi a disposable computer?

The ARM Chip & Instruction Sets

At the heart of the SoC on the Raspberry Pi is the ARM core. SoCs are not limited to ARM chips but they are the processor of choice due to the use of RISC which offers power saving advantages. The ARM chip itself has been around for over 30 years now and it has gone through continual development. The ARM11 used in the original Raspberry Pi was launched in 2003 and is built around the ARMv6 architecture. The ARMv7 chip used in the Raspberry Pi 2 is a few years older and is one of the fastest, most energy efficient chips available. The ARM v8 in the Raspberry Pi 3 is yet another step and its speed now make it possible to run popular Operating Systems such as Windows 10 and Ubuntu. The chip has a quad-core which means that it can multi-task, ie do several things at once, that was not previously possible on the original single-core chip.

We have seen two of the instruction sets that ARM provides on the Raspberry Pi, namely ARM and Thumb. Historically, there was a third instruction set called Jazelle. It was primarily intended to assist in mobile phone software development, and since release of the ARMv7 architecture has been de-emphasised.

Co-processors

The ARM design allows for additional processing hardware to be connected to it. (Interestingly this was a unique design structure introduced by Acorn as early as 1983 with the launch of its Second Processor Tube interface which allowed additional CPUs to be bolted onto the side of the BBC Micro. This would allow other processor dependent Operating Systems such as CP/M to be run. An ARM Second Processor unit was one of the last released for the BBC Micro!)

As these are designed to support the ARM, they are called co-processors. Up to 16 can be connected and are numbered from 0-15. Instructions such as MCR and MRC can be used to communicate with them, and many co-processors add their own instruction sets which are worth investigating.

We have already examined one co-processor in detail: The Vector Floating-Point co-processor which provides real number management to the otherwise integer-orientated ARM chip. In fact, the VFP occupies two slots, being CP10 and CP11 in the system. CP14 and CP15 are also reserved for system use, but the others are all free for use.

Pipeline

We examined the pipeline in Chapter 13. At that point we looked at the original generic three-stage process and hinted then that ARMv6 has an 8-stage operation. The eight stages are described in Figure 27b. During operation, dependent on the instruction being performed the pipeline will route one of three different ways to process stages 5, 6 and 7 and so will further maximise the instruction process prowess of the chip.

There are three blocks of operation that can be switched in at stages 5, 6 and 7 depending on the operation taking place. For example, if a multiply instruction is being processed then these stages are induced in place of the other parallel stages. This allows the ARM to deliver just about one instruction for each cycle.

The Fetch stages can hold up to four instructions, whist the Execute, Memory, and Write stages can contain a predicted branch, an ALU or multiply instruction, a load/store multiple instruction and a co-processor instruction in parallel execution.

It would be possible to increase the length of the pipeline, but it is impractical to do so as it would increase power consumption and create heat. This would have a devastating effect on small systems such as the Raspberry Pi meaning bigger power supplies and more space between components and perhaps even aided cooling! This is much less of a problem with the energy efficient Raspberry Pi 2 which has four cores it can utilise.

Stage	Name	Description
1	Fe1	This is first stage of the instruction fetch where the address is sent to memory and an instruction returned.
2	Fe2	Second stage of instruction fetch. The ARM will try to predict the destination of any branch at this point.
3	De	Decode instruction.
4	Iss	Read registers and issue instruction action.
5	Sh	Perform shift operations as required.
6	ALU	Perform integer operations
7	Sat	Saturate integer results
5	MAC1	First stage of the multiply-accumulate pipeline.
6	MAC2	Second stage of the multiply-accumulate pipeline.
7	MAC3	Third stage of the multiply-accumulate pipeline.
5	ADD	Address generation stage.
6	DC1	First stage of data cache access.
7	DC2	Second stage of data cache access.
8	WBi	Write back of data from the multiply or main execution pipelines (Load Store Unit).

Figure 30b. The eight-stage pipeline of the ARMv11 includes sub-pipelines which can be banked in for maximum efficiency.

Memory & Caches

Depending on what model Raspberry Pi you have it will come with a certain amount of memory. This memory is part of the SoC, and this sits on top of the ARM chip in an arrangement called 'package on package'.

The ARM also has an area of amazingly fast memory called a memory cache that it can use for its own purposes. These are for instruction and data storage and are respectively known as Icache and Dcache. Incidentally, these caches are controlled by the System control co-processor (CP15), as is all memory, thus enabling the ARM to get on with processing instructions. A second cache called L2 is also on-board. However, this is used exclusively by the VideoCore.

The GPU

The Graphics Processing Unit is the other major component of the SoC configuration. It is a Broadcom VideoCore IV unit that provides 1080 high resolution graphics using a combination of Open software and hardware accelerated computing. Although information on this proprietary system has been thin on the ground, several groups have been working at supplying information through GitHub sites. Example files in C can now be downloaded and bindings for other languages such as Python and Java exist.

ARMv8 Overview

The ARMv8 architecture was introduced to Raspberry Pi users with the release of Raspberry PI 2B v1.2 utilising the Broadcom chip BCM2837. The underlying architecture of the BCM2837 is identical to the BCM2836. The only significant difference is the replacement of the ARMv7 quad-core cluster with a quad-core ARM Cortex A53 (ARMv8) cluster. This was then carried on into the various iterations of the Raspberry Pi 4 utilising a different quad-core based on the Cortex-A72. These iterations also included VFPv4 and Neon. Also, significantly with the Raspberry Pi 4, the redesign of the boards allowed for an 8Mb memory version, which should better enable Linux usage and the porting and application of the Raspberry Pi OS in a 64-bit environment.

The original concept behind ARMv8 was to provide ARM with a clean slate with which to design and encode an entirely new instruction set. The brief was for it to be 64-bit instruction set whist adhering as much as possible to keeping mnemonics and processes familiar. A64 provides a new start. Hopefully, the new instruction set will remain consistent across architectures to allow stability for the development and continuity in implementation. And as already mentioned, Custom Instructions are a real possibility going forward with future core releases.

Because of the sheer weight of numbers, (units in the market, not processing power!) 32-bit ARM will remain accessible and a processor of choice for existing designers and developers. Not least because the programmers have vast experience in 32-bit code and there is a sea of AArch32 legacy applications in use. While there are some 64-bit only ARM processors (Cortex A34 for instance), dual compatibility remains a high priority. For this reason, part of the brief was, as much as possible, to maintain compatibility with older architectures whist streamlining both ARM and Thumb instruction sets. Thus, the Unified Assembler Language concept was developed for backward compatibility, plus improved operation in the FPU.

As we saw at the start of this book in Figure 1c, the latest Raspberry Pi ARM chips can run in both 32-bit (AArch32) and 64-bit (AArch64) state. Going forward it should be possible to run AArch32 and Arch64 apps within a AArch64 OS. However, an AArch32 OS could only run AArch32 apps. This means is that you could host a mix of 32-bit and 64-bit applications under the same 64-bit kernel. How this pans out though remains to be seen.

Raspberry Pi OS 64-Bit

In May 2020, a beta version of Raspberry Pi OS was released, and this largely featured an updated version of the standard 32-bit version. This can be installed on the Raspberry Pi 3 and Raspberry Pi 4. At the time of writing, it is available in Beta version so may contain bugs as much as the original development of Raspbian did on the 32-bit version. It worked fine when I installed it on a dedicated SD Card and there is an active community moving forward with it.

In Summary

This has been a quick look at the technology that drives your Raspberry Pi, at the core of which is the ARM chip that this book has shown you how to program. It is by no means definitive, but it does show that there are exciting new technologies still emerging on your Raspberry Pi that you can investigate and be at the cutting edge of exploring. The Raspberry Pi with quad-core chips opens-up even more possibilities for those willing to investigate.

Archimedes Principle

Figure 30c. The Acorn Archimedes boasting an ARM2 cpu.

The Acorn Archimedes was designed by Acorn Computers Ltd in Cambridge, England. The system was based on Acorn's own ARM architecture processors and proprietary Operating System – RISC OS. The first model was introduced in 1987, and systems in the Archimedes family were sold until the mid-1990s.

Powered by an ARM2 it provided better performance than Intel's 286 despite having 245,000 less transistors than Intel's big chip. (In fact, ARM2 had only 25,000 transistors!) This 'lack' of transistors told a lot about the relative simplicity of the ARM. The design, utilised a 32-bit CPU (with 26-bit addressing), running at 8Mhz, a significant upgrade from 8-bit home computers.

Raspberry Pi OS Assembly Language

APPENDICES

A: ASCII Character Set

Binary	Dec	Hex	ASC	Binary	Dec	Hex	ASC
00100000	32	20		00111111	63	3F	?
00100001	33	21	!	01000000	64	40	@
00100010	34	22	"	01000001	65	41	A
00100011	35	23	#	01000010	66	42	B
00100100	36	24	$	01000011	67	43	C
00100101	37	25	%	01000100	68	44	D
00100110	38	26	&	01000101	69	45	E
00100111	39	27	'	01000110	70	46	F
00101000	40	28	(	01000111	71	47	G
00101001	41	29	)	01001000	72	48	H
00101010	42	2A	*	01001001	73	49	I
00101011	43	2B	+	01001010	74	4A	J
00101100	44	2C	,	01001011	75	4B	K
00101101	45	2D		01001100	76	4C	L
00101110	46	2E	.	01001101	77	4D	M
00101111	47	2F	/	01001110	78	4E	N
00110000	48	30	0	01001111	79	4F	O
00110001	49	31	1	01010000	80	50	P
00110010	50	32	2	01010001	81	51	Q
00110011	51	33	3	01010010	82	52	R
00110100	52	34	4	01010011	83	53	S
00110101	53	35	5	01010100	84	54	T
00110110	54	36	6	01010101	85	55	U
00110111	55	37	7	01010110	86	56	V
00111000	56	38	8	01010111	87	57	W
00111001	57	39	9	01011000	88	58	X
00111010	58	3A	:	01011001	89	59	Y
00111011	59	3B	;	01011010	90	5A	Z
00111100	60	3C	<	01011011	91	5B	[

Binary	Dec	Hex	ASC	Binary	Dec	Hex	ASC
00111101	61	3D	=	01011100	92	5C	\
00111110	62	3E	>	01011101	93	5D	]
01011110	94	5E	^	01101111	111	6F	o
01011111	95	5F	_	01110000	112	70	p
01100000	96	60	`	01110001	113	71	q
01100001	97	61	a	01110010	114	72	r
01100010	98	62	b	01110011	115	73	s
01100011	99	63	c	01110100	116	74	t
01100100	100	64	d	01110101	117	75	u
01100101	101	65	e	01110110	118	76	v
01100110	102	66	f	01110111	119	77	w
01100111	103	67	g	01111000	120	78	x
01101000	104	68	h	01111001	121	79	y
01101001	105	69	i	01111010	122	7A	z
01101010	106	6A	j	01111011	123	7B	{
01101011	107	6B	k	01111100	124	7C	|
01101100	108	6C	l	01111101	125	7D	}
01101101	109	6D	m	01111110	126	7E	~
01101110	110	6E	n				

B: ARM Instruction Set

The following pages contain a summary of the ARM instruction set arranged by operation type. It is not definitive nor complete in anyway and it is intended simply as an aid memoir, and includes many of the instructions covered herein. Remember that instructions may vary with architecture, with some being depreciated or adapted.

The guides at www.arm.com are an excellent way of learning about new ARM processors and the architecture detail of the instructions for each of them.

The following abbreviations and their meanings are used:

- Rn — Destination Register, where 'n' is register number.
- Rm — Operator Register, where 'n' is register number.
- Rdn — Destination register is Rd or Rn, depending on if optional {Rd,} is specified.
- N — Negative condition code. Set to 1 if result is negative.
- Z — Zero condition code. Set to 1 if the result of the instruction is 0.
- C — Carry condition code. Set to 1 if the instruction results in a carry.
- V — Overflow condition code. Set to 1 if the instruction results in an overflow.
- # — Immediate constant
- { } — Optional parameters
- { | } — Alternative optional parameters
- (|) — Alternative required parameters

Load/Store Suffixes:

- B — Zero extended byte.
- H — Zero extended half-word: 16-bits.
- SB — Sign extended byte.
- SH — Sign extended half-word: 16-bits.
- S — Optional S indicates the Status Register is updated.

No suffix for Load/Store indicates four-byte transfer.

Compare and Test Instructions

Format		Description
CMP	Rn,Rm	Compare registers, update status
CMP	Rn,#K	Compare 8-bit K, update status
TST	Rn,Rm	Test registers, update status
TST	Rn,#K	Test with 8-bit K, update status
TEQ	Rn,Rm	Test Equivalent, update status
TEQ	Rn,#K	Test Equivalent 8-bit K, update status

Branch Instructions

Format		Description
B	label	Unconditional branch to label
BEQ	label	Branch if EQual
BNE	label	Branch if Not Equal
BLT	label	Branch if Less Than (Signed)
BLE	label	Branch if Less than Equal (Signed)
BGT	label	Branch if Greater Than (Signed)
BGE	label	Branch if Greater than Equal (Signed)
BLO	label	Branch if LOwer (Unsigned)
BLS	label	Branch if LOwer or Same (Unsigned)
BHI	label	Branch if HIgher (Unsigned)
BHS	label	Branch if Higher or Same (Unsigned)
BL	label	Update Link Register and Branch
BX	Rn	Branch to address in register Rn

Arithmetic Instructions

Format		Description
ADD{S}	{Rd,} Rn,Rm	Add two registers
ADD{S}	{Rd,} Rn,#K	Add register with 8-bit constant K
ADC{S}	{Rd,} Rn,Rm	Add two registers with Carry (C) C
ADC{S}	{Rd,} Rn,#K	Add register with 8-bit K & Carry(C)
SUB{S}	{Rd,} Rn,Rm	Subtract two registers
SDIV		Signed Divide
SUB{S}	{Rd,} Rn,#K	Subtract 8-bit constant K
SBC{S}	{Rd,} Rn,Rm	Subtract two registers with Carry
SBC{S}	{Rd,} Rn,#K	Subtract 8-bit K from reg with Carry
MUL	{Rd,} Rn,Rm	Multiple regs (Signed or Unsigned)
MLA		Multiple and Accumulate
MLS		Multiply and Subtract
NOP		No Operation
UMULL	RdL,RdH,Rn,Rm	Unsigned multiple (64-bit result)
SMULL	RdL,RdH,Rn,Rm	Signed multiple (64-bit result)

Logical Instructions

Format	Description
AND{S} {Rd,} Rn,(Rm|#K)	AND registers or 8-bit constant K
BIC{S} {Rd,} Rn AND NOT Rm	Bit Clear
ORR{S} {Rd,} Rn,(Rm|#K)	OR registers or 8-bit constant K
EOR{S} {Rd,} Rn,(Rm|#K)	Exclusive OR register or 8-bit constant K
NEG{S} {Rd,} Rn	Negate a register
LSL{S} {Rd,} Rn,(Rm|#K)	Logical Shift Left
LSR{S} {Rd,} Rn,(Rm|#K)	Logical Shift Right
ASR{S} {Rd,} Rn,(Rm|#K)	Arithmetic Shift Right
ROR{S} {Rd,} Rn,(Rm|#K)	ROtate Right

Data Movement Instructions

Format		Description
MOV{S}	Rd,Rm	Copy value from Rm to Rd
MOVW	Rd,#K	Copy 16-bit constant K to Rd (Zero Ext)
MOVT	Rd,#K	Copy 16-bit constant K to Rd [31:16]P
PUSH	Rn	Place Rn on top of the Stack
POP	Rn	Place the top of Stack into Rn
SVC	n	Supervisor Call (Software Interrupt SWI)

STR{B|H}   Rt,[Rn,#+/-K]
           Store: Regular Immediate Offset Addr (8-bit K)
STR{B|H}   Rt,[Rn,#+/-K]!
           Store: Pre-index Immediate Offset Addr (8-bit K)
STR{B|H}   Rt,[Rn],#+/-K
           Store: Post-index Immediate Offset[Rn]
STR{B|H}   Rt,[Rn,Rm {,LSL #s}]
           Store: Register Offset Addressing

LDR{B|H|SB|SH} Rt,[Rn,#+/-K]
           Load: Regular Immediate Offset Addr (8-bit K)
LDR{B|H|SB|SH} Rt,[Rn,#+/-K]!
           Load: Pre-index Immediate Offset Addr (8-bit K)
LDR{B|H|SB|SH} Rt,[Rn],#+/-K
           Load:Post-index Immediate Offset Addr (8-bit K)
LDR{B|H| SB|SH} Rt,[Rn,Rm {,LSL #s}]
           Load: Register Offset Addressing

C: ROS Syscalls

The first 192 System calls are listed below including a brief description of the call function. There is no official source or documentation of Linux System Calls therefore documentation is limited to voluntary sources.

Sys	Action	Function
0	restart-syscall	Restart a System call.
1	exit	Terminate the current process
2	fork	Create child process
3	read	Read from file descriptor
4	write	Write to file descriptor
5	open	Open / create file or device
6	close	Close a file descriptor
7	waitpid	Wait for process termination
8	creat	Create child process
9	link	Assign new name to a file
10	unlink	Delete name & file it refers to
11	execuve	Execute program
12	chdir	Change working directory
13	time	Get time in seconds
14	mknod	Create directory or special/ordinary file
15	chmod	Change permissions of a file
16	lchown	Change ownership of a file
18	oldstat	(Abandoned)
19	lseek	Reposition read/write file offset
20	getpid	Get process identification
21	mount	Mount filesystems
22	umount	Unmount filesystems
23	setuid	Set user identity
24	getuid	Get user identity
25	stime	Set time
26	ptrace	Process trace
27	alarm	Set alarm clock for delivery of signal
28	oldfstat	
29	pause	Wait for signal
30	utime	Change access and/or modification times
33	access	Check user's permissions for a file
34	nice	Change process priority
35	ftime	Return date and time

Sys	Action	Function
36	sync	Commit buffer cache to disk
37	kill	Send signal to a process
38	rename	Change the name or location of a file
39	mkdir	Create directory
40	rmdir	Delete (an empty) directory
41	dup	Duplicate a file descriptor
42	pipe	Create pipe
43	times	Get process times
45	brk	Change data segment size
46	setgid	Set group identity
47	getgid	Get group identity
48	signal	ANSI C signal handling
49	geteuid	Get user identity
50	getegid	Get group identity
51	acct *	Switch process accounting on or off
52	umount2	Mount and unmount filesystems
54	ioctl	Control device
55	fcntl	Manipulate file descriptor
57	setpgid	Set/get process group
58	ulimit :	Getrlimit(2)
60	umask	Set file creation mask
61	chroot	Change root directory
62	ustat	Get file system statistics
63	dup2	Replace second uplicate of first file descriptor
64	getppid	Get process identification
65	getpgrp	Set/get process group
66	setsid	Create session, set process group ID
67	sigaction	Examine and change signal status
70	setreuid	Set real and / or effective user ID
71	setregid	Set real and / or effective group ID
72	sigsuspend	POSIX signal handling functions
73	sigpending	POSIX signal handling functions
74	sethostname	Set host name
75	setrlimit	Get/set resource limits and usage
76	getrlimit	get/set resource limits and usage
77	getrusage	Get/set resource limits and usage
78	gettimeofday	Get time
79	settimeofday	Get time
80	getgroups	Get list of supplementary group IDs
81	setgroups	Set list of supplementary group IDs
82	select+K4:	Synchronous I/O multiplexing
83	symlink	Make new name for a file
84	oldlstat	
85	readlink	Read value of a symbolic link
86	uselib	Select shared library
87	swapon	Start swapping to file/device
88	reboot	Reboot or enable/disable Ctrl-Alt-Del
89	readdir	Read directory entry
90	mmap	Map files or devices to memory (defunct)

Sys	Action	Function
91	munmap	unmap files or devices to memory
92	truncate	Truncate file to specified length
93	ftruncate	Truncate file to specified length
94	fchmod	Change permissions of a file
95	fchown	Change ownership of a file
96	getpriority	Get program scheduling priority
97	setpriority	Set program scheduling priority
98	profil	Execution time profile
99	statfs	Get file system statistics
100	fstatfs	Get file system statistics
101	ioperm	Set port input/output permissions
102	socketcall	Socket system calls
103	syslog	Read/clr kernel msg buffer; loglevel
104	setitimer	Set an erval timer
105	getitimer	Get value of an erval timer
106	stat	Get file status
107	lstat	Get file status
108	fstat	Get file status
110	iopl	Change I/O privilege level
111	vhangup	Virtually hang-up the current process
112	idle	Make process 0 idle
113	vm86old	Enter virtual 8086 mode
114	wait4	Wait for process termination, BSD
115	swapoff	Stop swapping to file/device
116	sysinfo	Info on overall system statistics
117	ipc	System V IPC system calls
118	fsync	Sync complete in-core state with disk
119	sigreturn	Ret from sig so cleanup stack
120	clone	Create child process
121	setdomainname	Get/set domain name
122	uname	Get name & info about current kernel
123	modify_ldt	Get or set ldt
124	adjtimex	Tune kernel clock
125	mprotect	Control allowable accesses to memory
126	sigprocmask	POSIX signal handling functions
127	create_module	Create module entry
128	init_module	Initiate loadable module entry
129	delete_module	Delete module entry
130	get_kernel_syms	Retrieve kernel & module syms
131	quotactl	Manipulate disk quotas
132	getpgid	Set/get process group
133	fchdir	Change working directory
134	bdflush	Start/flush/tune buffer
135	sysfs	Get file system type information
136	personality	Set process execution domain
138	setfsuid	set user id for file system checks
139	setfsgid	set group id for file system checks
140	llseek	R/W file offset
141	getdents	Get directory entries

Sys	Action	Function
142	newselect+K4:	Sync I/O multiplexing
143	flock	Apply/remove advisory file lock
144	msync	Synchronize file with a memory map
145	readv	Read a vector
146	writev	Write a vector
147	getsid	Det session ID
148	fdatasync	Synchronize in-core data with disk
150	mlock	Disable paging for parts of memory
151	munlock	Re-enable paging for parts of memory
152	mlockall	Disable paging for calling process
153	munlockall	Re-eenable paging for calling process
154	sched_setparam	Set scheduling parameters
155	sched_getparam	Get scheduling parameters
156	sched_setscheduler	Set scheduling algo/param
157	sched_getscheduler	Get scheduling algo/param
158	sched_yield	Yield processor
159	sched_get_priority_max	Get static priority rng
160	sched_get_priority_min	Get static priority rng
161	sched_rr_get_erval	Fetch SCHED_RR erval
162	nanosleep	Pause execution for specified time
163	mremap	Re-map a virtual memory address
164	setresuid	Set real, eff. and saved user ID
165	getresuid	Get real/effective/saved user ID
166	vm86 s	Enter virtual 8086 mode
167	query_module	For bits pertaining to modules
168	poll	Wait for event on file descriptor
169	nfsservctl	Kernel nfs daemon
170	setresgid	Set real,effective,saved group ID
171	getresgid	Get real/effective/saved group ID
172	prctl	Operations on a process
173	rt_sigreturn	Cleanup stack after return from signal
174	rt_sigaction	Examine/change a signal action
175	rt_sigprocmask	Examine/change block signals
176	rt_sigpending :	Examine pending signals
177	rt_sigtimedwait	Wait for queued signals
178	rt_sigqueueinfo	Queue a signal and data
179	rt_sigsuspend	Wait for signal
180	pread	Read from file descriptor at given offset
181	pwrite	Write to file descriptor at given offset
182	chown	Change ownership of a file
183	getcwd	Get current working directory
184	capget	Get process capabilities
185	capset	Set process capabilities
186	sigaltstack	Set/Get signal stack context
187	sendfile	Transfer data between file descriptors
190	vfork	Create child process & block parent
191	getrlimit	Get resources limit
192	mmap2	Map file or devices to memory

INDEX

.align directive 169
.arm directive 283
.ascii directive 151, 167
.asciz directive 151, 167
.byte directive 169
.data directive 181
.equ directive 169
.macro directive 171
.syntax unified directive 295
.thumb directive 283
.word directive 169
32-bit 59
64-Bit 20
64-bit OS 312
64-bit 59

A
AArch.. 311
ADD 47
ADD 68
addition instructions 68
addition, binary 54
addition, matrices 271
address write back 150
addressing mode 143
addressing modes, Neon 261
addressing, indirect 91
addressing, indirect 143
addressing, pc relative 153
addressing, post indexed 143
addressing, post indexed 150
addressing, pre-indexed 143
addressing, pre-indexed 147
ADR 144, 147
AL 101
always 101
acronyms 28
AND 87
Apple Computers 22
applications, of neon 264
Archimedes 312
arithmetic shift right 113
ARM chip 308
ARM instructions 28
ARM programmers model 301
ARM2 312
ARMv8 34

ARMv8 architecture 61, 311
arrays, neon 265
as command 39
ASR 113
assembler comments 42
assemble for debugging 131
assembler errors 40
assembler source, from C 208
assembler start point 41
assembling 39
assembly language program 27
attributes, file 183

B
B 105
BAL 45, 106
base, GPIO 218
bash 36
BCM 217, 307
BEQ 64
BIC 91
big endian numbers 78
binary 48
binary addition 54
binary to decimal 51
binary to hex 52
binary, signed 55
binary subtraction 55
binary, weight 50
bit clear 91
bit numbering 50
bit rotations 114
bits 49
bits and flags 64
block transfer, memory 155
BLX 110
BNE 64
Branch 64
branch calculation 127
branch instructions 105
branch with link 110
breakpoint commands 138
breakpoint labels 137
breakpoints 135
Broadcom datasheet 216
bubble sort 202
bugs 71, 117
BX 110
byte accessed memory 60
bytes 49

C

C function library 185
C, generating assembler source 208
calculator, desktop 58
carry clear 101
Carry Flag 63
carry set 101
CBX 289
CC 101
Centre for Computing History 24
character, control 81
character case differences 90
character case conversion 90
CISC 21
clear bit 91
close file 177
CMN 64, 77
CMP 64, 77
column major order, tables 270
command line 35
commands, VIM 38
comments 42, 46
compare instruction 64, 76
compare instructions, using 106
compare negative instruction 64
compare, improving program size 108
compare, using effectively 108
compiler, cross 33
Compute Modules 22
condition codes, VFP 247
conditional execution 97
conditional execution, VFP 245
condition codes 98
constant range, immediate 115
control characters 81
controller, gpio 217
conversion, binary to decimal 51
conversion, binary to hex 52
conversion, decimal to binary 52
conversion, hex to decimal 53
conversion sources, floating point 243
coprocessors 309
coprocessor, VFP 245
Cortex processors 311
CPSR 63
CPU 27
create file 177
creating directories 46
cross compiler 33

CS 101
CubeSats 31
Current Program Status Register 63

D

D Registers 239, 257
data lanes, Neon 260
data processing instructions 67
debugging 129
debugging VFP 238
decimal to binary 52
decimal weight 50
deleting files 46
directives 82, 167
directory, creating 46
disassembler 133
divide instructions 75
division 122
double number 112
double precision numbers 235

E

eax 84
echo 42
eight stage, pipeline 310
endian numbers 78
entering thumb mode 283
EOR 88
EQ 99
equal 99
error codes, gpio 226, 281
error messages 44
errors 33
errors, assembly 40
executable file 46
executing, machine code program ... 39
extended rotate 114

F

fast interrupt mode 304
fetch, decode, execution pipeline .. 126
file attributes 183
file permissions 182
file, executable 46
files, deleting 46
files, object 46
FIQ 298
flag tests 92
flags 63
floating point, conversions 243

flush file 177
Frame Pointer variables 213
Frame Pointer, R11 .... 166, 210
functions, data through stack 197
functions 187, 195
functions, preserving flags 199
functions, thumb 289

G
GCC 205
gdb 131
GDB make 140
gdb, listing program 132
gdb, shortcuts 139
GE 103
Geany Programmer's Editor 36, 47
GNC Compiler 17
GOTO, GOSUB 66
GPCLR 219
GPFSEL 227
gpio 215
GPIO base 218
GPIO functions 230
GPIO pins 220, 231
GPIO registers 218
gpiomem 216
GPSEL 218
GPSET 219
GPU 216, 310
greater or equal 103
greater than 103
GT 103
GVIM 36

H
hex to decimal 53
hexadecimal 48
HI 102
high-level languages 30
higher 102
i/o devices 215
IDE 48
indirect addressing 91, 143, 147
instruction sets 308
instructions, addition 68
instructions, ARM 28
instructions, branch 105
instructions, compare 76
instructions, data processing 67
instructions, divide 75

instructions, logical 89
instructions, long multiplication ... 119
instructions, move 76
instructions, multiplication 73
instructions, shift 111
instructions, subtraction 71
instructions, using compare 106
integrated development environment 48
interleaving 255
interrupt disable bits 64
interrupt modes 298
interrupt register arrangements 300
interrupt request mode 304
interrupt, return from 306
interrupts, priority order 305
interrupts, writing routines 306
inter working 286
IRQ 298
ITE 290

J
Jet Propulsion Laboratory 16

K
keyboard, reading from 82

L
labels 41
languages, high level 30
last in, first out 161
ld command 39
LDM 155
LDR 62, 147
LE 103
left shift 112
LEN 249, 250
length, word 59
less than or equal to 103
libc 185
LIFO 161
Link Register, R14 .... 66, 106, 210
linking 39
linking files 44
list files 182
little endian numbers 78
location, cause of frozen program 130
logical AND 87
logical EOR 88
logical instructions 89
logical OR 88

logical shifts.................................... 111
long accumulation 121
long multiplication 119
lower than or same........................ 102
LS... 102
LSL.. 93, 111, 112
LT 103

M

machine code program.....................27
macros... 170
macros, matrix examples................ 279
make...85
make, gdb 140
makefile...84
matrix addition 271
matrix multiplication...................... 274
matrix rotation 266
memory arrangement 60
memory dump................................ 138
memory mapping 215
memory, block transfer 155
MI 100
minus set... 100
mixed vector operations................. 251
mixing, thumb and ARM 286
mkdir..46
MLA 74
mnemonics..28
Mode bits...64
mode changes, CPSR..................... 302
mode, addressing............................ 143
MOV 66, 76
move instructions..............................76
MOVT 118
MSR.. 303
MUL 73
multi file syndrome 47
multiplication instructions 73
multiplication, long 119
multiplication, matrices 274
multiplication, smarter.................... 123
multitasking..................................... 255
multiple flag conditions................. 102

N

NE 99
Negative Flag 63
Neon addressing modes................. 261
Neon applications 264

Neon arrays.................................... 265
Neon assembly 257
Neon data lanes............................. 260
Neon instructions data types......... 259
nested calls 106
never... 102
NEG 244
NOP.. 289
Not a Number, NaN 235
not equal 99
numbers, ones complement.............56
numbers, ordering............................77
numbers, twos complement 56
NV... 102

O

object files 46
octal number 181
ones complement numbers 56
open file 177
operands 67
ordering numbers............................77
ORR 88
Overflow Flag 63
overflow set......................................99
overflow, clear 100

P

parallel computing......................... 255
pc relative addressing.................... 153
PC register..63
pinout command 217
pins, GPIO...................................... 220
pipeline.................................. 126, 309
PL 100
plus clear.. 100
post-indexed addressing......... 143, 150
pre-indexed addressing........... 143, 147
pre-processor 206
preserving flags, functions 199
print result..42
print routines 200
printf... 211
printf, libc functions 187
printf, passing parameters............. 189
Program Counter, R15 63
program structure 32
program, single stepping............... 137
programmers model 61

programmers model, ARM 301

Q
Q registers 257
quad-core 34
quotient 122

R
R11, Frame Pointer 166
R14, Link Register 66
R15, Program Counter 63, 125
RASPBIAN 16
Raspberry Pi OS 20
Raspberry Pi chips 34
Raspberry Pi development 25
read file 177
reading from keyboard 82
register bank wrapping 249
register designations, functions 196
registers 41
registers, GPIO 218
registers, system call 95
registers, thumbs 282
Register, status 63
remainder 122
right shift 105, 113
right, arithmetic shift 113
RISC 21, 32
RISC OS 312
rm 46
ROR 114
rotations 114
routines, print 200
row major order, tables 270
RRX 114
RSB 71
RSC 71

S
S registers 239
S Suffix 65, 98, 104
SBC 71
scalar register banks 236
scanf 190
screen, writing to 80
SDIV 75
Second Processor, BBC Micro 16
shift instructions 111
shift, left 112

shift, right 113
shifts, logical 111
signed binary 55
signed divide 75
single precision numbers 235
Single Instruction, Multiple Data . 255
Single Instruction, Single Data 255
single-stepping, program 137
SISD 255
SMID 255
SMLALS 121
SMULL 119
SoC 233, 307
sort, bubble 202
sorting 202
source file, creation 36
SP, stack pointer 161
stack , ascending 162
stack frame 166
stack growth, order of 163
Stack Pointer, R13 161
stack, descending 162
stacks 161
standards, functions 195
Status Register 63
STM 155
STR 62
start point, machine code 41
STRIDE 250
structured programming 32
SUB 71
subtraction instructions 71
subtraction, binary 55, 65
sudo 37
suffix, S 65, 98, 104
SVC 79
SWI 79
sync file 177
sys_close 177
sys_create 177
sys_open 177
sys_read 177
sys_sync 177
sys_write 177
syscall 4 81
syscall, disassembling 213
Syscalls 79
system call registers 95
system calls 79
System on Chip 34

T

T bit 64, 281
tables, column major order 270
tables, row major order 270
TEQ 92
terminal 37
Terminology 24
tests, flags 92
text editors 36
thumb functions 289
thumb mode, entering 283
thumb registers 282
thumb, stack operations 288
TST 92
twos complement numbers 56

U

UDIV 75
UMALAS 121
UMULL 119
unsigned divide 75
User Mode 59, 64
using compare effectively 108

V

VABD 244
VADD 244
VC 100
VCMP 246
VCVT 243
vector floating point 209, 233
vectoral register banks 236
vectors 298
VFP 209, 233
VFP condition codes 247
VFP conditional execution 245
VFP co-processor 245
VFP register file 236
VFP rounding errors 240
VideoCore 216, 310
VIM 36
VIM commands 38
virtual memory 216
VLD 261
VLDM 241
VLDR 241
VMOV 242
VMRS 246
VPOP 242
VPUSH 242
VREV 269
VS 99
VSQRT 244
VST 261
VSTR 241
VSUB 244
VSWP 268
VTRN 268

W

wrapping, register bank 249
weight, binary 50
weight, decimal 50
word accessed memory 60
word aligned blocks 60
word lengths 59
writing to screen 80

Z

Zero Flag 63

www.brucesmith.info

Printed in Great Britain
by Amazon